EFFECTIVE NOTETAKING

Also by Fiona McPherson

Easy Russian Alphabet: A Visual Workbook

Indo-European Cognate Dictionary

Mnemonics for Study (2nd ed.)

My Memory Journal

How to Approach Learning: What teachers and students should know about succeeding in school

Successful Learning Simplified: A Visual Guide

How to Learn: The 10 principles of effective practice and revision

Planning to Remember: How to remember what you're doing and what you plan to do

Perfect Memory Training

The Memory Key

Effective Notetaking

3rd Edition

Fiona McPherson, PhD

Wayz Press
Wellington, New Zealand

Published 2018 by Wayz Press, Wellington, New Zealand.

ISBN 978-1-927166-52-9

To report errors, please email errata@wayz.co.nz

For additional resources and up-to-date information about any errors, go to the Mempowered website at www.mempowered.com

Contents

Lists

A quick reference to rules or lists of various kinds.

Introduction

1

First tip! Students (and indeed readers in general) are inclined to ignore Introductions. But these are usually valuable guides to how to read the text and what to expect from it. As you'll learn in later chapters, knowing what to expect is a vital factor in getting the most from both books and lecturers.

Being a successful student is far more about being a **smart user** of **effective strategies** than about being 'smart'. Indeed, we can predict how well a student will do simply on the basis of their use of study strategies. Forget intelligence. Forget hours put in. What is important is your use of effective study strategies.

To use a strategy effectively you need to understand how it works. You need to understand:

- *Why* it works
- *How* it works
- *When* it works
- When it *doesn't*
- *How* to use it effectively

You also need to understand your own learning style, to help you assess whether a particular strategy is right for *you*.

The effective and long-term use of any memory strategy requires two things:

- that you understand why and how and when the strategy works

- that you practice the strategy enough to achieve mastery.

This workbook is the first in a series of workbooks on study skills. The workbooks build on the information about memory and memory strategies provided in my book *The Memory Key* (and its later edition, *Perfect Memory Training*), which sets out the principles of how memory works, and how those principles relate to memory strategies. Because *The Memory Key* aimed to provide an overview of memory strategies across the board, it couldn't go into depth about specific memory strategies. These workbooks aim to do that for study strategies. They provide more detailed instruction about specific strategies, examples to help you understand more fully how and when to use them, and exercises to provide practice in using them.

This workbook looks at the most important group of study strategies — taking notes. note-taking encompasses many strategies, not simply the obvious ones such as how to format your notes, use headings and highlighting, how to summarize, how to review your notes, but also the more complex ones of how to evaluate text to work out which strategy is appropriate, and how to ask the right questions.

The distinction between note-taking and active reading (discussed in the next book in the series) is somewhat arbitrary. Reading actively often involves taking notes; taking notes often requires you to read. Some strategies are common to both. One such strategy involves activating prior knowledge in preparation for reading about / taking notes about a subject. This is called priming, and it really does help, especially when the subject matter is difficult or unfamiliar.

So let's get you primed, to help you get the most out of this book. Think about your answers to the following questions:

When do you take notes?

Why do you take notes?

Do you have different strategies for taking notes in a lecture and taking notes from a book?

Do you realize notes can be formatted in different ways?

Do you re-write your notes?

If you re-write your notes, do you simply copy them out again, or do you write them in different words, or in a different format?

Do you review your notes?

How do you review your notes?

Do you think skimming is a good strategy or something poor readers do?

Do you have a clear idea of what you want to get out of a text or a lecture beforehand?

In a lecture, do you try to take down everything?

Do you have trouble picking out what is important in a text or lecture?

Do you believe that successful students are simply more intelligent than less successful students?

Do you 'cram' before an exam rather than study regularly?

Do you find information only seems to stay in your memory for a short time?

Do you have trouble concentrating?

Do you have trouble sitting still in one place for long?

Do you have trouble holding sufficient information in your head to understand what's being said?

Do you have different strategies you use for different types of information or when you have different purposes?

When you started this book, did you study the Table of Contents for a few minutes, reflecting on the various topics indicated there?

The last question is also a hint! If you didn't study the Table of Contents (and most people don't, believing that it is only provided as a type of index — a place to direct you if you're looking for something specific), then I recommend you go back and look at it. I've deliberately provided a lot of sub-headings, so you can get a reasonable idea of what is covered in this book.

I'm not suggesting you pick and choose what interests you, because I think you will be surprised by some of the information for topics you may think are 'beneath' you (like highlighting), and the chapters do build on each other. But as I've just suggested, preparing your mind before reading a text is an important part of successful learning, and the Table of Contents is a good place to start.

Okay. I hope these questions and the Table of Contents have got you thinking about your current note-taking style, your problems, and what you want from this book. Let's dive in.

Making note-taking an effective strategy

If you don't understand how note-taking helps you — what its purpose really is — then you won't be able to properly direct your efforts to making your note-taking effective. If you don't understand the factors that can limit that effectiveness, then you won't be dealing with those factors effectively. In this brief chapter, I look at the purposes of note-taking, and why the limitations of working memory need to be taken into account.

Note-taking is probably the most common study strategy. Everyone takes notes — not everyone knows how to do it well. Research into the effectiveness of note-taking has found — surprise, surprise — that sometimes note-taking helps you remember information, and sometimes it doesn't[1].

So what factors make note-taking an effective strategy? Let's start by looking at what note-taking is all about. First, a couple of distinctions to help define what note-taking is.

The first distinction is that between note-taking from note-*making*. We *take* notes from a book or a lecture; we *make* notes as preparation for an essay or presentation or exam, or to clarify our thoughts. Although this book is mainly about note-taking (about which most research has been done), some of the discussion — especially the section on concept maps — is relevant to note-making.

The other distinction we need to make is one within note-taking — the difference between taking notes from a lecture and taking notes from a book.

Again, following the research, I talk mostly about note-taking from books. It is much easier to practice effective note-taking strategies from written texts before moving on to the much more challenging situation of a lecture. I discuss recommendations for taking lecture notes in chapter 10.

Okay, now we've got that out of the way, let's look at what note-taking is about.

Note-taking is a strategy for making information meaningful

Most people believe notes are to provide a written record of information they want to remember, but although that is certainly important, research reveals the main value of note-taking is through its effect on how you encode the information in your brain. That is, the *act* of note-taking is more important than the result.

For this reason, note-taking is effective to the extent that you **paraphrase, organize and make sense of the information** while taking notes[2] — in other words, to the extent that you put the information in your own words. Verbatim notes (where you have recorded information word-for-word) are of minimal value, unless of course you are simply using them as a stepping stone and later paraphrase and reorganize them.

Several factors affect whether or not note-taking is effective:

- the density / complexity of the information
- the style of the presentation (for example, a very formal, 'dry' text is more likely to be recorded verbatim while a more informal passage is more likely to be paraphrased — and thus more effectively recorded)
- how well the information is organized by the presenter
- how skilled you are at taking notes (in particular, your skill at capturing the most important points)

And in the case of taking lecture notes, we must add another factor:

- how fast the information is presented (note-taking is more likely to aid recall if presentation rate is slow and you can review your notes)

Of course, all these factors interact. How well the material needs to be organized depends on your skill; how much complexity you can deal with depends on skill, prior knowledge, and working memory capacity; how much density/complexity is manageable depends on the style of the text and how well it's organized.

And all of these depend on a specific skill component: your knowledge of which strategy is most effective, for you, in the specific situation.

This book will teach you not only what strategies are effective and when, but how to assess the presented material in order to determine the most effective strategy, and how to choose the right strategy for *you*.

I don't want to over-emphasize the personality factor. Although personal styles and abilities are something you need to take into account when considering which strategies will be most effective for you, effective strategies are effective strategies, regardless of the user. Moreover, it's a mistake to simply go with the strategies you are most comfortable with. Indeed, research suggests that the most effective strategies are often those you are initially *not* most comfortable with.

But there is one personal attribute that you should take into account when considering your approach to learning and using these strategies, and that is your working memory capacity. So before we go any further, I want to discuss this.

The importance of working memory

Working memory governs your ability to comprehend what you are reading or hearing, your ability to learn new words, your ability to reason, your ability to plan and organize yourself, and much more.

Working memory capacity (the amount you can 'hold' in working memory) varies between people, and indeed, WMC correlates highly with fluid intelligence (fluid intelligence refers to general reasoning and problem-solving abilities, while crystallized intelligence refers to cognitive functions associated with knowledge).

In fact, a study[3] found that a student's ability to take good notes and benefit from them is better predicted by his working memory capacity than by his grade point average or his score on the American College Test. The notes of students with a high working memory capacity were fuller, with more complex propositions, more main ideas, and more words.

A student with a low working memory capacity also has more trouble understanding text. Part of the reason for this is a reduced ability to make inferences.

When reading, we make inferences all the time. Such inferences may require knowledge out of our memory, or may require us to make connections between statements within the text. To do this, we have to be able to hold all the relevant information in our mind at the same time — a task more difficult for those who can 'hold' less in working memory.

Indications are that students with a low working memory capacity use less effective strategies when reading because such strategies are less demanding[4].

So what is working memory, and why does it have this effect?

What working memory is

To put information into our long-term memory store, we must **encode** it, which means, for the most part, we must actively process it — work on it. This we term being "in working memory". Essentially, being in working memory is a way of saying information is currently being worked on. It's not necessary, by the way, for all of this to be conscious, although mostly it will be.

Similarly, when we retrieve information — get it out of the memory store / "remember" it — the information again passes through this state of consciousness, this working memory.

But here we come to the nub of the issue. Our long-term memory store is incredibly large, but the amount we can process at any one time — the amount we can "hold" in working memory — is very very small.

Working memory capacity and the magic number seven

Probably the most widely known 'fact' about working memory is that it can only hold around seven chunks of information (between 5 and 9). Actually, the situation is even worse than that. Recent research is now converging on the idea that working memory can only hold four items, of which only one is in your 'focus of attention' at any one time. But it seems likely that you can also hold another three or so items in a state of readiness, ready to jump into working memory. So, as long as you keep all these items circulating (by, for example, muttering them under your breath, or just by keeping your mind circling through them all) then you have your effective capacity of seven.

Regardless, this tells us little about the limits of working memory because the size of a chunk is indeterminate.

1 2 3 4 5 6 7 are seven different chunks — if you remember each digit separately (as you would, for example, if you were not familiar with the digits — as a young child isn't). But for those of us who are only too well-versed in our numbers, 1 through to 7 could be a single chunk.

In any case, recent research suggests that it is not so much the *number* of chunks that is important. What may be more important is how long it takes you to say the words (information is usually held in working memory in the form of an acoustic, sound-based, code). It appears that you can only hold in working memory what you can say in 1.5 — 2 seconds. Slow speakers are therefore penalized. (This also explains why we tend to talk very fast when we have a lot of information we want to disgorge).

There's more than one working memory

But what we term "working memory" is not a single entity. It contains several functions, including the "central executive" which coordinates and manages the various tasks needed.

The extent to which working memory is domain-specific (different "working memories", if you like, for different sensory and cognitive systems, such as language, spatial memory, number) is still very much debated. However, there is a reasonable consensus that verbal and visuospatial information have different "stores". This is important, because it means you can increase the amount of information you're currently holding by using both systems. For example, when I need to remember, say, a phone number and a name, I'll repeat one while holding the other as a visual image — writing the name, as it were, on a mental whiteboard.

But the most important part of working memory, it now appears, is the executive control — your ability to control attention; your ability to concentrate and not be distracted by competing demands.

Working memory is about attention

We tend to focus on the more deliberate concentration ability when we think of attention, but these two aspects of attention are both important, and indeed, it may be that the ability to ignore irrelevant information is the more important.

In fact, it may be that working memory capacity is *only* critical when there's interference[5] — suggesting that the ability to ignore competing demands is the really critical part of attention.

Of course, interference comes from many sources — not just distractions in the environment, but things happening in your mind. Anxiety[6] or any strong emotion (love!) is distracting. Thoughts about what you plan to do later, or decisions you haven't made yet, can be distracting. Trying to do two things at once can be distracting. But these are just the obvious sources of distraction. Simply having dual goals can be a source of interference — for example, taking notes for an essay, while simultaneously thinking you might as well include information you might need for a future exam.

Most importantly and least obviously, conflicting, inconsistent, or merely different, information is a source of interference. For example, holding your goal in mind while you study is a possible source of interference. Reading about one thing and going on to another, if you're not completely sure how they're connected (if indeed they are connected), is a possible source of interference. Think of information gathering as rolling a snowball. As long as the information all sticks together in a coherent, consistent, meaningful ball, you're fine. But anything that doesn't fit into your ball is going to cause problems.

This has important implications for note-taking. One of these has to do with the cognitive load of your text or lecture. The cognitive load is the extent to which the material makes demands on working memory. There are two parts to it: intrinsic (how difficult the material is) and extrinsic (how it's presented). Research suggests[7] that the format of the material is only important when the intrinsic load is high — that is, when the material is reasonably difficult. Of course, what is difficult for one person may be easy for another — difficulty level is entirely subjective.

What all this means is that there is no one "best" strategy for taking notes. Which strategy will be the most effective depends on your working memory capacity, the distractions in your mind or the environment (your temporary functional WMC as it were), the (subjective) difficulty of the text, and the way the information is presented. Which is why it takes me a whole book to lay it all out!

Conditions for effective note-taking

Skill at note-taking

Slow or self-determined rate of presentation

Well-organized material

Material that is not too difficult for the strategy and the student's skill

Main points

Taking notes is only effective if the student has sufficient note-taking skill to deal with the learning material.

Note-taking is primarily a tool to encode information effectively in your memory.

Your working memory capacity affects your ability to take notes.

You can hold more information in working memory by forming information into cohesive 'chunks', and by using both verbal and visual memory systems.

How much information you can 'hold' in working memory is affected by your ability to ignore irrelevant information.

Cognitive load is the extent to which the material makes demands on working memory.

Review questions

1. The main value of taking notes is

    a.   to provide a written record

    b.   to help you organize your material

    c.   to provide a verbatim record

    d.   to help you understand your material

    e.   to help you put the information into your own words, in a way that helps you understand it

2. Whether or not your note-taking is effective depends on

    a.   the writer's / lecturer's skill at organizing the material

    b.   how well you can adapt to the way in which the material is presented

    c.   how difficult the material is

    d.   your skill at picking out the most important points

    e.   your knowledge of note-taking strategies, and your skill at applying them appropriately

3. Your working memory capacity affects

    a.   how much you can think about

    b.   how well you can organize yourself

    c.   how much you can understand of what you're reading or listening to

    d.   how easily you learn

    e.   how smart you are

4. You can't do anything about the limitations of your working memory capacity   T / F

5. Working memory capacity is

    a.   crucial for academic achievement

    b.   just another way of thinking about attention

    c.   crucial when there are competing demands on your attention

    d.   affected by the amount of distraction in your environment

    e.   affected by the amount of distraction in your own thoughts

    f.   affected by how well you know what you're doing

PART I

Selection strategies

The first and most crucial part of effective note-taking is about selecting what information is important.

Anything that helps you select the most important information is good.

Distinguishing the important from the unimportant information is arguably the most critical skill in successful studying. It is the foundation upon which all the other skills rest. Unfortunately, no-one has yet come up with an effective way of teaching this skill. Many people might indeed argue that it is not a skill, but an ability.

Although I agree that the ability to pick out what is important is in many ways the essence of intelligence, I certainly don't agree that it can't be taught. It is merely that, like any other skill, some people will learn it easily (in some cases without any direct instruction), while others will need more help and more practice.

But even those who may have "picked up" their selection skills without obvious effort, would benefit from some direct instruction and focused practice.

I say that no-one knows how to teach the ability to select the most important information, and in the most fundamental sense that is true. But information that is expressed in writing or in speech, in textbooks and lectures, commonly contains clues to what the writer or speaker regards as important. Reading these cues is certainly something that can be taught.

There are also conditions that make selection more difficult, and if you understand these, you will know when to apply a greater degree of attention to the material.

Successful selection requires understanding, but you don't have to understand the information completely in order to select what is most important. You do, however, need a certain degree of background knowledge. This is why most students take lots of notes when they are new to the subject and become more selective with time. It's also why it helps to read relevant material before a lecture.

There are a number of strategies which may be considered selection strategies:

- highlighting
- headings
- summaries

Let's look at these in turn.

Highlighting important information

Most students regard a set of colorful highlighter markers as essential tools, and I'm not denying their usefulness. But using those markers effectively is not as simple as it appears. There are a few guidelines that will help you become a more effective user. This brief chapter looks at when highlighting is a useful strategy, and what you should highlight.

Highlighting refers to any way of emphasizing key words or phrases, such as underlining, framing, using bold type, using a colored marker, etc.

When it's done *for* you, highlighting cues you to the most important information. But its effectiveness depends not only on the one doing the highlighting competently identifying the important details, but also on whether that person has the same goals as you.

When *you* are the one doing the highlighting, its value is mainly as an aid to focus your attention.

When you're considering whether to use highlighting in a particular situation, you need to ask yourself: will highlighting help me pick out the most important information?

If there are too many important points in the text, or the ideas are too complex to be conveyed in a brief phrase, then highlighting is not an effective strategy.

An example

The Conference of the Parties to the FCCC has regularly met since 1995. The "Berlin Mandate" negotiating process concentrated on strengthening emission reduction commitments of Annex 1 Parties in the period after 2000. It concluded in 1997 with the adoption of the Kyoto Protocol. The Protocol established legally binding emission constraints for Annex 1 Parties including New Zealand. Different percentage reductions relative to 1990 emissions were set for different countries such that total global emissions are reduced by more than 5 %. New Zealand's commitment is not to exceed 1990 emission levels, on average, during 2008-2012. Demonstrable progress towards meeting commitments is to be achieved by 2005. Forest sinks can be included as changes in forest carbon storage since January 1990. Countries may participate in emissions trading to meet their commitments as well as undertaking joint implementation to reduce emissions or planting forests. The "clean development" mechanism provides for a system of credits for projects in developing countries to reduce emissions and can lead to increase in the overall level of allowed emissions.

[from Hughes, P. & Gebbie, E. 2000. Getting More From Less: A Review Of Progress On Energy Efficiency And Renewable Energy Initiatives In New Zealand. Wellington: Office of the Parliamentary Commissioner For The Environment, p15]

Let's see what happens when we highlight proper names and "significant" phrases.

The Conference of the Parties to the FCCC has regularly met since 1995. The "Berlin Mandate" negotiating process concentrated on strengthening emission reduction commitments of Annex 1 Parties in the period after 2000. It concluded in 1997 with the adoption of the Kyoto Protocol. The Protocol established legally binding emission constraints for Annex 1 Parties including New Zealand. Different percentage reductions relative to 1990 emissions were set for different countries such that total global emissions are reduced by more than 5 %. New Zealand's commitment is not to exceed 1990 emission levels, on average, during 2008- 2012. Demonstrable progress towards meeting commitments is to be achieved by 2005. Forest sinks can be included as changes in forest carbon storage since January 1990. Countries may participate in emissions trading to meet their commitments as well as undertaking joint implementation to reduce emissions or planting forests. The "clean development" mechanism provides for a system of credits for projects in developing countries to reduce emissions and can lead to increase in the overall level of allowed emissions.

An effort such as this is not completely pointless. It forces you to actually read the words, and therefore is better than simply letting your eyes passively drift over the text as you would if you were reading without engagement. However, there are far too many items highlighted to make this an effective use of the strategy.

Does it help if you use different colors to highlight different types of material? See for yourself (you can see this in full color in the printable document available at my website, at mempowered.com/books/effective-notetaking/resources):

> The Conference of the Parties to the FCCC has regularly met since 1995. The "Berlin Mandate" negotiating process concentrated on strengthening emission reduction commitments of Annex 1 Parties in the period after 2000. It concluded in 1997 with the adoption of the Kyoto Protocol. The Protocol established legally binding emission constraints for Annex 1 Parties including New Zealand. Different percentage reductions relative to 1990 emissions were set for different countries such that total global emissions are reduced by more than 5 %. New Zealand's commitment is not to exceed 1990 emission levels, on average, during 2008- 2012. Demonstrable progress towards meeting commitments is to be achieved by 2005. Forest sinks can be included as changes in forest carbon storage since January 1990. Countries may participate in emissions trading to meet their commitments as well as undertaking joint implementation to reduce emissions or planting forests. The "clean development" mechanism provides for a system of credits for projects in developing countries to reduce emissions and can lead to increase in the overall level of allowed emissions.

If you were using this strategy in order to create three types of notes — picking out all the names / terms for a vocabulary list, constructing a timeline, plus your 'ordinary' notes — then there might be some utility in this. But there is still far too much highlighted to make this an effective strategy, and for the most part, having different colors simply adds to the information overload.

Part of the reason is that the material is *dense* — that is, it has many important details. There's also another reason which may not be so evident: while I'm familiar with the term "Kyoto Protocol", I don't know any more about this than any casual newspaper reader. Why does that matter so much? Let's look at another example.

Wang, Q., Leichtman, M.D. & White, S.H. 1998. Childhood memory and self-description in young Chinese adults: the impact of growing up an only child. Cognition, 69(1), 73-103.

This study examined the relationship between self-description and childhood memory in 255 Chinese young adults. Ninety-nine participants were from only child families and 156 had siblings. All participants completed two questionnaires: a version of the Twenty Statements Test of Kuhn and McPartland (Kuhn, M.H., McPartland, T.S., 1954. An empirical investigation of self-attitudes. American Sociological Review 19, 68-76) eliciting self-descriptions, and an instrument asking for earliest and other childhood memories. Based on theories positing a relationship between autobiography and the organization of the self, we predicted differences on both measures between only- and sibling-child participants. Findings indicated that compared with sibling children, only children had more private and fewer collective self-descriptions, earlier first memories, more specific and more self-focused memories. In addition, autobiographical measures were influenced by cohort, gender, preschool attendance, and urban/rural family effects. Findings are discussed in terms of literature on autobiography, the self and childhood in China.

This is the abstract from an academic paper. Although this material is also dense, I am familiar with the topic. I am not only familiar with it, I have specific interests — I know what I want from the material. Accordingly, I only need to highlight a relatively small amount of detail.

But what about if I had followed the principle I used in the first example? Namely, that of highlighting any name and significant-sounding phrase. In the text on the next page, you can see how a novice might deal with this material.

It's hardly surprising that almost all the material is highlighted, because you would expect that only the essential points would be mentioned in the abstract of an academic paper.

For the most part, then, highlighting is only a useful strategy when the material is relatively simple. However, what constitutes 'simple' depends on your knowledge of a topic.

Wang, Q., Leichtman, M.D. & White, S.H. 1998. Childhood memory and self-description in young Chinese adults: the impact of growing up an only child. Cognition, 69(1), 73-103.

This study examined the relationship between self-description and childhood memory in 255 Chinese young adults. Ninety-nine participants were from only child families and 156 had siblings. All participants completed two questionnaires: a version of the Twenty Statements Test of Kuhn and McPartland (Kuhn, M.H., McPartland, T.S., 1954. An empirical investigation of self-attitudes. American Sociological Review 19, 68-76) eliciting self-descriptions, and an instrument asking for earliest and other childhood memories. Based on theories positing a relationship between autobiography and the organization of the self, we predicted differences on both measures between only- and sibling-child participants. Findings indicated that compared with sibling children, only children had more private and fewer collective self-descriptions, earlier first memories, more specific and more self-focused memories. In addition, autobiographical measures were influenced by cohort, gender, preschool attendance, and urban/rural family effects. Findings are discussed in terms of literature on autobiography, the self and childhood in China.

Whether highlighting is an effective strategy in a particular situation also depends on how you are using it (i.e., in the context of what other strategies), and on your particular goals.

To see what I mean, here's a passage from a text on Benjamin Franklin. Go through it and highlight what you think is important [all the example texts are available from my website as a pdf, for you to easily print out. Go to mempowered.com/books/effective-notetaking/resources}.

BENJAMIN FRANKLIN was born in Milk Street, Boston, on January 6, 1706. His father, Josiah Franklin, was a tallow chandler who married twice, and of his seventeen children Benjamin was the youngest son. His schooling ended at ten, and at twelve he was bound apprentice to his brother James, a printer, who published the "New England Courant." To this journal he became a contributor, and later was for a time its nominal editor. But the brothers quarreled, and Benjamin ran away, going first to New York, and thence to Philadelphia, where he arrived in October, 1723. He soon obtained work as a printer, but after a few months he was induced by Governor Keith to go to London, where, finding Keith's promises empty, he again worked as a compositor till he was brought back to Philadelphia by a merchant named Denman, who gave him a position in his business. On Denman's death he returned to his former trade, and shortly set up a printing house of his own from which he published "The Pennsylvania Gazette," to which he contributed many essays, and which he made a medium for agitating a variety of local reforms. In 1732 he began to issue his famous "Poor Richard's Almanac" for the enrichment of which he borrowed or composed those pithy utterances of worldly wisdom which are the basis of a large part of his popular reputation. In 1758, the year in which he ceases writing for the Almanac, he printed in it "Father Abraham's Sermon," now regarded as the most famous piece of literature produced in Colonial America.

Meantime Franklin was concerning himself more and more with public affairs. He set forth a scheme for an Academy, which was taken up later and finally developed into the University of Pennsylvania; and he founded an "American Philosophical Society" for the purpose of enabling scientific men to communicate their discoveries to one another. He himself had already begun his electrical researches, which, with other scientific inquiries, he called on in the intervals of money-making and politics to the end of his life. In 1748 he sold his business in order to get leisure for study, having now acquired comparative wealth; and in a few years he had made discoveries that gave him a reputation with the learned throughout Europe. In politics he proved very able both as an administrator and as a controversialist; but his record as an office-holder is stained by the use he made of his position to advance his relatives. His most notable service in home politics was his reform of the postal system; but his fame as a statesman rests chiefly on his services in connection with the relations of the Colonies with Great Britain, and later with France. In 1757 he was sent to England to protest against the influence of the Penns in the government of the colony, and for five years he remained there, striving to enlighten the people and the ministry of England as to Colonial conditions. On his return to America he played an honorable part in the Paxton affair, through which he lost his seat in the Assembly; but in 1764 he was again despatched to England as agent for the colony, this time to petition the King to resume the government from the hands of the proprietors. In London he actively opposed the proposed Stamp Act, but lost the credit for this and much of his popularity through his securing for a friend the office of stamp agent in America. Even his effective work in helping to obtain the repeal of the act left him still a suspect; but he continued his efforts to present the case for the Colonies as the troubles thickened toward the crisis of the Revolution. In 1767 he crossed to France, where he was received with honor; but before his return home in 1775 he lost his position as postmaster through his share in divulging to Massachusetts the famous letter of Hutchinson and Oliver. On his arrival in Philadelphia he was chosen a member of the Continental Congress and in 1777 he was despatched to France as commissioner for the United States. Here he remained till 1785, the favorite of French society; and with such success did he conduct the affairs of his country that when he finally returned he received a place only second to that of Washington as the champion of American independence. He died on April 17, 1790.

Eliot, C.W. 1909. The Autobiography Of Benjamin Franklin. New York: P F Collier & Son Company. http://www.infomotions.com/etexts/literature/american/1700-1799/franklin-autobiography-244.txt

A lot of information there, wasn't there? Did you have trouble deciding what was important? It's hard to know what's important when you don't know what you're supposed to be interested in. A specific purpose — a goal — makes it much easier. In this case, let's see how much easier it is when your goal is to answer the question: why is Benjamin Franklin famous?

Have another try at highlighting the text with that in mind, before looking at my highlighted text (note I've used underlining this time).

BENJAMIN FRANKLIN was born in Milk Street, Boston, on January 6, 1706. His father, Josiah Franklin, was a tallow chandler who married twice, and of his seventeen children Benjamin was the youngest son. His schooling ended at ten, and at twelve he was bound apprentice to his brother James, a printer, who published the "New England Courant." To this journal he became a contributor, and later was for a time its nominal editor. But the brothers quarreled, and Benjamin ran away, going first to New York, and thence to Philadelphia, where he arrived in October, 1723. He soon obtained work as a printer, but after a few months he was induced by Governor Keith to go to London, where, finding Keith's promises empty, he again worked as a compositor till he was brought back to Philadelphia by a merchant named Denman, who gave him a position in his business. On Denman's death he returned to his former trade, and shortly set up a printing house of his own from which he published "The Pennsylvania Gazette," to which he contributed many essays, and which he made a medium for agitating a variety of local reforms. In 1732 he began to issue his famous "<u>Poor Richard's Almanac</u>" for the enrichment of which he borrowed or composed those pithy utterances of worldly wisdom which are the basis of a large part of his popular reputation. In 1758, the year in which he ceases writing for the Almanac, he printed in it "<u>Father Abraham's Sermon</u>," now regarded as the most famous piece of literature produced in Colonial America.

Meantime Franklin was concerning himself more and more with public affairs. He set forth a scheme for an Academy, which was taken up later and finally developed into the University of Pennsylvania; and he founded an "American Philosophical Society" for the purpose of enabling scientific men to communicate their discoveries to one another. He himself had already begun his electrical researches, which, with other scientific inquiries, he called on in the intervals of money-making and politics to the end of his life. In 1748 he sold his business in order to get leisure for study, having now acquired comparative wealth; and in a few years he had made discoveries that gave him a reputation with the learned throughout Europe. In politics he proved very able both as an administrator and as a controversialist; but his record as an office-holder is stained by the use he made of his position to advance his relatives. His most notable service in home politics was his reform of the postal system; but his fame as a statesman rests chiefly on his services in connection with the relations of the Colonies with Great Britain, and later with France. In 1757 he was sent to England to protest against the influence of the Penns in the government of the colony, and for five years he remained there, striving to enlighten the people and the ministry of England as to Colonial conditions. On his return to America he played an honorable part in the Paxton affair, through which he lost his seat in the Assembly; but in 1764 he was again despatched to England as agent for the colony, this time to petition the King to resume the government from the hands of the proprietors. In London he actively opposed the proposed Stamp Act, but lost the credit for this and much of his popularity through his securing for a friend the office of stamp agent in America. Even his effective work in helping to obtain the repeal of the act left him still a suspect; but he continued his efforts to present the case for the Colonies as the troubles thickened toward the crisis of the Revolution. In 1767 he crossed to France, where he was received with honor; but before his return home in 1775 he lost his position as postmaster through his share in divulging to Massachusetts the famous letter of Hutchinson and Oliver. On his arrival in Philadelphia he was chosen a member of the Continental Congress and in 1777 he was despatched to France as commissioner for the United States. Here he remained till 1785, the favorite of French society; and with such success did he conduct the affairs of his country that when he finally returned he received a place only second to that of Washington as the champion of American independence. He died on April 17, 1790.

So although highlighting is mainly useful for information that doesn't have too many important points, clearly this is not a property of the text itself, but also depends on what you want from it.

To help you determine whether highlighting is a useful strategy in a particular situation, you should understand how highlighting works.

What highlighting does

Highlighting separates selected words from the rest of the text, and causes you to direct more attention to the selected words. Such words are more likely to be recalled[1]. However, there are a number of provisos:

- if the material is familiar to you, it won't be affected by highlighting

- if the text is brief, particular details won't be helped by highlighting

- highlighting should be simple — using different methods (bolding, underlining, coloring text) to indicate different categories of information (such as key terms, examples, dates, key statements) doesn't improve recall and may even harm it2.

In other words, you should only highlight details you don't already know, and only when the text is long enough to benefit from it.

Highlighting acts to direct attention. It does not improve recall as such. What it does is improve recall for those parts highlighted — at the expense of the rest of the text. It is therefore vital that the right information be highlighted.

What should be highlighted?

Selection can be a problem when the teacher or writer is doing the highlighting, because the details that should be selected will be different depending on the goals of the reader and their familiarity with the material.

The *density* of the text is another critical factor. Density refers to the number of important ideas in the text. In high-density text, a large proportion may be core information. If this was all highlighted, you might create a situation where the material *not* highlighted is more visually distinctive!

So how much highlighting is 'right', then?

Well, in one study, highlighting was ineffective when answers to 22 questions in a 210 word passage were selected, but it *was* helpful when answers to 30 questions in a 6000 word passage were emphasized[3]. In another study, students who underlined sentences they considered of high structural importance, recalled no better than students who simply read the text — but those students who restricted their underlining to only one sentence per paragraph, recalled more[4].

There's no hard-and-fast rule, but the following guidelines may help:

- restrict your highlighting to no more than 10% of the text — i.e., one line in ten

- select those details that you want to remember, and don't think you will (don't highlight facts simply because they are important, if you already know them, or believe you will remember them without help)

- in information-dense text, or where the text is difficult, use highlighting only as an adjunct to other strategies

Highlighting is also likely to be ineffective when you are working under severe time constraints. The main value of highlighting (as a strategy) appears to lie in its encouragement to spend more time with the material.

Highlighting is an effective strategy

- as an aid to concentration

- when you are not pressed for time

- when the text is of relatively low-density (which depends not only on the text itself, but also on your goal, your familiarity with the material).

Review questions

1. The first, and arguably most important, note-taking skill is

    a.   organizing the material

    b.   putting the information into your own words

    c.   knowing what to ignore

    d.   summarizing

    e.   highlighting the important information

2. Highlighting is most effective when

    a.   you use lots of colors

    b.   there's lots of important details

    c.   the text is short

    d.   there aren't too many important details

    e.   you're in a hurry

3. How much text should be highlighted?

    a.   20%

    b.   less than 30%

    c.   no more than 10%

    d.   no more than half

4. If the text is difficult or too full of important information

    a.   use highlighting to help you select what really matters

    b.   never use highlighting

    c.   use highlighting only in conjunction with other strategies

5. When the teacher or textbook writer has highlighted material

    a. always use their highlights

    b. always ignore their highlights

    c. ignore their highlights when the information is already familiar to you

    d. ignore their highlights when the information isn't relevant to you and your study goal

Headings highlight structure

4

Few readers give headings due attention. Of course, not all headings are as useful as they could be, but in textbooks at least, they should be providing valuable information for taking good notes and understanding the text. In this chapter, you will (if you work through the examples) see how good headings can make a big difference. An important part of that is how headings signal the way the text is structured, so we'll spend some time looking at different topic structures and how you can use them.

Headings can help you select the main ideas. I say "can", because a lot of headings are 'cute' rather than informative.

To the extent that a heading — whether done by yourself or another — encapsulates the main idea of the following section, it is an effective strategy.

Let's look at an example. It is, deliberately, a fairly difficult text, but do actually read it, even if you find it largely incomprehensible. We're going to spend some time during the course of this book going over this example (during the course of which, I trust, it will become much more comprehensible!).

> NIH scientists have shown that a common gene variant influences memory for events in humans by altering a growth factor in the brain's memory hub. On average, people with a particular version of the gene that codes for brain derived neurotrophic factor (BDNF) performed worse on tests of episodic memory - tasks like recalling what happened yesterday. They also showed differences in activation of the hippocampus, a brain area known to mediate memory, and signs of

decreased neuronal health and interconnections. These effects are likely traceable to limited movement and secretion of BDNF within cells, according to the study, which reveals how a gene affects the normal range of human memory, and confirms that BDNF affects human hippocampal function much as it does animals'.

Long known to be critical for the growth and survival of neurons, BDNF has also recently been shown to play a key role in memory and hippocampal function in animals. To find out if it works similarly in humans, the researchers explored the consequences of a tiny variance in the human BDNF gene, where its molecular makeup differs slightly across individuals. People inherit two copies of the BDNF gene - one from each parent - in either of two versions. Slightly more than a third inherit at least one copy of a version nicknamed "met," which the researchers have now linked to poorer memory. It's called "met" because its chemical sequence contains the amino acid methionine in a location where the more common version, "val," contains valine.

"We are finding that this one amino acid substitution exerts a substantial influence on human memory, presumably because of its effects on the biology of the hippocampus," said Weinberger.

Despite its negative effect on memory, the "met" version's survival in the human genome suggests that it "may confer some compensatory advantage in other biological processes," note the researchers. Although they found that it does not confer increased susceptibility to schizophrenia, they suggest that the "met" variant might contribute to risk for - or increase functional impairment in - other disorders involving hippocampal dysfunction, such as Alzheimer's disease or mood disorders.

Drawing on participants in the NIMH intramural sibling study of schizophrenia, Egan and colleagues first assessed their hippocampal function and related it to their BDNF gene types.

Among 641 normal controls, schizophrenia patients, and their unaffected siblings, those who had inherited two copies of the "met" variant scored significantly lower than their matched peers on tests of verbal episodic (event) memory. Most notably, normal controls with two copies of "met" scored 40 percent on delayed recall, compared to 70 percent for those with two copies of "val." BDNF gene type had no significant effect on tests of other types of memory, such as semantic or working memory.

The researchers then measured brain activity in two separate groups of healthy subjects while they were performing a working memory task that normally turns off hippocampus activity. Functional magnetic resonance imaging (fMRI) scans revealed that those with one copy of "met" showed a pattern of activation along the sides of the hippocampus, in contrast to lack of activation among those with two copies of "val."

Next, an MRI scanner was used to measure levels of a marker inside neurons indicating the cell's health and abundance of synapses - tiny junctions through which neurons communicate with each other. Again, subjects with one copy of "met" had lower levels of the marker, N-acetyl-aspartate (NAA), than matched individuals with two copies of "val." Analysis showed that NAA levels dropped as the number of inherited "met" variants increased, suggesting a possible "dose effect."

Unlike other growth factors, hippocampal BDNF is secreted, in part, in response to neuronal activity, making it a likely candidate for a key role in synaptic plasticity, learning and memory. To explore possible mechanisms underlying the observed "met"- related memory effect, the researchers examined the distribution, processing and secretion of the BDNF proteins expressed by the two different gene variants within hippocampal cells. When they tagged the gene variants with green fluorescent protein and introduced them into cultured neurons, they discovered that "val" BDNF spreads throughout the cell and into the branch-like dendrites that form synapses, while "met" BDNF mostly clumps inside the cell body without being transported to the synapses. To regulate memory function, BDNF must be secreted near the synapses.

"We were surprised to see that 'met' BDNF secretion can't be properly regulated by neural activity," said Lu.

The observed memory decrements are likely traceable to the failure of "met" BDNF to reach the synapses, as well as its inability to secrete in response to neuronal activity, say the researchers.

"Our study provides direct in vivo data that the molecular mechanisms related to activity dependent BDNF secretion and signaling, such as synaptic plasticity, may underlie humans' greatly expanded verbally-mediated memory system, just as it does for more rudimentary forms of memory in animals," said Egan.

In following-up their leads, the researchers are searching for a possible BDNF connection with the memory problems and hippocampal changes of Alzheimer's disease, depression and normal aging.

Adapted from a National Institutes of Health press release, January 2003, http://www.nih.gov/news/pr/jan2003/nimh-23.htm

Without looking back at the text, see if you can answer these questions:

1. What does BDNF stand for?

2. What are the nicknames for the two versions of the BDNF gene?

3. Which variant is associated with poorer episodic memory?

4. What disorders may be affected by this gene?

5. Does the BDNF gene type affect working memory?

Don't check back to see if you're right — let's look first at the same text with headings.

Human Gene Affects Memory

NIH scientists have shown that a common gene variant influences memory for events in humans by altering a growth factor in the brain's memory hub. On average, people with a particular version of the gene that codes for brain derived neurotrophic factor (BDNF) performed worse on tests of episodic memory - tasks like recalling what happened yesterday. They also showed differences in activation of the hippocampus, a brain area known to mediate memory, and signs of decreased neuronal health and interconnections. These effects are likely traceable to limited movement and secretion of BDNF within cells, according to the study, which reveals how a gene affects the normal range of human memory, and confirms that BDNF affects human hippocampal function much as it does animals'.

BDNF plays a key role in memory

Long known to be critical for the growth and survival of neurons, BDNF has also recently been shown to play a key role in memory and hippocampal function in animals. To find out if it works similarly in humans, the researchers explored the consequences of a tiny variance in the human BDNF gene, where its molecular makeup differs slightly across individuals.

Two versions of BDNF gene

People inherit two copies of the BDNF gene - one from each parent - in either of two versions. Slightly more than a third inherit at least one copy of a version nicknamed "met," which the researchers have now linked to poorer memory. It's called "met" because its chemical sequence contains the amino acid methionine in a location where the more common version, "val," contains valine.

"We are finding that this one amino acid substitution exerts a substantial influence on human memory, presumably because of its effects on the biology of the hippocampus," said Weinberger.

Met variant

Despite its negative effect on memory, the "met" version's survival in the human genome suggests that it "may confer some compensatory advantage in other biological processes," note the researchers. Although they found that it does not confer increased susceptibility to schizophrenia, they suggest that the "met" variant might contribute to risk for - or increase functional impairment in - other disorders involving hippocampal dysfunction, such as Alzheimer's disease or mood disorders.

Schizophrenia study

Drawing on participants in the NIMH intramural sibling study of schizophrenia, Egan and colleagues first assessed their hippocampal function and related it to their BDNF gene types.

Among 641 normal controls, schizophrenia patients, and their unaffected siblings, those who had inherited two copies of the "met" variant scored significantly lower than their matched peers on tests of verbal episodic (event) memory. Most notably, normal controls with two copies of "met" scored 40 percent on delayed recall, compared to 70 percent for those with two copies of "val." BDNF gene type had no significant effect on tests of other types of memory, such as semantic or working memory.

The researchers then measured brain activity in two separate groups of healthy subjects while they were performing a working memory task that normally turns off hippocampus activity. Functional magnetic resonance imaging (fMRI) scans revealed that those with one copy of "met" showed a pattern of activation along the sides of the hippocampus, in contrast to lack of activation among those with two copies of "val."

Next, an MRI scanner was used to measure levels of a marker inside neurons indicating the cell's health and abundance of synapses - tiny junctions through which neurons communicate with each other. Again, subjects with one copy of "met" had lower levels of the marker, N-acetyl-aspartate (NAA), than matched individuals with two copies of "val." Analysis showed that NAA levels dropped as the number of inherited "met" variants increased, suggesting a possible "dose effect."

How BDNF works

Unlike other growth factors, hippocampal BDNF is secreted, in part, in response to neuronal activity, making it a likely candidate for a key role in synaptic plasticity, learning and memory. To explore possible mechanisms underlying the observed "met"- related memory effect, the researchers examined the distribution, processing and secretion of the BDNF proteins expressed by the two different gene variants within hippocampal cells. When they tagged the gene variants with green fluorescent protein and introduced them into cultured neurons, they discovered that "val" BDNF spreads throughout the cell and into the branch-like dendrites that form synapses, while "met" BDNF mostly clumps inside the cell body without being transported to the synapses. To regulate memory function, BDNF must be secreted near the synapses.

"We were surprised to see that 'met' BDNF secretion can't be properly regulated by neural activity," said Lu.

The observed memory decrements are likely traceable to the failure of "met" BDNF to reach the synapses, as well as its inability to secrete in response to neuronal activity, say the researchers.

"Our study provides direct in vivo data that the molecular mechanisms related to activity dependent BDNF secretion and signaling, such as synaptic plasticity, may underlie humans' greatly expanded verbally-mediated memory system, just as it does for more rudimentary forms of memory in animals," said Egan.

Possible connection with memory problems in old age

In following-up their leads, the researchers are searching for a possible BDNF connection with the memory problems and hippocampal changes of Alzheimer's disease, depression and normal aging.

Better? See if you can answer these questions:

1. What does BDNF do?

2. What distinguishes the two variants chemically?

3. How common is the variant associated with poorer episodic memory?

4. If you have only one copy of the variant associated with poorer episodic memory is that as bad as having two?

5. In what ways do the variant genes act differently in the cells?

One last version:

Human gene affects memory for events

People with a particular variant of the gene controlling the brain factor BDNF have reduced hippocampal function

NIH scientists have shown that a common gene variant influences memory for events in humans by altering a growth factor in the brain's memory hub. On average, people with a particular version of the gene that codes for brain derived neurotrophic factor (BDNF) performed worse on tests of episodic memory - tasks like recalling what happened yesterday. They also showed differences in activation of the hippocampus, a brain area known to mediate memory, and signs of decreased neuronal health and interconnections. These effects are likely traceable to limited movement and secretion of BDNF within cells, according to the study, which reveals how a gene affects the normal range of human memory, and confirms that BDNF affects human hippocampal function much as it does animals'.

BDNF plays a key role in memory

Long known to be critical for the growth and survival of neurons, BDNF has also recently been shown to play a key role in memory and hippocampal function in animals. To find out if it works similarly in humans, the researchers explored the consequences of a tiny variance in the human BDNF gene, where its molecular makeup differs slightly across individuals.

Two variants: "Met" variant linked to poorer episodic memory; "Val" variant more common

People inherit two copies of the BDNF gene - one from each parent - in either of two versions. Slightly more than a third inherit at least one copy of a version nicknamed "met," which the researchers have now linked to poorer memory. It's called "met" because its chemical sequence contains the amino acid methionine in a location where the more common version, "val," contains valine.

"We are finding that this one amino acid substitution exerts a substantial influence on human memory, presumably because of its effects on the biology of the hippocampus," said Weinberger.

"Met" variant might increase risk of Alzheimer's and other disorders involving the hippocampus

Despite its negative effect on memory, the "met" version's survival in the human genome suggests that it "may confer some compensatory advantage in other biological processes," note the researchers. Although they found that it does not confer increased susceptibility to schizophrenia, they suggest that the "met" variant might contribute to risk for - or increase functional impairment in - other disorders involving hippocampal dysfunction, such as Alzheimer's disease or mood disorders.

Study finds those with two copies of "met" perform dramatically worse on tests of episodic memory but not on other memory tests

Drawing on participants in the NIMH intramural sibling study of schizophrenia, Egan and colleagues first assessed their hippocampal function and related it to their BDNF gene types.

Among 641 normal controls, schizophrenia patients, and their unaffected siblings, those who had inherited two copies of the "met" variant scored significantly lower than their matched peers on tests of verbal episodic (event) memory. Most notably, normal controls with two copies of "met" scored 40 percent on delayed recall, compared to 70 percent for those with two copies of "val." BDNF gene type had no significant effect on tests of other types of memory, such as semantic or working memory.

Two copies of "met" worse than one, but any "met" variant is associated with hippocampal dysfunction

The researchers then measured brain activity in two separate groups of healthy subjects while they were performing a working memory task that normally turns off hippocampus activity. Functional magnetic resonance imaging (fMRI) scans revealed that those with one copy of "met" showed a pattern of activation along the sides of the hippocampus, in contrast to lack of activation among those with two copies of "val."

Next, an MRI scanner was used to measure levels of a marker inside neurons indicating the cell's health and abundance of synapses - tiny junctions through which neurons communicate with each other. Again, subjects with one copy of "met" had lower levels of the marker, N-acetyl-aspartate (NAA), than matched individuals with two copies of "val." Analysis showed that NAA levels dropped as the number of inherited "met" variants increased, suggesting a possible "dose effect."

"Met" variant less successful in distributing BDNF proteins to the synapses

Unlike other growth factors, hippocampal BDNF is secreted, in part, in response to neuronal activity, making it a likely candidate for a key role in synaptic plasticity, learning and memory. To explore possible mechanisms underlying the observed "met"- related memory effect, the researchers examined the distribution, processing and secretion of the BDNF proteins expressed by the two different gene variants within hippocampal cells. When they tagged the gene variants with green fluorescent protein and introduced them into cultured neurons, they discovered that "val" BDNF spreads throughout the cell and into the branch-like dendrites that form synapses, while "met" BDNF mostly clumps inside the cell body without being transported to the synapses. To regulate memory function, BDNF must be secreted near the synapses.

"We were surprised to see that 'met' BDNF secretion can't be properly regulated by neural activity," said Lu.

The observed memory decrements are likely traceable to the failure of "met" BDNF to reach the synapses, as well as its inability to secrete in response to neuronal activity, say the researchers.

"Our study provides direct in vivo data that the molecular mechanisms related to activity dependent BDNF secretion and signaling, such as synaptic plasticity, may underlie humans' greatly expanded verbally-mediated memory system, just as it does for more rudimentary forms of memory in animals," said Egan.

Possible connection with memory problems in old age

In following-up their leads, the researchers are searching for a possible BDNF connection with the memory problems and hippocampal changes of Alzheimer's disease, depression and normal aging.

Can you answer these?

1. Which variant is more common?

2. Does the BDNF gene type affect semantic memory?

3. Is the BDNF gene type associated with a higher risk of schizophrenia?

4. What appears to be the problem with the variant associated with poorer episodic memory?

5. Are people with two "met" genes more likely to get Alzheimer's?

Now I do realize that the second set of questions should have been easier to answer than the first, and the third set should have been easiest of all, simply because you have increased your familiarity with the material. But my purpose in setting these questions is not to conduct an experiment, but simply to help you judge your grasp of the material.

Was the text with headings easier to understand and remember than the first text? Was the final text, with its longer, more specific headings, easier still? I hope so. Let's look at why.

Do headings help memory?

The presence of headings has been found to produce better summaries[1], better outlines[2], and better memory for the main points of a text[3].

Headings are organizational signals

Headings are classified as **organizational signals**. Other organizational signals are overviews and topical summaries (which we'll look at in the next chapter). The difference between these and other types of signal, such as highlighting, is that organizational signals emphasize the topics of a text and their organization.

Such signaling devices usually improve the reader's recall for the information which is emphasized, although at the expense, perhaps, of the rest of the information in the text. So headings usually help readers remember more topics, but less about each topic. Details that support the signaled information are more likely to be remembered than other details.

A comparison of the effects of an overview, a topical summary, and headings, found no difference in the amount of information remembered without specific prompts$_4$ (free recall). In other words, all these aids to memory — overviews, topical summaries, headings — are about as good as each other, and seem to work in the same way.

However, signaling doesn't always help your ability to recall information. Moreover, while recognition has been the subject of much less research and results are inconsistent, on balance it would seem that signals are much less helpful to recognition (which is the type of memory you may be relying on in multi-choice tests).

Main points

Headings have the same function as summaries — to emphasize topics and the organizational structure.

Headings usually, but not invariably, improve recall for the information they emphasize.

Headings may help you remember details that support the emphasized information.

The recall of emphasized information is usually at the expense of those details that are *not* emphasized.

How do headings help memory?

To understand how headings help memory, you need to understand how you process text. Read the Benjamin Franklin passage again and write a summary of it. When you've done that, look at the two summaries below.

BENJAMIN FRANKLIN

born Boston 1706

schooling ended at ten

apprenticed at 12 to a printer

went to Philadelphia in 1723

eventually set up a printing house, publishing "The Pennsylvania Gazette"

began "Poor Richard's Almanac" in 1732

lasted till 1758, the same year he printed in it "Father Abraham's Sermon," regarded as the most famous piece of literature produced in Colonial America.

set forth a scheme for an Academy, which later developed into the University of Pennsylvania

founded the "American Philosophical Society"

studied electricity

sold his business in 1748

reform of the postal system

in England 1757–1762

returning to America, lost his seat in the Assembly in the Paxton affair

1764 sent back to England to petition the King to resume the government from the hands of the proprietors

actively opposed the proposed Stamp Act, but lost the credit for this and much of his popularity through his securing for a friend the office of stamp agent in America

In France 1767-1775

lost his position as postmaster through his share in divulging to Massachusetts the famous letter of Hutchinson and Oliver

returning to Philadelphia, chosen a member of the Continental Congress

1777-1785 commissioner for the United States in France

returned to America he received a place only second to that of Washington as the champion of American independence

died 1790.

BENJAMIN FRANKLIN

early life

schooling ended at ten

apprenticed at 12 to a printer

printer

1723 went to Philadelphia

eventually set up a printing house, publishing "The Pennsylvania Gazette"

1732-1758 published "Poor Richard's Almanac"

1758 published "Father Abraham's Sermon" — the most famous piece of literature produced in Colonial America.

inventions

studied electricity

public affairs

education

set forth a scheme for an Academy, which later developed into the University of Pennsylvania

founded the "American Philosophical Society"

postal

reform of the postal system

actively opposed the proposed Stamp Act, but lost the credit for this and much of his popularity through his securing for a friend the office of stamp agent in America

lost his position as postmaster through his share in divulging to Massachusetts the famous letter of Hutchinson and Oliver

diplomatic

1757–1762; 1764-1766 in England

1767-1775 in France

1777-1785 commissioner for the United States in France

ups and downs

?1763 lost his seat in the Assembly in the Paxton affair

1775 chosen a member of the Continental Congress

1785 received a place only second to that of Washington as the champion of American independence

dates

1706-1790

1723 went to Philadelphia

1732-1758 "Poor Richard's Almanac"

1758 "Father Abraham's Sermon"

1757–1762 in England

1767-1775 in France

1777-1785 commissioner for the United States in France

Which of these two summaries best reflects the summary you made? Which one do you think is more effective (easier to understand and remember)?

How easily you remember details you've read in a text depends heavily on the degree to which the details have been integrated with the rest of the material. Narrative texts are remembered so easily because stories (and most particularly "traditional" stories, like folk tales) are a chain of causal events: this happens, so this happens. In expository texts (texts that explain and describe), the connection between items is usually less predictable.

The difficulty you experience in remembering a text is directly a consequence of the extent to which the information flows in a "logical" order.

Expository texts are organized around topics. A good reader is sensitive to the topic structure of a text. But texts vary considerably in the degree to which they make the topic structure clear to the reader, and transitions between topics are particularly problematic — which is where headings can be of great value.

The first summary in my Benjamin Franklin example represents a processing strategy that is not particularly sensitive to the text structure — a linear or listing strategy. It simply lists each point as it appears in the original text. The second summary reflects a strategy that is more sensitive to text structure. Note how the ideas are no longer simply listed in the order in which they appeared, but instead have been reorganized to reflect the presumed hierarchical organization of topics and sub-topics that underlies the passage.

Organizational signals like headings appear to help recall by encouraging you to choose the more effective topic structure strategy. They do this by emphasizing the transitions between topics, and by articulating the topics (that is, summing them up in a pithy phrase). This suggests that you can counteract the failure of many texts to provide headings, or to provide effective headings, by using a topic structure strategy.

This is supported by evidence that headings are most beneficial to those students who are capable of using the topic structure strategy but tend not to do so unless prompted.

Learning to use the topic structure strategy

To effectively use a topic structure strategy you need to understand the different types of text structure. Most texts will belong to one of these six types:

- **Description**: the extension or clarification of main ideas through explanations, examples, or information about attributes.

- **Collection**: a list of facts or elements.

- **Classification**: where items are grouped in classes.

- **Sequence**: a connecting series of events or steps, possibly causally related.

- **Comparison**: where two or more things are compared or contrasted.

- **Problem**: discussion of a problem and its solution, or a question and its answer.

Knowing the type of structure helps you predict how the ideas in the text will be related, which will not only help you understand the text more easily, and ask the right questions, but also enable you to choose the most appropriate format for your notes. Here's a more detailed description and an example for each of these structures:

Description

In description, a paragraph always has a main idea. Other sentences in the paragraph either clarify the main idea by giving examples or illustrations, or extend the main idea by explaining it in more detail. Here's an example:

Irritability is defined as an organism's capacity to respond to conditions outside itself. ... The organism's response is the way it reacts to stimulus. For example, a plant may have a growth response. This happens when ...

Collection

Collection passages may be a bulleted or numbered list, or a list of items in paragraph form, for example:

There are four general properties of solids. Tenacity is a measure of ... Hardness is ... Malleability refers to ... Ductility is ...

Classification

In classification, items are grouped into categories. For example:

Experimental variables can be grouped into one of two categories, either a manipulated variable or a controlled variable. A variable that can ...

Sequence

A sequence describes a series of steps in a process. For example:

Hearing can be described in five separate stages. First, ...

Comparison/contrast

This type of text looks at relationships between items. In comparison, both similarities and differences are studied. In contrast, only the differences are noted. For example:

There are two different hypotheses for the origin of the earth: the nebular hypothesis and the comet-produced hypothesis. The nebular hypothesis maintains ... In contrast, the comet-produced hypothesis states ... The first hypothesis assumes ... The latter hypothesis asserts ...

Problem

This type of text can resemble a sequence structure, in that it may include cause and effects. Typically, a text with this structure will state a problem and its causes and effects, then suggest one or more solutions; sometimes solutions might be suggested first, followed by problem, causes, effects. For example:

The problem of stress today ... Many factors contribute to stress ... The consequences of prolonged stress include ... How can we reduce the problem of stress ...

[first five examples adapted from Cook & Mayer 1988]

To identify which structure is being used, you need to pay attention to the cues in the text, most particularly signal words and phrases, and titles and headings. Here are some of the most common signal words/phrases:

Description: *in particular, for instance, for example, is defined*

Collection: *in addition to, and ... and ... and, a number of, many, one ... two ... three*

Classification: *belongs to, types, classes, categories, group*

Sequence: *first ... second ..., finally, therefore, consequently, the next, if ... then, leads to, causes, because*

Comparison: *likewise, similarly, same, in comparison*

Contrast: *in contrast, but, on the other hand, on the contrary, different*

But bear in mind that texts will often not provide such obvious cues. In the absence of clear signals such as these, you need to think about the overall theme of the text.

> ### The text structure
>
> - cues you to what is important
> - helps you ask the right questions
> - tells you how the ideas in the text are related
> - provides a structure for your notes
> - cues you to the best format for your notes.

Exercise 4.1

Below are three lengthy passages. Identify the type of structure and create headings where you think appropriate (I have put a space between each paragraph to enable headings to be written in, but that doesn't mean a heading is required in each space).

Text 1

"Consolidation" is a term that is bandied about a lot in recent memory research. Here's my take on what it means.

Initially, information is thought to be encoded as patterns of neural activity - cells "talking" to each other. Later, the information is coded in more persistent molecular or structural formats (e.g., the formation of new synapses). It has been assumed that once this occurs, the memory is "fixed" — a permanent, unchanging, representation.

With new techniques, it has indeed become possible to observe these changes. Researchers found that the changes to a cell that occurred in response to an initial stimulation lasted some three to five minutes and disappeared within five to 10 minutes. If the cell was stimulated four times over the course of an hour, however, the synapse would actually split and new synapses would form, producing a (presumably) permanent change.

How to detect

The hypothesis that new memories consolidate slowly over time was proposed 100 years ago, and continues to guide memory research. In modern consolidation theory, it is assumed that new memories are initially 'labile' and sensitive to disruption before undergoing a series of processes (e.g., glutamate release, protein synthesis, neural growth and rearrangement) that render the memory representations progressively more stable. It is these processes that are generally referred to as "consolidation".

assumption in modern. Consolidation. theory

Re Consolidation

Recently, however, the idea has been gaining support that stable representations can revert to a labile state on reactivation.

In a way, this is not surprising. We already have ample evidence that retrieval is a dynamic process during which new information merges with and modifies the existing representation — memory is now seen as reconstructive, rather than a simple replaying of stored information.

Researchers who have found evidence that supposedly stable representations have become labile again after reactivation, have called the process "reconsolidation", and suggest that consolidation, rather than being a one-time event, occurs repeatedly every time the representation is activated.

This raises the question: does reconsolidation involve replacing the previously stable representation, or the establishment of a new representation, that coexists with the old?

Whether reconsolidation is the creating of a new representation, or the modifying of an old, is this something other than the reconstruction of memories as they are retrieved? In other words, is this recent research telling us something about consolidation (part of the encoding process), or something about reconstruction (part of the retrieval process)?

The principal player in memory consolidation research, in terms of brain regions, is the hippocampus. The hippocampus is involved in the recognition of place and the consolidation of contextual memories, and is part of a region called the medial temporal lobe (MTL), that also includes the perirhinal, parahippocampal,and entorhinal cortices. Lesions in the medial temporal lobe typically produce amnesia characterized by the disproportionate loss of recently acquired memories. This has been interpreted as evidence for a memory consolidation process.

Some research suggests that the hippocampus may participate only in consolidation processes lasting a few years. The entorhinal cortex, on the other hand, gives evidence of temporally graded changes extending up to 20 years, suggesting that it is this region that participates in memory consolidation over decades. The entorhinal cortex is damaged in the early stages of Alzheimer's disease.

There is, however, some evidence that the hippocampus can be involved in older memories — perhaps when they are particularly vivid.

A recent idea that has been floated suggests that the entorhinal cortex, through which all information passes on its way to the hippocampus, handles "incremental learning" — learning that requires repeated experiences. "Episodic learning" — memories that are stored after only one occurrence — might be mainly stored in the hippocampus.

This may help explain the persistence of some vivid memories in the hippocampus. Memories of emotionally arousing events tend to be more vivid and to persist longer than do memories of neutral or trivial events, and are, moreover, more likely to require only a single experience.

Whether or not the hippocampus may retain some older memories, the evidence that some memories might be held in the hippocampus for several years, only to move on, as it were, to another region, is another challenge to a simple consolidation theory.

So where does all this leave us? What is consolidation? Do memories reach a fixed state?

My own feeling is that, no, memories don't reach this fabled "cast in stone" state. Memories are subject to change every time they are activated (such activation doesn't have to bring the memory to your conscious awareness). But consolidation traditionally (and logically) refers to encoding processes. It is reasonable, and useful, to distinguish between:

the initial encoding, the "working memory" state, when new information is held precariously in shifting patterns of neural activity,

the later encoding processes, when the information is consolidated into a more permanent form with the growth of new connections between nerve cells,

the (possibly much) later retrieval processes, when the information is retrieved in, most probably, a new context, and is activated anew

I think that "reconsolidation" is a retrieval process rather than part of the encoding processes, but of course, if you admit retrieval as involving a return to the active state and a modification of the original representation in line with new associations, then the differences between retrieval and encoding become less evident.

When you add to this the possibility that memories might "move" from one area of the brain to another after a certain period of time (although it is likely that the triggering factor is not time per se), then you cast into disarray the whole concept of memories becoming stable.

Perhaps our best approach is to see memory as a series of processes, and consolidation as an agreed-upon (and possibly arbitrary) subset of those processes.

Text 2

At the height of the Ice Age, between 34,000 and 30,000 B.C., much of the world's water was locked up in vast continental ice sheets. As a result, the Bering Sea was hundreds of meters below its current level, and a land bridge, known as Beringia, emerged between Asia and North America. At its peak, Beringia is thought to have been some 1,500 kilometers wide. A moist and treeless tundra, it was covered with grasses and plant life, attracting the large animals that early humans hunted for their survival.

The first people to reach North America almost certainly did so without knowing they had crossed into a new continent. They would have been following game, as their ancestors had for thousands of years, along the Siberian coast and then across the land bridge.

Once in Alaska, it would take these first North Americans thousands of years more to work their way through the openings in great glaciers south to what is now the United States. Evidence of early life in North America continues to be found. Little of it, however, can be reliably dated before 12,000 B.C.; a recent discovery of a hunting lookout in northern Alaska, for example, may date from almost that time. So too may the finely crafted spear points and items found near Clovis, New Mexico.

Similar artifacts have been found at sites throughout North and South America, indicating that life was probably already well established in much of the Western Hemisphere by some time prior to 10,000 B.C. Around that time the mammoth began to die out and the bison took its place as a principal source of food and hides for these early North Americans. Over time, as more and more species of large game vanished whether from overhunting or natural causes plants, berries, and seeds became an increasingly important part of the early American diet. Gradually, foraging and the first attempts at primitive agriculture appeared. Native Americans in what is now central Mexico led the way, cultivating corn, squash, and beans, perhaps as early as 8,000 B.C. Slowly, this knowledge spread northward.

By 3,000 B.C., a primitive type of corn was being grown in the river valleys of New Mexico and Arizona. Then the first signs of irrigation began to appear, and, by 300 B.C., signs of early village life.

By the first centuries A.D., the Hohokam were living in settlements near what is now Phoenix, Arizona, where they built ball courts and pyramid like mounds reminiscent of those found in Mexico, as well as a canal and irrigation system.

The first Native-American group to build mounds in what is now the United States often are called the Adenans. They began constructing earthen burial sites and fortifications around 600 B.C. Some mounds from that era are in the shape of birds or serpents; they probably served religious purposes not yet fully understood.

The Adenans appear to have been absorbed or displaced by various groups collectively known as Hopewellians. One of the most important centers of their culture was found in southern Ohio, where the remains of several thousand of these mounds still can be seen. Believed to be great traders, the Hopewellians used and exchanged tools and materials across a wide region of hundreds of kilometers.

By around 500 A.D., the Hopewellians disappeared, too, gradually giving way to a broad group of tribes generally known as the Mississippians or Temple Mound culture. One city, Cahokia, near Collinsville, Illinois, is thought to have had a population of about 20,000 at its peak in the early 12th century. At the center of the city stood a huge earthen mound, flattened at the top, that was 30 meters high and 37 hectares at the base. Eighty other mounds have been found nearby.

Cities such as Cahokia depended on a combination of hunting, foraging, trading, and agriculture for their food and supplies. Influenced by the thriving societies to the south, they evolved into complex hierarchical societies that took slaves and practiced human sacrifice.

In what is now the southwest United States, the Anasazi, ancestors of the modern Hopi Indians, began building stone and adobe pueblos around the year 900. These unique and amazing apartment-like structures were often built along cliff faces; the most famous, the "cliff palace" of Mesa Verde, Colorado, had more than 200 rooms. Another site, the Pueblo Bonito ruins along New Mexico's Chaco River, once contained more than 800 rooms.

Perhaps the most affluent of the pre-Columbian Native Americans lived in the Pacific Northwest, where the natural abundance of fish and raw materials made food supplies plentiful and permanent villages possible as early as 1,000 B.C. The opulence of their "potlatch" gatherings remains a standard for extravagance and festivity probably unmatched in early American history.

The America that greeted the first Europeans was, thus, far from an empty wilderness. It is now thought that as many people lived in the Western Hemisphere as in Western Europe at that time -- about 40 million. Estimates of the number of Native Americans living in what is now the United States at the onset of European colonization range from two to 18 million, with most historians tending toward the lower figure. What is certain is the devastating effect that European disease had on the indigenous population practically from the time of initial contact. Smallpox, in particular, ravaged whole communities and is thought to have been a much more direct cause of the precipitous decline in the Indian population in the 1600s than the numerous wars and skirmishes with European settlers.

Indian customs and culture at the time were extraordinarily diverse, as could be expected, given the expanse of the land and the many different environments to which they had adapted. Some generalizations, however, are possible. Most tribes, particularly in the wooded eastern region and the Midwest, combined aspects of hunting, gathering, and the cultivation of maize and other products for their food supplies. In many cases, the women were responsible for farming and the distribution of food, while the men hunted and participated in war.

By all accounts, Native-American society in North America was closely tied to the land. Identification with nature and the elements was integral to religious beliefs. Their life was essentially clan-oriented and communal, with children allowed more freedom and tolerance than was the European custom of the day.

Although some North American tribes developed a type of hieroglyphics to preserve certain texts, Native-American culture was primarily oral, with a high value placed on the recounting of tales and dreams. Clearly, there was a good deal of trade among various groups and strong evidence exists that neighboring tribes maintained extensive and formal relations — both friendly and hostile.

The first Europeans to arrive in North America — at least the first for whom there is solid evidence — were Norse, traveling west from Greenland, where Erik the Red had founded a settlement around the year 985. In 1001 his son Leif is thought to have explored the northeast coast of what is now Canada and spent at least one winter there.

While Norse sagas suggest that Viking sailors explored the Atlantic coast of North America down as far as the Bahamas, such claims remain unproven. In 1963, however, the ruins of some Norse houses dating from that era were discovered at L'Anse-aux-Meadows in northern Newfoundland, thus supporting at least some of the saga claims.

In 1497, just five years after Christopher Columbus landed in the Caribbean looking for a western route to Asia, a Venetian sailor named John Cabot arrived in Newfoundland on a mission for the British king. Although quickly forgotten, Cabot's journey was later to provide the basis for British claims to North America. It also opened the way to the rich fishing grounds off George's Banks, to which European fishermen, particularly the Portuguese, were soon making regular visits.

Columbus never saw the mainland of the future United States, but the first explorations of it were launched from the Spanish possessions that he helped establish. The first of these took place in 1513 when a group of men under Juan Ponce de León landed on the Florida coast near the present city of St. Augustine.

With the conquest of Mexico in 1522, the Spanish further solidified their position in the Western Hemisphere. The ensuing discoveries added to Europe's knowledge of what was now named America — after the Italian Amerigo Vespucci, who wrote a widely popular account of his voyages to a "New World." By 1529 reliable maps of the Atlantic coastline from Labrador to Tierra del Fuego had been drawn up, although it would take more than another century before hope of discovering a "Northwest Passage" to Asia would be completely abandoned.

Among the most significant early Spanish explorations was that of Hernando De Soto, a veteran conquistador who had accompanied Francisco Pizarro in the conquest of Peru. Leaving Havana in 1539, De Soto's expedition landed in Florida and ranged through the southeastern United States as far as the Mississippi River in search of riches.

Another Spaniard, Francisco Vázquez de Coronado, set out from Mexico in 1540 in search of the mythical Seven Cities of Cibola. Coronado's travels took him to the Grand Canyon and Kansas, but failed to reveal the gold or treasure his men sought. However, his party did leave the peoples of the region a remarkable, if unintended, gift: Enough of his horses escaped to transform life on the Great Plains. Within a few generations, the Plains Indians had become masters of horsemanship, greatly expanding the range and scope of their activities.

While the Spanish were pushing up from the south, the northern portion of the present-day United States was slowly being revealed through the journeys of men such as Giovanni da Verrazano. A Florentine who sailed for the French, Verrazano made landfall in North Carolina in 1524, then sailed north along the Atlantic Coast past what is now New York harbor.

A decade later, the Frenchman Jacques Cartier set sail with the hope — like the other Europeans before him — of finding a sea passage to Asia. Cartier's expeditions along the St. Lawrence River laid the foundation for the French claims to North America, which were to last until 1763.

Following the collapse of their first Quebec colony in the 1540s, French Huguenots attempted to settle the northern coast of Florida two decades later. The Spanish, viewing the French as a threat to their trade route along the Gulf Stream, destroyed the colony in 1565. Ironically, the leader of the Spanish forces, Pedro Menéndez, would soon establish a town not far away — St. Augustine. It was the first permanent European settlement in what would become the United States.

[taken from the Outline of U.S. History, published by the U.S. Department of State. http://usinfo.state.gov/products/pubs/histryotln/index.htm]

Text 3

Ozone?
UV?

In this section, we will explore what is ozone and what is ultraviolet radiation. We then will explore the relationship between ozone and ultraviolet radiation from the sun. It is here that ozone plays its essential role in shielding the surface from harmful ultraviolet radiation. By screening out genetically destructive ultraviolet radiation from the Sun, ozone protects life on the surface of Earth. It is for this reason that ozone acquires an enormous importance. It is why we study it so extensively.

About 90% of the ozone in our atmosphere is contained in the stratosphere, the region from about 10 to 50 km (32,000 to 164,000 feet) above Earth's surface. Ten percent of the ozone is contained in the troposphere, the lowest part of our atmosphere where all of our weather takes place. Measurements taken from instruments on the ground, flown on balloons, and operating in space show that ozone concentrations are greatest between about 15 and 30 km.

Although ozone concentrations are very small, typically only a few molecules O^3 per million molecules of air, these ozone molecules are vitally important to life because they absorb the biologically harmful ultraviolet radiation from the Sun. There are three different types of ultraviolet (UV) radiation, based on the wavelength of the radiation. These are referred to as UV-a, UV-b, and UV-c. UV-c (red) is entirely screened out by ozone around 35 km altitude, while most UV-a (blue) reaches the surface, but it is not as genetically damaging, so we don't worry about it too much. It is the UV-b (green) radiation that can cause sunburn and that can also cause genetic damage, resulting in things like skin cancer, if exposure to it is prolonged. Ozone screens out most UV-b, but some reaches the surface. Were the ozone layer to decrease, more UV-b radiation would reach the surface, causing increased genetic damage to living things.

Because most of the ozone in our atmosphere is contained in the stratosphere, we refer to this region as the stratospheric ozone layer. In contrast to beneficial stratospheric ozone, tropospheric ozone is a pollutant found in high concentrations in smog. Though it too absorbs UV radiation, breathing it in high levels is unhealthy, even toxic. The high reactivity of ozone results in damage to the living tissue of plants and animals. This damage by heavy tropospheric ozone pollution is often manifested as eye and lung irritation. Tropospheric ozone is mainly produced during the daytime in polluted regions such as urban areas. Significant government efforts are underway to regulate the gases and emissions that lead to this harmful pollution, and smog alerts are regular occurrences in polluted urban areas.

To appreciate the importance of stratospheric ozone, we need to understand something of the Sun's output and how it impacts living systems. The Sun produces radiation at many different wavelengths. These are part of what is known as the electromagnetic (EM) spectrum. EM radiation includes everything from radio waves (very long wavelengths) to X-rays and gamma rays (very tiny wavelengths). EM radiation is classified by wavelength, which is a measure of how energetic is the radiation. The energy of a tiny piece or "packet" of radiation (which we call a photon) is inversely proportional to its wavelength. $E \uparrow \quad \partial \downarrow$

The human eye can detect wavelengths in the region of the spectrum from about 400 nm (nanometers or billionths of a meter) to about 700 nm. Not surprisingly, this is called the visible region of the spectrum. All the colors of light (red, orange, yellow, green, blue, and violet) fall inside a small wavelength band. Whereas radio waves have wavelengths on the order of meters, visible light waves have wavelengths on the order of billionths of a meter. Such a tiny unit is called a nanometer (1 nm= 10-9 m). At one end of the visible "color" spectrum is red light. Red light has a wavelength of about 630 nm. Near the opposite end of the color spectrum is blue light, and at the very opposite end is violet light. Blue light has a wavelength of about 430 nm. Violet light has a wavelength of about 410 nm. Therefore, blue light is more energetic than red light because of its shorter wavelength, but it is less energetic than violet light, which has an even shorter wavelength. Radiation with wavelengths shorter than those of violet light is called ultraviolet radiation.

The Sun produces radiation that is mainly in the visible part of the electromagnetic spectrum. However, the Sun also generates radiation in ultraviolet (UV) part of the spectrum. UV wavelengths range from 1 to 400 nm. We are concerned about ultraviolet radiation because these rays are energetic enough to break the bonds of DNA molecules (the molecular carriers of our genetic coding), and thereby damage cells. While most plants and animals are able to either repair or destroy damaged cells, on occasion, these damaged DNA molecules are not repaired, and can replicate, leading to dangerous forms of skin cancer (basal, squamous, and melanoma).

Solar flux refers to the amount of solar energy in watts falling perpendicularly on a surface one square centimeter, and the units are watts per cm2 per nm. Because of the strong absorption of UV radiation by ozone in the stratosphere, the intensity decreases at lower altitudes in the atmosphere. In addition, while the energy of an individual photon is greater if it has a shorter wavelength, there are fewer photons at the shorter wavelengths, so the Sun's total energy output is less at the shorter wavelengths. Because of ozone, it is virtually impossible for solar ultraviolet to penetrate to Earth's surface. For radiation with a wavelength of 290 nm, the intensity at Earth's surface is 350 million times weaker than at the top of the atmosphere. If our eyes detected light at less than 290 nm instead of in the visible range, the world would be very dark because of the ozone absorption!

To appreciate how important this ultraviolet radiation screening is, we can consider a characteristic of radiation damage called an action spectrum. An action spectrum gives us a measure of the relative effectiveness of radiation in generating a certain biological response over a range of wavelengths. This response might be erythema (sunburn), changes in plant growth, or changes in molecular DNA. Fortunately, where DNA is easily damaged (where there is a high probability), ozone strongly absorbs UV. At the longer wavelengths where ozone absorbs weakly, DNA damage is less likely. If there was a 10% decrease in ozone, the amount of DNA damaging UV would increase by about 22%. Considering that DNA damage can lead to maladies like skin cancer, it is clear that this absorption of the Sun's ultraviolet radiation by ozone is critical for our well-being.

While most of the ultraviolet radiation is absorbed by ozone, some does make it to Earth's surface. Typically, we classify ultraviolet radiation into three parts, UV-a (320-400 nm), UV-b (280-320 nm), and UV-c (200-280 nm). Sunscreens have been developed by commercial manufacturers to protect human skin from UV radiation. The labels of these sunscreens usually note that they screen both UV-a and UV-b. Why not also screen for UV-c radiation? When UV-c encounters ozone in the mid-stratosphere, it is quickly absorbed so that none reaches Earth's surface. UV-b is partially absorbed and UV-a is barely absorbed by ozone. Ozone is so effective at absorbing the extremely harmful UV-c that sunscreen manufacturers don't need to worry about UV-c. Manufacturers only need to eliminate skin absorption of damaging UV-b and less damaging UV-a radiation.

The screening of ultraviolet radiation by ozone depends on other factors, such as time of day and season. The angle of the Sun in the sky has a large effect on the UV radiation. When the Sun is directly overhead, the UV radiation comes straight down through our atmosphere and is only absorbed by overhead ozone. When the Sun is just slightly above the horizon at dawn and dusk, the UV radiation must pass through the atmosphere at an angle. Because the UV passes through a longer distance in the atmosphere, it encounters more ozone molecules and there is greater absorption and, consequently, less UV radiation striking the surface.

[adapted from the Stratospheric Ozone Electronic Textbook, produced by NASA's Goddard Space Flight Center Atmospheric Chemistry and Dynamics Branch. http://www.ccpo.odu.edu/SEES/ozone/oz_class.htm]

The usefulness of classifying the text structure is something that will become more apparent as we work through the different ways of summarizing and formatting notes.

A further effect of signals

The topic structure strategy and listing strategy are encoding strategies, that is, they are strategies for putting information into memory. But remembering is not only about putting information in; it's also about getting it out again. While signals such as headings appear to mainly affect encoding strategy (whether in helping you decide which encoding strategy to use, or in making your encoding easier), they are also potentially helpful in your recall strategy.

This is revealed by the evidence that when signals are not present, recall tends not to follow the text's structure as well as it does when signals are present[5]. When there are no signals, recall tends to be strongly affected by standard memory factors such as:

- **serial position** (items mentioned first or last are remembered better than items in the middle),

- **familiarity** (items you are already familiar with are recalled more easily), and

- **elaboration** (items discussed at greater length are remembered better).

In other words, if you don't use the text structure to encode and recall the information, you're most likely to preferentially remember the information that you already knew, information that appeared at the start or end of the text, and information that was discussed a lot.

It's not surprising that we use these as guidelines to what is important, but serial position and familiarity in particular are quite indirect indicators to an item's relative importance. When you use more accurate signals to guide you instead, the influence of these factors is considerably lessened[6] (although elaboration is most likely to still be influential — unsurprisingly, because the length of discussion is a clear signal of importance (although it may simply reflect the writer's whim!)).

I've said that, although headings and other signals usually improve your recall of the topics, they may reduce the amount of detail you remember. I say 'may', because research has produced particularly inconsistent findings. It may well be that the inconsistency results from students' very variable ability to use the topic structure to guide their recall.

In other words, to benefit most fully from organizational signals such as headings, you probably need to make a deliberate effort not only to use that information in your encoding (note-taking), but also when you practice retrieving the information[7].

Do some individuals benefit more from headings than others?

Effect of reading ability

As has been suggested, "mature" readers are thought to routinely use a topic structure strategy when processing informative text, while less skilled readers are more likely to rely on a listing strategy. If this is the case, we would expect headings to make little difference to skilled readers.

At the other end of the scale, some poor readers may fail to use a structure strategy even when encouraged to do so — for these, too, headings should make little difference.

According to this logic then, headings should be of greatest benefit to those students in the middle — those capable of using a structure strategy, but not inclined to do so without prompting. And there is indeed, some evidence to support this[8].

Nevertheless, the evidence suggests that even experienced readers are relatively insensitive to structure in the absence of signals.

> ## Characteristics of a skilled reader
>
> Skilled readers demonstrate their sensitivity to topic structure in several ways:
>
> - they read topic-introducing sentences more slowly
> - they read topic sentences that are difficult to relate to the topic more slowly[1]
> - they recall more superordinate items than subordinate (e.g., categories rather than category members).

Readiness to think

Level of reading ability is not the only personal attribute that has an impact. Another attribute is your inclination for effortful processing — that is, the pleasure you take in engaging your mind. In one study, organizational signals (an overview and summary as well as headings) were of greater benefit to those students who were not inclined to engage in effortful processing.

In other words, the signals effectively eliminated the differences in recall performance between students who enjoyed effortful processing (who usually remember more) and those who didn't[9].

It's assumed that this occurs because students who readily engage in effortful processing are more inclined to use the structure strategy when confronted with a text without signals.

It's has also been suggested that headings only help when students already have a high knowledge of the subject discussed in the text. This is consistent with the theory that headings work by activating prior knowledge.

Headings may, however, have other benefits for students with little prior knowledge — in helping them organize the information contained in the text, and in helping them search for specific items[10].

> ## When are headings most useful?
>
> When the text has several topics and is not clearly organized.
>
> When other cues to the structure of the text and the relative importance of details aren't available.
>
> When the reader needs assistance in understanding the organization of the text, or the relative importance of details.

The bottom line is, if you find a text confusing, with too many topics and poorly organized, then writing headings through the text is a helpful strategy. This is particularly true if you find it hard to hold all the information you need in your head, whether because you have a low working memory capacity (permanently or temporarily) or because the text holds too much detail.

If headings are provided in the text, pay attention to them, but don't hesitate to re-write them if they are not useful to you (either because they're not very good headings, or because the author's goals and perspectives don't match yours).

Main points

How easily text is remembered depends on the extent to which the sequence of statements is clear and logical.

Recall depends heavily on how well-connected the information is.

Headings are one of the strategies used to help emphasize changes of topic and the organizational structure of the text.

To assess whether headings used in a text are of value to you, ask yourself the following questions:

- Do they highlight the main points and themes?
- Do they provide meaningful connections between topics?
- Do they provide good retrieval cues?

Good headings help you select the most important information.

Good headings help you see the structure of the text.

Text structure helps you organize your notes.

In the absence of good headings, use signal words to identify the text structure.

Review questions

1. Organizational signals are strategies that

    a. show you what details are important

    b. show you how the material is organized

    c. help you identify the topics covered

    d. help you remember the material

2. Organizational signals include

    a. highlighting

    b. summaries

    c. headings

    d. some kinds of summary

3. Headings

    a. are more useful than summaries

    b. help you remember all the details

    c. are most useful for helping you remember the topics covered

    d. are always useful

    e. are useful as guides to the organizational structure of the text

4. Expository texts are harder to remember than story texts because

    a. stories are much more entertaining

    b. story texts usually have a predictable chain of events

    c. we're much more familiar with story patterns

    d. expository texts are organized in ways that are less familiar to most readers

    e. expository texts lack interesting characters

5. There are only 6 types of expository text structure   T / F

6. Identifying the text structure helps you

    a. organize your thoughts

    b. pick an appropriate structure for your notes

    c. identify which details are unimportant

    d. create the right questions for review

    e. remember the details

7. Poor readers read important sentences more slowly than other sentences   T / F

8. Headings are most useful when

    a. the text is really well organized

    b. the text is poorly organized

    c. important topics and details are clearly signaled in the text

    d. other signals to what is important aren't available

59

Summaries

5

Let's face it, summarizing is the heart of note-taking. In this lengthy chapter, I work through a difficult text in considerable detail to show how to create good summaries — a hint: it's a lot more complicated than just copying out the important sentences! This is the most important study skill you can learn.

Again, as with highlighting and headings, we must distinguish between summaries you create and summaries that are provided for you.

Taking notes is, of course, largely about summarizing, so we're going to spend quite a while on this skill. But first, because summaries are usually provided in textbooks, and are a very useful tool in preparing you for your own summary, let's talk briefly about summaries that are provided for you.

There are a number of different types of summary. The simplest kind is a topical summary, which is a straightforward string of factual statements. This is the kind that you are most likely to see provided. Topical summaries summarize the main points without adding any new information or offering a new perspective.

More complex summaries may re-organize text into a different format (graphic summaries) — for example, in the form of outlines, graphic organizers, multimedia summaries or maps. These are most likely to be provided to illustrate sections of the text. Topical summaries appear at the end of the passage they summarize.

Sometimes a passage is preceded, rather than followed, by a summary. Although this takes the same form as a topical summary, it's called an overview.

A passage may also be preceded by an advance organizer, which strictly speaking is not a summary at all, but it is a useful tool, in the same way that summaries are.

Let's begin by looking at topical summaries and overviews.

Topical summaries and overviews

In the discussion of headings, I grouped headings with topical summaries and overviews, labeling them organizational signals. The discussion of organizational signals in the chapter on headings thus applies equally to topical summaries. Accordingly, it won't surprise you to learn that the value of a summary of this kind is to provide a structure to help you understand the material and take effective notes. If you have a topical overview in front of you as you listen to a lecture or work your way through a text, then you have a guide to help you understand where any particular topic stands in the larger context.

Topical overviews make reading of the text faster[1] (a prepared reader is a speedy reader), and, if the text is difficult or poorly organized, more easily understood[2]. But like headings, although topical overviews and summaries may help you remember more topics, they may not help you remember the details that belong to those topics.

Using overviews and summaries

You may regard summaries that are provided for you as a substitute for taking your own notes, but the problem with this is twofold: first, taking notes is about putting things in your own words, so someone else's summary isn't going to do much for you; and second, the writer's goals are not necessarily (in fact, will almost certainly not be!) the same as yours.

But provided summaries are very useful as *guides* to what is important. A summary can also be a great priming tool. I mentioned priming at the beginning of this book; let's look at it in a little more detail.

The first step in taking notes is *not* to read the text, but to prepare yourself for it. Your mind needs to be primed; you need to have the right context in mind. If the teacher or writer has set the scene for you, perhaps with an overview or an advance organizer, then you should start by reading this. Then reflect on what you've been told. Give your mind time to gather up the relevant information, get into the right head-space. Not only that, but sort out in your mind what you need from the text. What do you expect to learn? What do you need to know?

I can't emphasize this last question enough. *What do you need to know?*

What is your goal in reading this text? Do you have specific questions that need answering? Perhaps you're preparing an essay. If so, before you start, you should spend time working out exactly what you are going to talk about. If you simply start reading in the vague hope that what you need (something you're rather foggy on) will pop out at you, you're going to spend a great deal of time to little purpose. Some thought beforehand will save you a lot of time and effort.

But perhaps you are taking notes with no more specific purpose than that the text is required reading. That's where reading an overview is particularly helpful.

Let's look at an example. Consider our familiar passage on the gene for episodic memory. Do you remember how you felt the first time you read that? Perhaps a little overwhelmed? Not sure what it all meant? Consider how you might have felt if the passage had been preceded by an overview, like this:

> Brain derived neurotrophic factor (BDNF) plays a key role in neuron growth and survival and, it now appears, memory. We inherit two copies of the BDNF gene - one from each parent - in either of two versions. Slightly more than a third of us inherit at least one copy of a version nicknamed "met," which the researchers have now linked to poorer memory. Those who inherit the "met" gene appear significantly worse at remembering events that have happened to them, probably as a result of the gene's effect on hippocampal function. Most notably, those who had two copies of the "met" gene scored only 40% on a test of episodic (event) memory, while those who had two copies of the other version scored 70%. Other types of memory did not appear to be affected. It is speculated that having the "met" gene might also increase the risk of disorders such as Alzheimer's and Parkinson's.

Now after you read a summary such as this, you should try to articulate the essence of the matter to yourself, that is, frame it in your own words.

Imagine you are telling a friend what it's about. Ignore, for the moment, any details you don't understand. Do you understand the *heart* of the matter? What is it? Don't be satisfied with your own feeling that you understand what it's going on about — if you can't put it into words, it doesn't count!

Okay, the essence of this passage is that there is a gene that's linked to a poorer memory for events. That's all. The rest is detail.

Now you've articulated the essence — described the topic — you can start to worry about the details (still looking just at the overview).

First detail: BDNF.

Do you know what that is? If you do, you've got a connection to your existing knowledge. But chances are you don't — otherwise, this would be a much easier topic! (I chose it because the material is not likely to be familiar.) So, there's something — and it's important, or it wouldn't be in the overview — that you don't understand, and you need to. You don't need to do anything with that yet. Chances are it will be explained in the text. What you do now is simply make a note (mental or actual) — *BDNF, what is it?* — to look for the answer in the text.

Now, what's the next detail? — "neuron growth and survival". Do you know what a neuron is? Do you understand what it means by "growth and survival"? If so, think on the knowledge that's dragged up — make the connections. If not, make another note.

This short passage has at least seven details that should give you pause. Here are the other five:

- "We inherit two copies" — do you understand why?

- "two versions" — do you understand what it means by "different versions"; are you confused by "two copies" and "two versions"? These are not the same thing. Read it again and make sure it's clear in your mind, or if it's not clear from the overview, make a mental note to clarify the matter when reading the text.

- "hippocampal function" — do you have any idea what this means? Maybe you've heard of the hippocampus, and guess it has something to do with that. If so, search your mind for what you know of the hippocampus. Even if all you know is that it's a structure in the brain, that's something that gives you a connection.

- "episodic (event) memory" — do you know what is meant by episodic memory? Can you guess? Guessing is good, if you don't know.

Guess, and make a note to check your guess in the text.

- "disorders such as Alzheimer's and Parkinson's" — you've probably heard of these disorders, at least the first one. Indeed, if you're naïve in this topic, this may well be the first thing that provides a real connection to what you know. Don't waste it, even though it's only peripheral to the subject of the text. It may not help you understand the topic, but because it's something familiar, it will help you remember. So make this a strong connection — dredge up what you know. Maybe a relative has Alzheimer's, or a relative of a friend. Maybe you remember that Ronald Reagan had Alzheimer's; that Michael J. Fox and Muhammad Ali have Parkinson's.

Now you're primed to read the text — you've activated any relevant knowledge, and you have a number of details you want explained.

But what about the situation when no overview is provided? Check for a summary at the end and read that. If no summary is provided, scan the text for headings. As we have seen, informative headings can provide a summary.

Advance organizers

Like overviews, advance organizers appear before the text they refer to, with the similar aim of preparing the student's mind. But advance organizers differ from overviews in that they are written at a higher level of abstraction. Overviews, like summaries, say nothing that is not in the text; advance organizers do. Advance organizers, like topical overviews, are technically something that needs to be provided by the writer or teacher. However, you can attempt to create your own *after* reading the text (technically, of course, it wouldn't be an *advance* organizer then).

Let's look at how an advance organizer for our gene-for-memory text would differ from the overview.

New research demonstrates that tiny and apparently innocuous differences in a single gene can significantly affect people's abilities. In this case, one tiny difference in a gene that is important for the growth and survival of brain cells has a dramatic effect on a person's ability to remember things that have happened to him. The finding helps explain why young, healthy people with no apparent memory problems don't all do the same on memory tests. The gene variant might also make a person more vulnerable to memory damage from age, depression, or Alzheimer's.

Compare this to the overview. The overview is much more detailed; the advance organizer isn't worried about details — it's attempting to put the study in context, to show why it is important.

Overviews and summaries act simply by selecting the important text and repeating it. Advance organizers do that too, but more importantly, they act by putting what you are about to read in context — and not everything in an advance organizer will necessarily appear in the text.

Hopefully, the advance organizer will connect the new facts and ideas you are about to learn to knowledge you already have. It follows from this that how effective any particular advance organizer is will depend on its success in doing that. This success clearly depends on the knowledge the student has.

Research has had mixed results in determining the effectiveness of advance organizers, and the very variable ability of students to use them effectively seems to be the cause[3]. Advance organizers seem to benefit able readers more than poor ones.

This doesn't mean that advance organizers are necessarily unhelpful to poor readers. Rather, it seems likely that the level of abstraction may be too high for some students, or the framework the organizer is trying to set in place refers to knowledge the student doesn't have. In other words, an advance organizer would, in principle, benefit poorer students, but the level needs to be more appropriate, with a greater emphasis on simple, concrete examples.

Interestingly, it seems that the benefit of an advancer organizer is greater if students don't read the text immediately after reading the organizer, but have a short delay before doing so[4]. Reflection time!

So, where does all this leave you? If an advance organizer is provided by the writer or your teacher, it's worth making an effort to — not simply read it — but think about it. The point of the advance organizer is to activate any existing relevant knowledge — to link the text you are going to read to the concepts already in your head — and to provide an organizing framework for the new material. It won't succeed in doing that if you don't give it some reflection time!

Moreover, you shouldn't immediately give up on it if the advance organizer is at too high a level for your current understanding. If it's a written text, try and see if any examples given in the organizer trigger other examples that are more comprehensible to you. Or see if your teacher can produce other examples that might have more meaning for you.

As for writing your own, you may well find this a valuable exercise. Rather than an advance organizer, think of this as a high-level abstract. Not a summary, but your attempt to give personal meaning to the text.

Main points

A topical summary is a straightforward string of factual statements.

Topical summaries summarize the main points without adding any new information or offering a new perspective.

Topical summaries have the same functions and disadvantages as headings.

An overview is a topical summary that precedes the text.

Overviews make it easier to read and understand text.

Like overviews, advance organizers precede the text.

Advance organizers are concerned with the big picture.

Advance organizers help you connect new facts and ideas to knowledge you already have.

Creating summaries

How useful a summary you create is depends entirely on your skill at distinguishing important information from less important.

Although summarizing is an effective strategy for learning from text, it's been estimated that perhaps half of all college students can't do it effectively[5]. Many students don't progress beyond the most basic (and ineffective) strategy: copy-delete, in which the student copies out those sentences he regards as important, leaving out the ones he doesn't regard as important.

This strategy, while relatively easy, ignores the fact that main ideas are rarely contained in a single significant sentence (otherwise, why did the author write all those words?). A main idea is contained in a *paragraph*, not a single sentence. Your goal in summarizing is to tease out all the important information contained in related sentences and combine them into a new sentence or sentences, that are as brief as can be.

In other words, your aim is to extract the *meaning* of the paragraph, the essence.

A good summary:

- is short,

- contains only, and all, the most important information, and

- is in your own words.

Here's an example, from a reasonably complex piece of text:

Human gene affects memory for events

People with a particular variant of the gene controlling the brain factor BDNF have reduced hippocampal function.

BDNF plays a key role in memory.

Two variants: "Met" variant linked to poorer episodic memory; "Val" variant more common.

"Met" variant might increase risk of Alzheimer's and other disorders involving the hippocampus.

Study finds those with two copies of "met" perform dramatically worse on tests of episodic memory but not on other memory tests.

Two copies of "met" worse than one, but any "met" variant is associated with hippocampal dysfunction.

"Met" variant less successful in distributing BDNF proteins to the synapses.

Possible connection with memory problems in old age.

Seem familiar? This is a summary from the earlier example we studied when considering headings. Because this particular example had headings that were unusually lengthy and informative, it was possible to construct a summary simply from these. But of course, headings like these are rare!

This summary could be constructed from headings because the headings were essentially topic sentences.

Identifying or creating topic sentences is a critical part of summarizing, and it is the most difficult. A researcher identified[6] five basic rules for note-taking that he used to measure the skill of students, which emphasizes this point. Here are his five "rules":

1. delete trivial material

2. delete redundant material

3. replace lists of items with a superordinate term

4. select a topic sentence

5. if no topic sentence given, create one

The researcher found that even fifth graders reliably excluded trivial and redundant details — clearly this is the easy part. But even college students only created topic sentences (when they weren't provided) half the time. Clearly the most difficult part of summarizing is to construct sentences that sum up a paragraph.

But a large part of the problem is perhaps that effective summarizing isn't achieved by rigidly following a paint-by-numbers approach. Notwithstanding all the instruction your English teacher gave you about the construction of an essay, out in the real world, text isn't necessarily so rigidly structured. More importantly, you can't simply start at the beginning of a chapter and steadily work through, paragraph by paragraph, discarding unimportant details and identifying or constructing topic sentences. The writer will say something in a later paragraph that will impact on earlier ones; emphasis will change; you'll realize that something that didn't seem important is in fact important.

So, if you're not to start at the beginning and work your way through to the end, what do you do?

Summarizing step-by-step

As I said earlier, before you start to take notes, before you even read the text, you need to prime yourself. You do this by reading any summaries provided, or studying the headings. But if none of these are provided, your last resort is to skim the text. Skimming is a skill I will discuss in more detail in my book on active reading, but basically it involves skimming your gaze lightly over a text, looking for signal words and phrases, and skipping all the information that provides background or supporting information (identifying the text structure helps with this).

Now you're prepared — you have previewed and reflected; you have some idea what you are going to find in the text and the information you are after — you can read the text.

Okay. You've read it. Now it's time to start summarizing. Let me just say again: don't start doing this until you have read the text! Some people want to 'save time' and start jotting down notes as they go. This reminds me of a boss I had way back when I was young and worked in a government department. It was the practice for us clerks to write the letters which needed to be written, the typists would then type them up (that dates me!), and then they would be passed up the chain of command to be approved — but usually amended by the bosses first, then re-typed. My boss would invariably start hacking away at the letter right from the beginning, without reading it first. What would happen, time and time again, with my letters (and it drove me wild), is that he would correct something I'd written, and then realize I'd said something in the next sentence which made his correction unnecessary. At which point he'd put a line through his comment, write "Sorry, Fiona" in the margin, and the whole thing would have to go back in the queue for the typing pool. He never learned.

So … be smart. You're in a better position because of the preparation you've done, but you still don't know how well your idea of the content matches the actual content, or how much your perspective might change when you read the complete text. Moreover, the best summaries are made without reference to the text (we'll get to that).

Now that you've read the complete text, you need to identify the main idea. Yes, you did that earlier, in your preparation. But now you check — were you right? Do you want to amend it at all? Re-word it?

It may be that the text has confused you. You thought you knew what the theme of the text was; now, drowning in details, you're not sure. If you're having trouble figuring out the main idea, look for repetition — references that are repeated throughout the text. How often a writer refers to an idea is a good clue to how important she thinks it is. Also look for opportunities for generalization. If there are lists of items, categorize them. Sometimes the main idea is hidden among the details.

Once you've worked out the main idea of the text, you need to identify the supporting ideas. Do that by grouping together paragraphs on the same topic and labelling them.

Do note that when I say "identify" the main or supporting ideas, I don't mean that the ideas will necessarily be lying around ready to be identified. You may well need to construct them from the text — that's what "working it out" means. Even if the ideas are described clearly in a single sentence, you should still try to put in your own words — only then will you know you understand it.

Finally, you should check you've done it right! On the next page you can see a checklist.

> ## Checklist
>
> Have you stated the main idea of the passage?
>
> Do you have all the important information?
>
> Have you included any information that is not important?
>
> Is it in your own words?

The most difficult part of this process is certainly constructing the main idea when it isn't succinctly expressed in a single topic sentence — remember, this is the step that even college students managed only half the time. The part students find easiest is deleting the unimportant information[7].

To summarize effectively really requires you to look beyond the surface words — to understand the text in more abstract terms than those in which the text is expressed. This may occur quite naturally when you are putting the writer's thoughts into your own words.

A simple example of a higher level of abstraction is the transformation of a list of items into a categorical grouping (as in 'rule 3': Replace lists of items with a superordinate term).

For example, if the text spoke of potatoes, peas, carrots, and broccoli, and you replaced them with the label 'vegetables'. Or to take a more complex example, you could replace hippocampus, perirhinal, parahippocampal,and entorhinal cortices, with 'brain regions involved in memory consolidation' — note that this is more specific than the broader and more standard category 'brain regions' — it is, in fact, a category created from the context of the text.

You will find it more difficult to express the ideas in the text in your own words if you keep yourself glued to the text. It is far easier to use your own words if you try and produce summaries without looking at the text.

This may account in part for why summaries are usually more effective if the student has written them after a short delay, and not immediately after reading the text.

It's worth noting, too, that summarizing after a delay has been shown to be dramatically more effective in terms of the student understanding how well they've learned the material[8]. This in turn is vitally important in enabling the student to effectively distribute his time.

> ## Rules for more effective summarizing
>
> 1. Preview and reflect
>
> 2. Read
>
> 3. Identify the main idea, and put it in your own words (without looking at the text)
>
> 4. Identify the important supporting ideas, and put them in your own words
>
> 5. Check

The "basic rules" I cited earlier can be useful to help you achieve these more abstract goals, if you're having trouble. Thus, if you can't identify the main and supporting ideas, try deleting trivial and redundant material, replacing lists of items with a superordinate (higher-level) term, and seeking out topic sentences.

Lets go back to our gene for memory example and go through it step by step. Prepare yourself — going through it step by step is a lengthy process, but nothing else will show you exactly how to tackle a difficult text.

Example

First step: Priming

We'll start by running through our preparation:

Main idea: there is a gene that's linked to poorer memory for events

Mental notes:

1. BDNF, what is it?

2. Is a neuron any cell in the brain, or is it a special type of cell? Am I right in thinking it's a cell?

3. What does it mean by "neuron growth and survival"? Do neurons grow?

4. I know we inherit a copy of each gene from our parents, so that makes two — but is "versions" the same as "copies" or something different?

5. I guess "hippocampal function" has something to do with brain function, but I don't know what kind of function they're talking about — have to check that.

6. I'm guessing "episodic memory" has to do with remembering things that have happened to you, but I better check, and I'm not sure exactly what's included in that — does it just mean events like going to a party, or everything, like remembering reading a book or meeting a person? And if so, doesn't that mean everything's episodic memory?

Look back at the text, and read it again with all this in mind.

Now, have you answered all your questions? The ones you haven't answered, or not been able to answer in any depth — does it matter? Just because you framed these questions in the beginning doesn't mean they have to be answered. You may find, on reading the text, that you don't need to answer all these questions to understand what the text is about. Don't get bogged down in details that don't matter! (On the other hand, do delve, if necessary, into details that do matter — telling which is which is half the battle.)

So, first question: BDNF, what does the text tell us about that?

It tells us that it is a growth factor, and because we are also told that it has to do with the growth and survival of neurons, we can guess that "growth factor" simply means some substance that affects cell growth. You may be happy with that level of explanation, or it may leave you still confused and uncertain. Since BDNF is a substantive part of the topic, it's worth seeking out some clarification. A simple check of Wikipedia, for those online, will bring up the information that BDNF is a neurotrophic factor — a chemical that stimulates neurogenesis, the growth of new neurons; that it's a protein that helps neurons survive and encourages new neurons to grow. (Note: I use Wikipedia as a reference source in this discussion because it is a quick and handy reference, particularly appropriate when searching for the sort of low-level information we are talking about here. You should always assess any information you find in terms of whether it's consistent with what you know from other sources — in this case, whether the information you dig out of Wikipedia is consistent with what's in the text.)

Second question: what is a neuron? If you understand it as a "brain cell", then that is really all you need to know to understand what's going on.

This brings up an important issue — judging how much detail you need. How much detail you need depends on your goal. If all you want to do is understand what this passage is about, then "neuron = brain cell" will be quite adequate. However, if you are keen to understand a broader topic than the very specific one discussed here — if, for example, this is part of a number of neurological reports you want to come to grips with — then you will want to delve more deeply into the question.

But try and keep focused. Expertise is better developed bit by bit. So for now, you might see what Wikipedia has to offer on the subject of neurons.

There's quite a lot there, so don't get bogged down. If you want to understand neuroscience, you'll need to understand neurons, but you don't need all this stuff now. Stick with what's relevant, and bookmark or print out the text for later reference. Picking out the bits that are relevant will familiarise you with the material, and gradually, as you pick out other relevant bits for different reports, you will develop your understanding of the neuron. In general, we remember best the information that is relevant to our focus.

Probably all you need to take away for now is the information that:

- a neuron is "a major class of cells in the nervous system" — which tells you that, yes, neurons are cells; no, they're not the only type of cells in the brain.

- there are different types of neurons.

- neurons are activated by electrical impulses and chemical substances.

- it is now known that new neurons can be created in the hippocampus of an adult brain.

This last point answers our third question: what does it mean by "neuron growth and survival"?

Fourth question: are "versions" and "copies" of genes the same thing? The text refers to people inheriting "at least one copy of a version", so, no, they can't be the same thing. The text also talks about "a tiny variance in the human BDNF gene, where its molecular makeup differs slightly across individuals", so from this we infer that genes can come in different versions, and which version you have depends on the copies you inherited from your parents.

Fifth question: what's meant by "hippocampal function"? The text tells us the hippocampus is "a brain area known to mediate memory", so clearly hippocampal function simply means the functioning of this brain area.

Sixth question: what's meant by "episodic memory"? The text describes tests of episodic memory as being "tasks like recalling what happened yesterday". Later on, the text refers to "other types of memory, such as semantic or working memory". So episodic memory is contrasted with semantic and working memory. Does this help? That depends on whether you know what these are!

If you're not comfortable with your level of understanding, check out Wikipedia again. That tells us that episodic memory includes autobiographical memory, that it records information about the time and place of events and your accompanying emotions, and that it contrasts with semantic memory, which is memory for facts (such as the capital of Turkey, and the characteristics of mammals). That's probably as much as you need.

Okay, by answering all those questions that were in your mind when you read the text, you hopefully have a better grasp of what the text is about. But although you understand the summary much better now, the text may have thrown up another host of questions.

Don't get bogged down in them! Ask yourself — do they matter? Is this particular detail important in helping me understand the main ideas?

Second step: Dissecting the text

Let's go through the text paragraph by paragraph, identifying and articulating the main supporting ideas. In this case, we already have a topic sentence for each set of related paragraphs, but let's see how they were created.

Here's the first paragraph:

> NIH scientists have shown that a common gene variant influences memory for events in humans by altering a growth factor in the brain's memory hub. On average, people with a particular version of the gene that codes for brain derived neurotrophic factor (BDNF) performed worse on tests of episodic memory — tasks like recalling what happened yesterday. They also showed differences in activation of the hippocampus, a brain area known to mediate memory, and signs of decreased neuronal health and interconnections. These effects are likely traceable to limited movement and secretion of BDNF within cells, according to the study, which reveals how a gene affects the normal range of human memory, and confirms that BDNF affects human hippocampal function much as it does animals'.

And here's the topic sentence that was created: **People with a particular variant of the gene controlling the brain factor BDNF have reduced hippocampal function.**

The first thing you should observe is that this sentence rather surprisingly doesn't include the important information that the gene variant affects memory for events. This is because that information is already included in the main idea: "there is a gene that's linked to a poorer memory for events". So we don't need to repeat that, even though it is an important part of this opening paragraph. We are looking for the supporting ideas.

The second thing that may surprise you is that a topic sentence needs to be created at all. You may feel that the writer has provided a topic sentence. And so he has — but is it one that suits your purposes? It misses out crucial information because it is, quite correctly, attempting to explain the main idea of the whole passage in terms simple enough for a novice to understand. But you're looking for important supporting details — "BDNF" and "hippocampus" are important details.

The third thing to notice is that this sentence mentions BDNF, but only describes it as a "brain factor", and doesn't provide any explanation at all of "hippocampal function". No one but you can decide how much of a reminder you need. You may want to expand "brain factor" to "brain growth factor", and "hippocampal function" to "function of the hippocampus (important brain region for memory)". You may need to add even more detail (e.g., "BDNF (chemical that encourages growth of new neurons)") — notice that this isn't detail that's in the paragraph you're supposedly summarizing; it's in the next.

And finally, I hope you noticed that the topic sentence took information from several sentences — here's the paragraph again, with the relevant bits highlighted:

> NIH scientists have shown that a common **gene variant** influences memory for events in humans by altering a **growth factor** in the brain's memory hub. On average, people with a particular version of the **gene that codes for brain derived neurotrophic factor (BDNF)** performed worse on tests of episodic memory — tasks like recalling what happened yesterday. They also showed **differences in activation of the hippocampus**, a brain area known to mediate memory, and signs of decreased neuronal health and interconnections. These effects are likely traceable to limited movement and secretion of BDNF within cells, according to the study, which reveals how a gene affects the normal range of human memory, and confirms that **BDNF affects human hippocampal function** much as it does animals'.

Here's the next paragraph:

> Long known to be critical for the growth and survival of neurons, BDNF has also recently been shown to play a key role in memory and

hippocampal function in animals. To find out if it works similarly in humans, the researchers explored the consequences of a tiny variance in the human BDNF gene, where its molecular makeup differs slightly across individuals.

Now the topic sentence for that was simply:

BDNF plays a key role in memory. You may feel you need more detail about how genes vary; if so, incorporate that into the next topic sentence, which covers the third and fourth paragraphs:

People inherit two copies of the BDNF gene - one from each parent - in either of two versions. Slightly more than a third inherit at least one copy of a version nicknamed "met," which the researchers have now linked to poorer memory. It's called "met" because its chemical sequence contains the amino acid methionine in a location where the more common version, "val," contains valine.

"We are finding that this one amino acid substitution exerts a substantial influence on human memory, presumably because of its effects on the biology of the hippocampus," said Weinberger.

The topic sentence for this was: **Two variants: "Met" variant linked to poorer episodic memory; "Val" variant more common**, and, again, you might find that this is insufficient detail for you. It all depends on how well you have understood the details.

In the discussion of highlighting, I said, "select those details that you want to remember and don't think you will (don't highlight facts simply because they are important, if you already know them, or believe you will remember them without help)". This is true for summarizing as well. You are not trying to record everything you read / hear — you are recording what *you need help to remember*. You should only write enough to cue you to remember all the other associated details. Which is why no-one can make a blanket rule about how much detail should be in 'good' notes — it depends on the individual's needs and abilities. Of course, if you are taking notes for other people to share, the notes will need to be fuller.

But whether or not you need to note the details, you do need to understand enough to judge what's important and what's not. For example, you may have been thrown by the sentence: "It's called 'met' because its chemical sequence contains the amino acid methionine in a location where the more common version, 'val', contains valine." If that leaves you completely bewildered, then it's probably a good idea to dig up some more information. The distinction between 'met' and 'val' is what this passage is all about.

But to dig further, you need to be able to recognize what the crucial word or phrase is. It's not methionine, or valine, or chemical sequence, or location. It's "amino acid". Put that into Wikipedia and, unless you are comfortable with chemistry, you will probably be a little overwhelmed. But don't run away! Just scan the text for something that makes sense.

Hopefully you will notice that "Amino acids are the basic structural building units of proteins. They form short polymer chains". What should have attracted your attention are the words "proteins" and "chains". We established earlier that BDNF was a protein, and the sentence we are trying to clarify used the word "sequence", which sounds like it might have something to do with a chain. So we might now be able to come to grips with the sentence "It's called 'met' because its chemical sequence contains the amino acid methionine in a location where the more common version, 'val', contains valine", by reminding ourselves that we're talking about two variants of a gene for BDNF, which is a protein, that must in one variant have methionine in one part of its chain of amino acids, and in the other variant, valine in the same place in the chain.

The next paragraph is interesting because the two sentences that comprise it do not really belong together, emphasizing the perils of assuming everything you read follows the rules you were taught about paragraphing.

> Despite its negative effect on memory, the "met" version's survival in the human genome suggests that it "may confer some compensatory advantage in other biological processes," note the researchers. Although they found that it does not confer increased susceptibility to schizophrenia, they suggest that the "met" variant might contribute to risk for - or increase functional impairment in - other disorders involving hippocampal dysfunction, such as Alzheimer's disease or mood disorders.

If you read this paragraph with insufficient care, you might be pardoned for believing that the second sentence expands on the first, leading to the following possible topic sentence: "evolutionary advantage of "met" gene may include increased risk of Alzheimer's and mood disorders, but not schizophrenia"!

You'll notice that I didn't include in my topic sentence the idea that the gene might give some sort of compensatory advantage, which is pure speculation, nor the negative finding that there was no link to schizophrenia.

The next paragraph is a necessary introduction to the section that follows, but contains nothing that needs to be included in your notes. This emphasizes why you shouldn't stick too literally to the instruction you may have been given, to find a topic sentence for each paragraph.

> Drawing on participants in the NIMH intramural sibling study of schizophrenia, Egan and colleagues first assessed their hippocampal function and related it to their BDNF gene types.

However, although you don't need to record anything, you do need to understand the essence of it. But remember, don't get bogged down in details that don't matter. Thus, you don't need to understand exactly what the "NIMH intramural sibling study of schizophrenia" is, but you do need to understand the nature of the study: that it was a study into schizophrenia, and the subjects' hippocampal function and BDNF gene type was assessed.

The next paragraph is a crucial one, giving us the main finding of the study:

> Among 641 normal controls, schizophrenia patients, and their unaffected siblings, those who had inherited two copies of the "met" variant scored significantly lower than their matched peers on tests of verbal episodic (event) memory. Most notably, normal controls with two copies of "met" scored 40 percent on delayed recall, compared to 70 percent for those with two copies of "val." BDNF gene type had no significant effect on tests of other types of memory, such as semantic or working memory.

If you're familiar with the language of experimental studies, this will be clear to you. If you're not, there will be a few 'jargon' terms that might give you pause: "controls"; "matched peers"; "delayed recall"; "significant effect". But it's not necessary to understand these terms exactly; you can probably guess enough of the meaning from the context to understand the essentials. Namely, that the **Study finds those with two copies of "met" perform dramatically worse on tests of episodic memory but not on other memory tests**.

The next paragraphs start to become more technical:

> The researchers then measured brain activity in two separate groups of healthy subjects while they were performing a working memory task that normally turns off hippocampus activity. Functional magnetic resonance imaging (fMRI) scans revealed that those with one copy of "met" showed a pattern of activation along the sides of the hippocampus, in contrast to lack of activation among those with two copies of "val."

> Next, an MRI scanner was used to measure levels of a marker inside neurons indicating the cell's health and abundance of synapses - tiny junctions through which neurons communicate with each other. Again, subjects with one copy of "met" had lower levels of the marker, N-acetyl-aspartate (NAA), than matched individuals with two copies of

"val." Analysis showed that NAA levels dropped as the number of inherited "met" variants increased, suggesting a possible "dose effect."

There will probably be a number of details that aren't crystal clear to you; the question is, do any of them matter?

The first paragraph talks about a "working memory task" that normally "turns off hippocampus activity", and "Functional magnetic resonance imaging (fMRI) scans" showing a "pattern of activation along the sides of the hippocampus". Again, you don't need to understand exactly what these all mean, but you do need to have a broad understanding of what's being talked about. The main message here is there is abnormal activity in the hippocampus in those carrying the "met" gene. The key words in the text that should have keyed you to this are: "**normally** turns **off** hippocampus activity" and "those with one copy of 'met' showed a pattern of activation" — i.e. activity when there should be none. This interpretation being confirmed by "lack of activation among those with two copies of 'val'."

The second paragraph is more puzzling, most particularly the second sentence. The first thing is that 'marker' isn't explained. A quick search using Google reveals that NAA is a "marker of neuronal loss", which fits with the reference in the text and is probably as much as you need to know. The really important point of this sentence is tied up with this phrase "dose effect". If you're not familiar with this, you may nevertheless be able to guess the meaning from the rest of the two sentences. "NAA levels dropped as the number of inherited "met" variants increased" indicates that the levels of NAA were highest when the number of "met" genes was zero; lower when the person had one "met" gene; and lowest for those people who had two "met" genes.

My topic sentence for these two paragraphs was: **Two copies of "met" worse than one, but any "met" variant is associated with hippocampal dysfunction**.

We've dealt with the heart of the matter. My next topic sentence encapsulated the next four paragraphs:

Unlike other growth factors, hippocampal BDNF is secreted, in part, in response to neuronal activity, making it a likely candidate for a key role in synaptic plasticity, learning and memory. To explore possible mechanisms underlying the observed "met"- related memory effect, the researchers examined the distribution, processing and secretion of the BDNF proteins expressed by the two different gene variants within hippocampal cells. When they tagged the gene variants with green fluorescent protein and introduced them into cultured neurons, they discovered that "val" BDNF spreads throughout the cell and into the branch-like dendrites that form synapses, while "met" BDNF mostly clumps inside the cell body without being transported to the synapses. To regulate memory function, BDNF must be secreted near the synapses.

"We were surprised to see that 'met' BDNF secretion can't be properly regulated by neural activity," said Lu.

The observed memory decrements are likely traceable to the failure of "met" BDNF to reach the synapses, as well as its inability to secrete in response to neuronal activity, say the researchers.

"Our study provides direct in vivo data that the molecular mechanisms related to activity dependent BDNF secretion and signaling, such as synaptic plasticity, may underlie humans' greatly expanded verbally-mediated memory system, just as it does for more rudimentary forms of memory in animals," said Egan.

You may have paused over "synaptic plasticity". Does it matter that you don't understand exactly what is meant by that? Here's a way to help you judge. Do you remember what I said earlier about repetition? If you scan the text for mention of "synaptic plasticity", you will see it mentioned twice; "synapses" — a clearly related word — is mentioned four times. This is a lot of repetition, and suggests you do need to have some understanding of synapses and synaptic plasticity.

But wait — synapses were mentioned for the first time in an earlier paragraph. We weren't interested then; now we are. Going back, we see synapses are defined as "tiny junctions through which neurons communicate with each other". So, if you understand from this that synapses are a part of the neuron that are critical for neuronal activity — processing information — that is probably all you need for now.

You may have also paused over "the distribution, processing and secretion of the BDNF proteins". A scan of the text reveals that secretion (in one of its verbal forms) is mentioned four times — looks like that's important too. But your own knowledge of the meaning of the word 'secretion' may be enough for you to understand its meaning in this context — you don't need to understand exactly how chemicals interact with neurons.

You probably don't understand what is meant by "tagged the gene variants with green fluorescent protein" or "cultured neurons", but these are only mentioned once. If you infer from the text that they must be particular techniques for finding out what's going on at the cellular level, that's all you need.

Now that we understand, broadly, what these paragraphs are about, we can reduce their complexity to a very simple sentence: **"Met" variant less successful in distributing BDNF proteins to the synapses**.

Last paragraph, very short:

> In following-up their leads, the researchers are searching for a possible BDNF connection with the memory problems and hippocampal changes of Alzheimer's disease, depression and normal aging.

Which I simply rendered as: **Possible connection with memory problems in old age**. And there we are!

Summarizing isn't just about the notes you take

That took a long time to work through. Did you notice that most of the time was spent in making sure you understood what the text was about, and that most of that understanding wasn't explicitly translated into notes?

This is a useful lesson, and points to something you should take to heart: the less you understand, the fuller your notes will tend to be — because you can't tell what's important and what's not. The more you understand, the more scanty your notes will be — because you have captured the gist, you have recorded only what is important.

Most of the texts you study, of course, will not be as difficult as the one we have just taken apart. Normally, the text you are studying will be on a topic that has some familiarity to you. But by choosing what was hopefully an unfamiliar topic, the process of taking notes and searching for meaning should be more clearly revealed.

Exercise 5.1

Here's a simpler text to practice on. Because this is a brief text, there are no headings or previews to study beforehand. This is a good text to practice your skimming on.

Skim the text, then put the main idea in your own words. Identify the structure of the text. Note down any questions or uncertainties you have. Read the text and write a brief summary. Remember your checklist when you're done.

How blood flows

We all know that blood flows through our body in continuous motion, and that our heart is the pump that drives this motion. But the circulatory system is best understood not as a single system but in terms of its three constituent parts — pulmonary circulation (involving the lungs), coronary circulation (involving the heart), and systemic circulation (involving the blood vessels).

Pulmonary circulation is the movement of blood from the heart to the lungs, and back to the heart again.

The heart has four chambers — the upper chambers are called atriums; the lower chambers are called ventricles. Blood, with all the waste products it has collected in its journey through the body (most particularly carbon dioxide), enters the heart through the right atrium, via two large veins — the inferior vena cava and the superior vena cava. The inferior vena cava carries the blood from the lower half of the body; the superior from the upper half.

When the right atrium is filled with blood, it contracts, pushing the blood into the right ventricle, which then likewise contracts, pushing the blood into the pulmonary artery. The pulmonary artery carries the blood to the lungs, where carbon dioxide and oxygen are exchanged. The blood, now cleaned of its waste and rich in oxygen (because the oxygen drawn into the lungs through breathing binds with blood), is then carried by the pulmonary veins back to the heart — to the left atrium this time. From whence, in the same process as before, it passes through to the left ventricle, and then leaves the heart through the main artery — the biggest artery in the body — the aorta. From there, it begins to circulate throughout the body.

Coronary circulation refers to the movement of blood *within* the heart. Heart tissue needs nourishment, and this nourishment comes through capillaries in the heart.

So the heart and lungs have their own systems; systemic circulation is the part of the circulatory system that supplies nourishment to the tissues throughout the rest of the body. It does this, of course, through the blood vessels —arteries, veins, and capillaries. Arteries carry blood *away* from the heart. Veins carry blood *to* the heart. Capillaries connect the arteries to veins.

Because the heart is a pump, blood comes out in spurts, causing the outflow to vary in volume and speed. This means that blood flow can occur at a high pressure, which is why the arteries need to have thick walls, and why they need to be able to expand and contract to accommodate the changes in pressure.

Veins, on the other hand, carry blood to the heart in a continuous, even flow, and are therefore thinner than arteries, and less elastic.

Systemic circulation begins with the aorta. The aorta branches into many smaller arteries (the smallest are called arterioles), which carry the fresh, oxygenated blood through the body. Finally, the blood reaches the capillaries, where the oxygen and nutrients carried by the blood are released. The de-oxygenated blood now enters the veins, to travel back to the heart and begin its journey once more.

Main points

How effective your summary is depends on your skill at distinguishing important information from less important.

A good summary:

- is short,

- contains only, and all, the most important information, and

- is in your own words.

Identifying or creating topic sentences is the most difficult part of summarizing.

The first step in summarizing is to prepare yourself for it. Read any overview, advance organizer, summary, or headings provided, or skim the text if none are provided.

Reflect. Try to articulate the main idea. Work out what you want from the text. Think of specific questions and uncertainties you have.

Read the text.

Identify the main idea. Without looking at the text, put it in your own words.

Identify the main supporting ideas. Without looking at the text, put them in your own words.

Check that you've answered your initial questions and clarified your uncertainties.

Only record what you need help to remember. The more you know, the less you need to record.

Review questions

1. Topical summaries
   a. offer a more abstract perspective on the material
   b. don't provide any information that is not in the text
   c. are the same as overviews
   d. offer new details, that aren't in the text being summarized
   e. help you remember all the details

2. Topical summaries that are provided in the text
   a. can be used for your own notes
   b. are useful guides to what's important in the text
   c. are usefully read first, to get you thinking about the text
   d. can't be understood until you've read the text
   e. aren't worth reading, because they won't be relevant to your goals

3. Advance organizers are the same as topical summaries   T / F

4. Advance organizers
   a. appear at the end of the text
   b. offer a more abstract perspective on the material
   c. don't provide any information that is not in the text
   d. are most useful to poor readers
   e. help you activate your relevant knowledge

5. To summarize well, you need to understand the material at a 'higher', more abstract level   T / F

6. To get the most out of advance organizers

    a.   read them *after* reading the text

    b.   allow time to reflect before reading the text

    c.   skim them quickly

    d.   spend more time on them than on the text itself

7. Summarizing involves

    a.   copying out important sentences or phrases

    b.   noting down all the interesting details

    c.   putting the important information into your own words

    d.   noting down all the complicated information

    e.   creating one sentence for each paragraph

8. When you're summarizing from a textbook

    a.   take notes as you read

    b.   read the text first

    c.   read any provided summaries first

    d.   read any headings before reading the text

    e.   skim the text, then take notes as you read

9. Summaries are most effectively created

    a.   without looking at the text

    b.   paragraph by paragraph, as long as you've studied the text first

    c.   from all the questions you thought of when trying to understand the text

    d.   from skimming, without getting bogged down in the details of the text

    e.   by rewriting summaries provided for you

10. The key to creating a good summary is

    a. knowing what to ignore

    b. finding the main idea

    c. recognizing what's important

    d. being able to put things into your own words

    e. knowing how to format the information appropriately

Graphic summaries

There are more types of summary than straightforward lists of factual statements, or indeed any sort of strictly verbal summary. In this chapter, I look at various types of summary that combine visual and verbal elements. I also go into some detail about the principles of visual language, and how these can help you construct good diagrams. Even if you're not interested in being able to make graphic summaries yourself, this discussion will help you better 'read' diagrams in your textbook — too many students fail to pay due attention to these. Finally, I touch on the issue of many students being intimidated by illustrations or by drawing.

Now a **topical summary** is, as I said, the simplest type of summary — a straightforward string of factual statements. Graphic summaries (which come in different types) re-organize the text.

Outlines and Graphic Organizers

In an outline, topics are listed with their subtopics in a linear format, like this one (next page):

Branches of Government (U.S.A.)		
I	Executive Branch	
	A. Represented by:	President
	B. Powers:	Can recommend legislation; veto legislation; appoint judges
	C. Length of Term:	4 years; maximum term 8 years
II	Legislative Branch	
	A. Represented by:	Congress
	B. Powers:	Can enact legislation; override veto, reject and impeach judges; impeach President
	C. Length of Term:	2 years (House of Representatives) or 6 years (Senate); no maximum term
III	Judicial Branch	
	A. Represented by:	Supreme Court and other federal courts
	B. Powers:	Can declare legislation unconstitutional
	C. Length of Term:	life

Graphic organizers show the same sort of information, but in a more visual format, like this tree diagram:

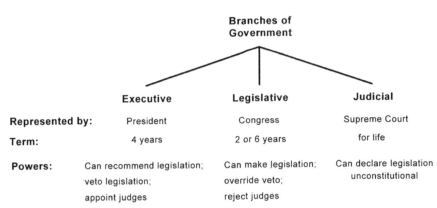

Although graphic organizers can come in many forms, most commonly they are either tree diagrams or matrices. Here is a matrix of the same information:

	Executive Branch	Legislative Branch	Judicial Branch
Represented by	President	Congress	Supreme Court
Term	4 years	2 or 6 years	Life
Powers	Can recommend legislation; veto legislation; appoint judges	Can enact legislation; override veto, reject and impeach judges; impeach President	Can declare legislation unconstitutional

Basically, graphic organizers are visual outlines showing relationships. Both outlines and graphic organizers are useful strategies for hierarchical information. However, while an outline does pick out the most important information and does show hierarchical relations (and, as you may have noticed, can include more detail more easily), it is not as effective in showing the relationships *between* concepts.

Compare the examples. In the outline, the clusters *within* a topic are clear, but the relations *between* topics — between the clusters — are not. That is, in the outline you can readily see the various attributes of each branch, but you can't so easily compare one branch to another.

The graphic organizer, on the other hand, allows connections between clusters to be more readily seen. Notice how much easier it is to grasp the similarities and differences between the different branches of the U.S. Government when looking at the tree diagram or the matrix, compared with looking at the outline.

In general, graphic organizers are more effective than outlines — but not invariably. In a study involving text summaries, graphic organizers were superior only when the students had enough time to study them properly[1] — but where the students did have enough time, those who had studied the graphic organizer tested just as well after two days as they had when tested immediately, while those who had studied the outline performed more poorly (and those who had only read the text were worst of all). In other words, graphic organizers are much better for long-term recall (which is, after all, what you usually want!). This appears even more true when the text is longer[2].

But sometimes graphic organizers are less effective than outlines, and this may be because graphic organizers can make it *too* easy to see the relations. Because of this, the reader doesn't need to work as hard to understand the material, with the consequence that the material isn't processed to the extent that it needs to be for lasting memory. This doesn't apply, of course, if you're constructing the graphic organizer yourself.

Graphic organizers have an advantage over outlines in terms of cognitive load. Remember how I said working memory is thought to have two sub-systems — one that is essentially visual, and one essentially auditory. When we read text, notwithstanding we are receiving the information through our visual sense, we tend to encode it through auditory working memory (because words are fundamentally sound-based). There is evidence that graphic organizers use visual working memory more than auditory, while outlines use auditory more than visual. The advantage of a graphic organizer, therefore, may lie partly in its reduction of cognitive load — that is, by spreading the load on working memory between both systems[3].

Additionally, the use of visual information in addition to verbal information creates more retrieval paths (paths along the connected links from initial cue to the memory you're looking for), increasing the chances of finding the information again.

All of this means that if outlines or graphic organizers are provided for you, even if the same information is also provided in the text, it's worth spending time studying the outline/graphic. If an outline is provided, consider re-drawing the information as a graphic organizer. If neither is provided, and the material is appropriate (we'll get to that), then consider formatting your notes in the form of a graphic organizer or outline.

As far as producing these yourself is concerned, outlines are easier to produce than graphic organizers, which is why they are much more popular. Although outlines are in general less effective than graphic organizers, both are generally more effective than conventional notes.

In two studies comparing note-taking formats in a lecture[4], both outlines and matrix notes were usually more detailed, better organized, and contained more ideas. Matrix notes were also slightly more coherent. But of course the material was compatible with a matrix format, which is not always the case.

Although a graphic organizer is more effective, an outline is certainly sufficient in the right circumstances. Because it is easier to construct than a graphic organizer, if the material can be adequately described in an outline, you should use it. This will depend partly on the material itself, and partly on your goal. If you're simply aiming to learn the "facts" (i.e., you're not trying to develop your understanding), then research indicates an outline will be just as productive as a graphic organizer[5]. If the text is short (1000 words or less), an outline is probably better[6]. But with longer and more complex material, it would seem that graphic organizers are worth the trouble. In such cases, research also suggests that several graphic organizers are most effective[7] — a warning that we shouldn't try to cram too much information into a graphic organizer.

Identifying the text structure can help you decide what sort of format is most appropriate. Remember, too, that graphic organizers, like outlines, are not designed to provide full notes — so you shouldn't be trying to include everything. It's all about selecting what's important.

Which to use

Graphic organizers

- need more time to process than outlines
- are of little value when the text is short and simple
- are helpful for constructing super-clusters
- are helpful for showing relationships between clusters

Outlines

- are easier and quicker to process than graphic organizers
- are better for shorter, simpler texts
- are effective for rote-learning facts
- are useful for showing hierarchical information and relationships *within* clusters, but not for displaying relationships *between* clusters

---

Constructing outlines or graphic organizers

As I said, these type of summaries are good for displaying hierarchical information; the reverse is true too — they're *only* good for displaying hierarchical information. Now, much of the text you study will be hierarchical, but this will be true to varying degrees. Some topics will be rigidly hierarchical (particularly in the sciences), but others will have only small portions of information that can be expressed in a hierarchical format. So the first question you have to ask yourself is: is this information best expressed in a hierarchical format? (If you've identified the text structure, you will know the answer to that.)

The second question is: if it is, what type of format? A tree, a matrix, a flowchart, or perhaps something more idiosyncratic?

Don't let yourself get too bogged down trying to work out the right format. Often (especially in the beginning, when you are still mastering these skills), you simply have to try out different formats. It's only through practice that you'll build up your sense of what format is right for your information.

Here is a step-by-step guide for you to use in your practice:

Constructing a graphic organizer

1. Divide your text into passages of around 1500 words

2. Outline the main ideas in the passage

3. Choose a graphical organizer format that fits the structure of the information

4. Fit your main ideas into the format

5. If it doesn't work, reconsider the structure of the information

6. Try again!

(Steps recommended by Horton & Lovitt 1989[8])

Exercise 6.1

Here's a text (less than 1000 words long) for you to practice on:

Introducing brain cells

The brain contains two types of nerve cell: **neurons** and **glia**. There are, roughly, some 100 billion neurons in the human brain. There are ten times as many glia. Yet it is neurons we talk about all the time. Of course, it is neurons that are important! But glia are the "glue" that hold the neurons together, and the latest research suggests that glia are more important than we have thought.

But neurons, although only 10% of our brain cells, do perform most of the information processing, which is why they have always been the principal focus of research.

Neurons, like glia, are a broad class of cells. There are several different types of neuron, but they all have certain attributes in common. They all have a **cell body / soma**, containing the **cell nucleus**. They all have thin tubes radiating from the cell body. These are called **neurites**, and come in two flavors: **axons** and **dendrites**. There is usually only one axon, and it is of uniform thickness, and very long by comparison with dendrites (axons can be over a meter in length). A neuron contains many dendrites, which are very short (rarely more than 2mm) and usually taper to a fine point.

It is the axon that carries the output of the neuron. It is the dendrites, which come in contact with many axons, that receive the incoming signals.

The soma, the cell body, is roughly spherical and contains the same organelles contained in any animal cell. The most important are the nucleus, the rough endoplasmic reticulum, the smooth endoplasmic reticulum, the Golgi apparatus, and the mitochondria.

The nucleus holds the chromosomes, which contain the DNA.

Endoplasmic reticulum are, very basically, folded membranes. Rough endoplasmic reticulum exist in all cells, but are particularly abundant in neurons. Rough ER contains **ribosomes**, tiny balls vitally involved in protein synthesis. Rough ER contrasts with smooth ER, which is just the same except that the membranes don't contain ribosomes. The function of smooth ER depends on its location within the cell. Most smooth ER plays no role in protein synthesis.

Yet another type of folded membrane is the Golgi apparatus, where processing of the proteins, after their assembly, takes place. It is thought that, among other functions, the Golgi apparatus is involved in sorting proteins for delivery to different parts of the neuron.

The last vital structure within the neuron is the mitochondrion. The function of this type of cell is to supply the energy the cell needs to function.

The shape of a neuron is governed by its **cytoskeleton**. The cytoskeleton consists of three types of element: **microtubules**, **microfilaments**, and **neurofilaments**.

Of these, by far the biggest are the microtubules, which may be thought of as hollow tubes that run through neurites. Neurofilaments are between microtubules and microfilaments in size. Similar filaments are found in cells other than neurons — one such is keratin, which, bundled together, makes hair. Unlike microtubules and microfilaments, both of which are made up of polymers, neurofilaments are made from single long protein molecules. This makes them very strong, and also very stable. However, neurofilaments can cause problems — the neurofibrillary tangles characteristic of Alzheimer's disease are neurofilaments gone wild.

Microfilaments are only about as thick as the cell membrane. Although they're found throughout the neuron, they're particularly abundant in the neurites.

These structures — the soma, the organelles within, the membrane, the cytoskeleton — exist in all cells, but now we come to a part of the neuron that is unique to neurons: the axon. As was mentioned, the axon is the means by which the neuron can send its message on — it's the output mechanism. The important thing to remember is that neurons, unlike other cells in the body, aren't in physical contact with each other. To communicate with each other they need something to leap the gap between them.

The synapse is the point of contact between the neurons, and information flows from across the gap between neurons in a process called **synaptic transmission**, which involves the release of chemicals called **neurotransmitters**.

The other type of neurite is the dendrites, which derive their name from the Greek for tree. This is because the dendrites, as they branch out from the soma in profusion, resemble the branches of a tree.

Neurons can be categorized in various ways. They can be classified by the number of neurites they have. A neuron with one neurite is **unipolar**; one with two is **bipolar**; one with more is **multipolar**. Most neurons are multipolar.

They can also be classified according to the shape and size of the dendritic tree, (e.g., pyramidal cells, stellate cells), or according to whether their dendrites have spines (**spiny** vs **aspinous**). They can also be classified according to the connections they make: **primary sensory neurons** connect with sensory surfaces; **motor neurons** connect with muscles; **interneurons** connect with other neurons. Most neurons are interneurons.

Neurons can also be classified according to axon length: **projection neurons** (or **Golgi Type I**) have long axons that extend from one part of the brain to another; **local circuit neurons** (or **Golgi Type II**) have short axons.

And finally, they can be classified according to chemistry, that is, on the particular neurotransmitters they release.

But most of the brain is taken up by glia, the support cells. Most glia are a type called **astrocytes**. It's the astrocytes that fill the spaces between neurons. **Oligodendroglia** provide the insulation for axons in the brain and spinal cord. **Schwann cells** are similar to the oligodendroglia, fulfilling the same function outside the brain and spinal cord, in the peripheral nervous system.

Multimedia summaries

What about information that isn't hierarchical?

Multimedia summaries are particularly appropriate (and valuable) for scientific explanations — for information that involves cause-&-effect relationships. In multimedia summaries, pictures and words are combined.

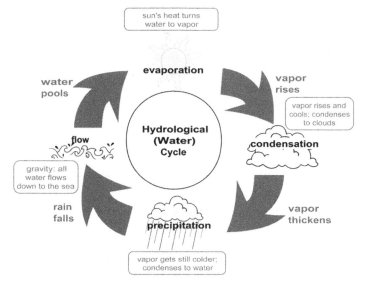

Research suggests a multimedia summary that combines both visual and verbal formats, but only has a small amount of text, is more effective than a purely verbal summary. It also indicates that illustrations are most useful when they portray a series of steps, in a cause-and-effect chain, with explanatory text that is integrated with the illustrations — as in the above example.

Notice how the words are tightly integrated with the images. Each image has a one-word label plus a brief description. Each arrow has its own explanatory label. Without the words, the pictures would lose much of their value, but without the images, the words would lose a significant amount of their memorability. Even if you have both, presented separately much of the help they give each other is lost.

Integration of text and illustration is critical. For example, a study that used computerized instruction found dramatic improvement in memory when the narration was synchronous with the animation, but no improvement when the narration was presented either before or after the text. This confirms other research using more conventional media (e.g., illustrations in textbooks).

Richard Mayer has carried out a number of experimental studies involving college students' understanding and recall of scientific material in various conditions. From this he tentatively concludes that there are four conditions under which illustrations can help learning:

- when the text contains a cause-and-effect chain rather than a list of facts

- when the illustration contain a series of frames showing the steps, together with integrated labels, rather than a one-frame static image

- when the students are unfamiliar with the subject

- when the students are tested on their understanding rather than their ability to simply regurgitate rote-learned material

When all of these conditions are met, the impact of illustrations can be dramatic.

Notice that of these four conditions, two concern the user and the use, while the third concerns the type of information being represented. Only one concerns the graphic itself. However, following Mayer, we can also say that the best multimedia summaries are[9]:

- **concise**: there's a small number of simple illustrations and only a small number of words

- **coherent**: illustrations are presented in a cause-and-effect sequence

- **coordinated**: text is presented together with the relevant illustration.

Obeying these rules can make all the difference between an effective and an ineffective summary (bearing in mind the need for the right context, in terms of user, use, and information type).

It's worth noting that these three strategies all have the effect of reducing the load on working memory, which is presumably why they are beneficial. Similarly, the main approach to constructing effective multimedia environments (discussion of which is outside the scope of this book) has been to try and reduce cognitive load.

This suggests not only that multimedia summaries may be of particular benefit to those with a low working memory capacity, but also that, regardless of your working memory capacity, such summaries will be of particular benefit if you are in circumstances which impact on working memory. For example, if you are stressed or anxious (which typically 'uses up' some of your working memory), or multitasking (such as listening to music or engaging in social media while you study).

Getting the most from multimedia summaries

Students who tend to ignore or neglect diagrams might find the following novel strategy helpful. Not usually thought of in a study context, this strategy involves implementation intentions. Implementation intentions are a strategy for helping you remember things you need or plan to do, such as picking up bread on the way home, or dropping off something next time you're in someone's neighborhood. They're often described in the form of if-then statements.

So, for example, in a study[10] investigating the benefits of such statements in learning from multimedia summaries, researchers used statements like these:

- "If I have finished reading a page, then I will carefully re-read all paragraphs!"
- "If I am looking at a picture, then I will search for its central elements with regard to content!"
- "If I have read a paragraph, then I will search the picture for the contents described therein!"

These three intentions each cover a different aspect of multimedia learning: processing the text, processing the image, and integrating the two.

You might think it sounds unnatural, and a bit silly, to say such things to yourself. In the study, students were instructed to transcribe the statements twice, and to imagine how they would later realize the intention. As with anything, a bit of practice will clear the awkwardness away, and eventually, if you train yourself to do this habitually, you won't need the explicit statements any more.

A thing to note is that there's no clear evidence that these particular intentions are better than any other. Here's the full set of statements used in the study:

- To encourage text processing:
    - "If I have opened a new page, then I will carefully study the title first!"
    - "If I have finished reading a page, then I will carefully re-read all paragraphs!"
    - "If I have read a paragraph, then I will search for references to previous paragraphs!"
- To encourage image processing:
    - "If I have opened a new page, then I will carefully study the picture first!"
    - "If I am looking at a picture, then I will search for its central elements with regard to content!"
    - "If I have looked at a picture, then I will put its central elements into context with each other!"
- To encourage integration:
    - "If I have read a paragraph, then I will search the picture for the contents described therein!"
    - "If I have looked at a picture, then I will search the text for explanations of the examined picture elements!"
    - "If I want to click to the next page, then I first carefully study the picture to verify my understanding of the text!"

It may even be better to come up with your own, so feel free to do so, or at least to tweak these. See what sits best for you. The only thing to remember is that you want one from each aspect — but only to the extent that you need the assistance. You might be confident of your text processing skills, for example, and so would only need to encourage image processing and integration. Choose statements in light of the tasks you feel you need to be reminded of.

And don't feel it has to be in the form of an if-then statement. It may be enough, for example, to have a simple reminder to look out for signals in the text that direct your attention to specific elements in the diagram. (Such signals are particularly useful for students with poor knowledge in the topic.)

Given that you've mastered the first step — that of actually paying attention to the image — how do you tackle it?

One strategy that has been shown to improve learning from multimedia summaries is self-explanation[11]. This essentially involves asking yourself why something might be so. I discuss this strategy, which is useful in a variety of situations, in the section on connection strategies.

Another strategy is to rewrite or add labels to the diagram. As with paraphrasing text, the action of putting things into your own words helps you understand, and shows you what you don't understand.

One problem with many illustrations is that they include a lot of irrelevant information, which gets in the way of learning. This is why it's important to develop your ability to read and evaluate pictures and diagrams. You need to learn when it's worth your while to put effort into an image, and what aspects should be attended to. You can use the rules I set out above to help you judge whether a summary is worth attending to, and 'fix' it if it isn't.

What do I mean by that? Here's an example of an ineffective (but quite typical) summary:

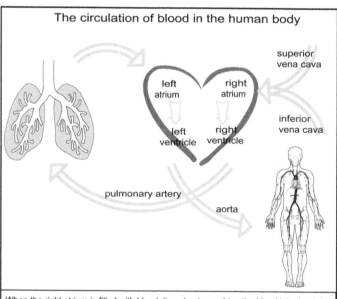

The circulation of blood in the human body

superior vena cava

left atrium right atrium

inferior vena cava

left ventricle right ventricle

pulmonary artery

aorta

When the right atrium is filled with blood, it contracts, pushing the blood into the right ventricle, which then contracts, pushing the blood into the pulmonary artery.
The pulmonary artery carries the blood to the lungs, where carbon dioxide and oxygen are exchanged.
The blood is then carried by the pulmonary veins back to the left atrium.
The left atrium fills with blood, then contracts, pushing the blood into the left ventricle, which then contracts, pushing the blood into the aorta.
The aorta branches into many smaller arteries, that carry the fresh, oxygenated blood through the body. Finally, the blood reaches the capillaries, where the oxygen and nutrients carried by the blood are released. The de-oxygenated blood now enters the veins, to travel back to the heart and begin its journey once more.

Looking at the information represented, we can see that it is appropriate for a graphic. However, it fails to meet the requirements of an effective multimedia summary.

Study it in the light of the principles I've laid out. What makes this graphic ineffective? What could you do to make it more helpful for learning?

The problem with this is that everything is happening at once, and the text is lumped together, separate from the illustrations. We need to break it down into steps, with the appropriate bits of text right next to the matching illustration.

Have a go at doing that yourself before looking at my version (page 104). Don't worry about anatomically accurate drawings; rough iconic shapes, or even words, are fine. The important thing is to integrate the text with the appropriate parts of the image.

Fixing poor multimedia summaries is considerably easier than creating your own, but in the right circumstances, producing a multimedia summary is an extremely good way of helping you understand and remember the material.

Multimedia summaries are an example of a broad class of strategies that might be termed visual language strategies. Later in the chapter, we'll discuss the principles of visual language.

> **Rules for effective multimedia summaries**
>
> Be very concise.
>
> Use a minimum of text.
>
> Coordinate words and images.

Maps

Geographical maps are probably not something you have thought of as a summary, but like graphic organizers, they are particularly appropriate for conveying spatial relationships, and in certain circumstances may also help with recall of other information.

There's quite a lot of evidence that when a geographic map is provided, students remember more of the text information that is referenced in the map than they would if only given the text[12] (but best if the map is examined before reading the text[13]).

Maps, it appears, can be useful not only for remembering spatial relations, but also help memory for any information embedded into them. In studies, maps have helped in learning word associations[14]. For example, say you had to remember the following information:

> Jerry is a truck driver. Stuart is a prison guard. Mary-Jo is a chemist. Sarah works at the hospital. Kevin works at the supermarket. Kim is a bartender. Jamie is a pilot.

One way to learn this is a list of paired associates (Jerry-truck; Stuart-prison; etc). But a better way would be to sketch out a map and place them on it, like this:

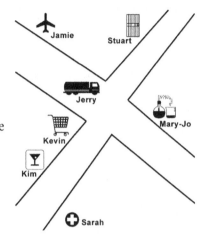

In this case, the spatial information is entirely arbitrary. But by arranging the names on a map, you have provided a visual arrangement that helps memory.

However, the key value of a map lies in the spatial information it provides. Because maps are all about relationships, paying attention to specific features on the map (which is the natural thing for an untrained student to do) turns out not to be very helpful[15]. What you need to pay attention to is the relationships *between* the features, rather than the features themselves. Let's look at an example.

This is a simple sketch of the lower portion of England and Wales, and I hope you take the point that a map doesn't have to be detailed and geographically accurate. Particularly when it's something you're constructing, a rough sketch is perfectly satisfactory.

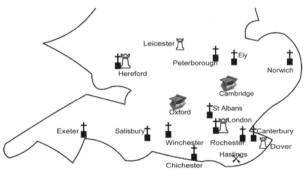

This rough sketch is entirely adequate to illustrate what I mean by paying attention to the relationships between features, rather than to the features themselves. This map shows the major castles, cathedrals, and universities after the Norman Conquest. The sort of things you should be noticing, looking at this map, are: how the thickest cluster is around London; that

Exeter and Norwich and Hereford are all some distance from any other major institution; that Oxford and Cambridge form a roughly equidistant triangle with London; that most of the castles and cathedrals are clustered in the lower right quadrant, radiating out, it might be thought, from Hastings (scene of the famous battle in 1066).

Maps seem to be particularly useful as a kind of visual advance organizer[16], suggesting that if a map is provided, you are advised to study it before reading the text. But you can also use maps as a means of taking notes. One study has found that students who drew a map as they read about a fictitious country understood and remembered much more. Copying details onto a blank map has also been found to be useful[17].

But research hasn't been entirely positive; the inconsistency in experimental results suggests that certain conditions are necessary for maps to be useful. The most important of these conditions, it has been suggested, is that the information can be chunked together in such a way as not to exceed working memory capacity.

This argument suggests that maps with only a limited number of features on them are useful. One study suggested the optimum number of features is between 12 and 16[18], but of course, as always, that depends on the individual, and also on the nature of the features and their relationships with each other.

Although I've said that you should pay attention to the relations between features rather than the features themselves, that doesn't mean you should ignore the features. Some features seem to be of greater value than others. For example, there have been a number of studies suggesting that icons (simple drawings, as in the examples) are more helpful than arbitrary geometric symbols[19].

But this does depend on how demanding the task is. If it's too tough, the complexity of drawings is just an additional burden on limited cognitive resources. On the other hand, if the drawings are familiar, they may ease the burden[20].

This emphasis on working memory isn't surprising. As I've already said, working memory may be the reason why graphic summaries tend to benefit recall. Maps clearly involve the visuospatial working memory system, thus reducing the load on the part of working memory which is busy processing the text[21].

Main points

Outlines and graphic organizers

Outlines and graphic organizers are useful strategies for hierarchical information.

Graphic organizers are better at showing the relationships *between* concepts.

Tree diagrams and matrices are the most common type of graphic organizer.

Graphic organizers are more effective for long-term recall and developing understanding.

Outlines are easier to produce than graphic organizers.

Graphic organizers are only needed for longer and more complex text.

Both outlines and graphic organizers are more effective than conventional notes.

Multimedia summaries

Multimedia summaries are useful for cause-&-effect relationships.

Multimedia summaries help develop understanding.

The best multimedia summaries are concise, coherent, and coordinated.

Maps

Maps help you remember spatial relations

To benefit from maps you need to pay attention to the relationships *between* the features.

The most effective maps have a limited number of features, and use simple, familiar icons.

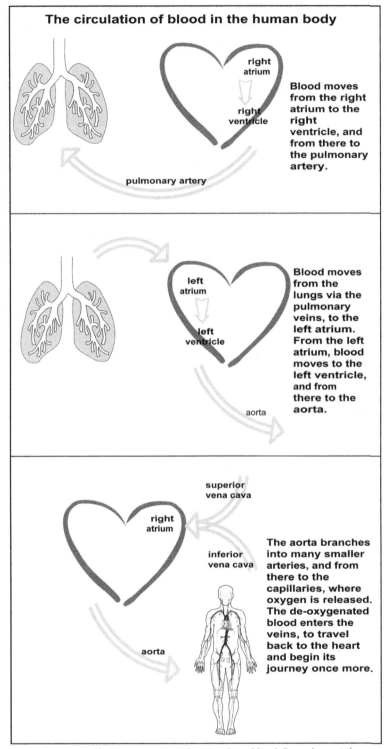

the more effective summary showing how blood flows (see p99)

Visual language

Multimedia summaries, maps, graphic organizers — and concept maps and mind maps, which we will look at later — all these can be considered examples of visual language.

Visual Language is a term Robert Horn[22] uses to refer to "language based on tight integration of words and visual elements". Horn has tried to create a grammar for this language, and given the number and usefulness of note-taking formats that use visual language, it's worth spending some time discussing the principles he's come up with.

Given how many people are intimidated by the idea of drawing, it's important to note that visual language requires little or no drawing ability — the approach encompasses shapes, and the images emphasize icons and symbols. For example:

If you use a computer, of course, you can produce quite artistic efforts using clipart!

Principles of visual language

Where do you start? Horn suggests[23] the first thing to do is to chunk the information into what he calls **information blocks**. You can think of this as the visual language equivalent of the paragraph — it's the fundamental building block of what Horn calls an **information map**.

Horn cites four principles for constructing information blocks:

- **Chunking**: group the information into small, manageable chunks (let the constraints of working memory guide you)

- **Relevance**: a chunk should only include information relating to a single main point

- **Consistency**: within a subject, be consistent in your use of words, labels, format, and ways of arranging your information (for example, you might always put definitions in a rectangular box, and examples in an oval)

- **Labeling**: label your chunks and groups of chunks according to specific criteria

Criteria for labeling:

- **Clear**: clearly describes what the block is about

- **Brief**: long enough to be clear, but no longer

- **Consistent**: the words you use should match those you use in the block (for example, if the text in the block talks about 'meat-eaters', don't then use the word 'carnivores' in the label)

- **Familiar**: Horn specifies the use of familiar words, rather than technical or difficult words that may not be familiar 'to your audience'. However, this is not such a consideration when the diagram is only for your own use. It's a good idea to prefer familiar words to ensure it's readily comprehensible, but if part of the purpose is to learn technical vocabulary, then using the to-be-learned terms as labels is helpful.

- **Appropriate**: the label should reflect the significance of the block — if the information is very important, or, on the contrary, merely interesting, the label should point to this.

- **Independent**: labels should act as advance organizers, preparing the reader for what's in the block; it should be able to stand alone — not require the associated block to make sense of it.

There is also a fifth principle, which comes into play when we are dealing with several information blocks on a topic: the **hierarchy principle**. Organizing related chunks into a hierarchy is a natural action — the thing to note here is Horn's requirement that groups of blocks be labeled.

It's also important to extend the basic principles to this growth. Thus, you don't want your groups to be too large either. If there are too many to grasp easily (and that precise limit will depend on your own working memory capacity and how comfortable you are with the material), subdivide into smaller groups.

Having chunked and labeled your information, the next consideration is how to arrange it. But before we move onto that, let's look at the chunking and labeling process in action. We'll use the chapter on headings as our text.

Here's a summary of the main points in that chapter (note that this summary refers to an earlier draft of this chapter, and some of the information in it no longer appears in the text):

Organizational signals include: overviews, topical summaries, headings.

- emphasize the **topics** of a text and their organization
- usually improve the reader's recall for the information which is emphasized
- are all about as good as each other, and seem to work in the same way. seem to help recall more than recognition, and cued recall more than free recall

Expository texts are texts that explain and describe; are organized around topics

Two types of text-processing strategies:

- linear or listing strategy: not particularly sensitive to the text structure
- topic structure strategy: more sensitive to text structure

two main theories about how organizational signals might affect recall:

- the **strategy selection hypothesis** postulates that signaling affects which text-processing strategy you use
- the **strategy implementation hypothesis** postulates that signaling makes it easier to use the topic structure strategy

more evidence for the selection hypothesis

this hypothesis implies a lack of effective headings doesn't matter if you use a topic structure strategy.

also implies headings are less important if other signals to text structure are available

also suggests that signals may be of no particular benefit when the text has few topics and a clear structure.

Although these are encoding strategies, research suggests signals may only help if you also use them in retrieving.

If recall doesn't follow the text's structure, it tends to be strongly affected by standard memory factors like:

- **serial position** (items mentioned first or last are remembered better than items in the middle),

- **familiarity** (items you are already familiar with will of course be recalled more easily), and

- **elaboration** (items discussed at greater length will be remembered better).

Headings might be of more benefit to some students than others.

- may be of greatest benefit to students who are neither skilled nor poor readers — those capable of using a structure strategy, but not inclined to do so without prompting.

- may be of greater benefit to those students who are not inclined to engage in effortful processing

- may be of greater benefit when students already have a high knowledge of the subject discussed in the text.

In summarizing, I've also done a certain 'natural' amount of grouping related information together and editing it so those groups have a fairly obvious theme. Having done that, the next step — chunking and labeling — is easy.

Organizational signals

- include: overviews, topical summaries, headings. [**Definition**]

- -

- emphasize the topics of a text and their organization. [**Function**]

- -

- usually improve the reader's recall for the information which is emphasized.

- are all about as good as each other, and seem to work in the same way.

- seem to help recall more than recognition, and cued recall more than free recall [**Benefits**]

Processing text

Expository texts

- texts that explain and describe
- are organized around topics [**Definition**]

Text-processing strategies: [**Definition**]

- linear or listing strategy: not particularly sensitive to the text structure.
- topic structure strategy: more sensitive to text structure

Organizational signals might affect recall by: [**Definition**]

- *encouraging* you to use a topic structure strategy (**strategy selection hypothesis**)
- making it *easier* to use a topic structure strategy (**strategy implementation hypothesis**)

More evidence for the strategy selection hypothesis.

Strategy selection hypothesis: [**Implications**]

- implies a lack of effective headings doesn't matter if you use a topic structure strategy.
- implies headings less important if other signals to text structure are available
- suggests that signals may be of no particular benefit when the text has few topics and a clear structure.

If recall doesn't follow the text's structure, it tends to be strongly affected by: [**Implications**]

- **serial position** (items mentioned first or last are remembered better than items in the middle),
- **familiarity** (items you are already familiar with will of course be recalled more easily), and
- **elaboration** (items discussed at greater length will be remembered better).

Individual differences

- may be of greatest benefit to students who are neither skilled nor poor readers — those capable of using a structure strategy, but not inclined to do so without prompting.

- may be of greater benefit to those students who are not inclined to engage in effortful processing

- may be of greater benefit when students already have a high knowledge of the subject discussed in the text.

Let's look at the ways we can arrange information.

Arranging the information

There are six principles known as Gestalt principles, which are useful to know if you wish to draw effective visual representations:

1. **Proximity**: people tend to group together elements that are physically close to each other
For example, in this figure, we can't help but see the first column as separate from the others, which clearly belong together.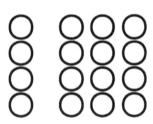

2. **Similarity**: people tend to group together elements that are similar in some way (e.g., same color or size)

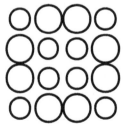 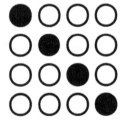

3. **Common region**: people tend to see elements enclosed by lines as one unit

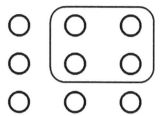

4. **Connectedness**: people tend to see connected elements as a single unit

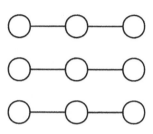

5. **Continuation**: people tend to group together elements that appear to be continuations of each other.
This figure, for example, is clearly seen as two lines crossing — as a wavy X — rather than four lines meeting in the middle.

6. **Closure**: people tend to make figures "complete" when some elements are missing.
This figure, for example, is usually seen as a square, rather than four unconnected circles.

These principles are useful to bear in mind when considering the various ways we can arrange information. Horn lists the following major arrangement classes:

- Matrix

- Concentric

- Level

- Proximity grouping

- Boundary

- Network

We've already looked at matrices — basically, they're tables. Here are examples of the other classes:

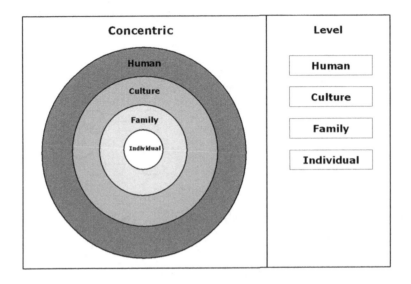

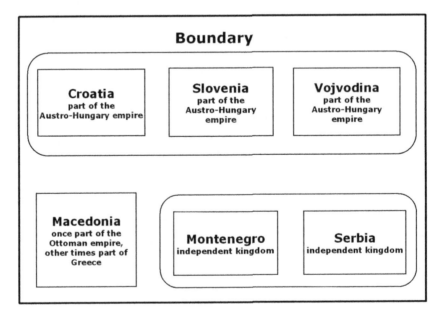

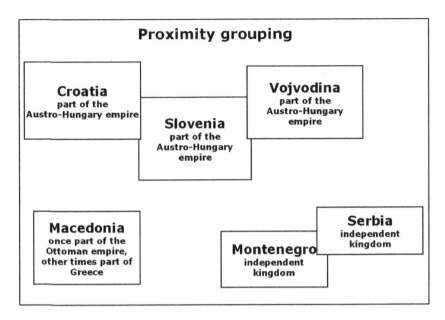

Networks come in a lot of varieties. Horn makes a fundamental distinction between those with directional flow, such as these:

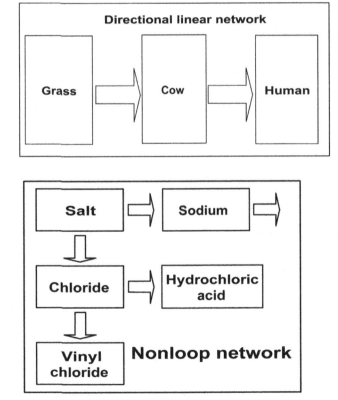

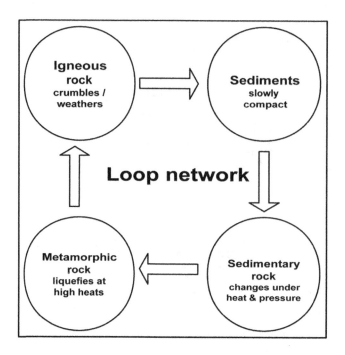

And those without, such as these:

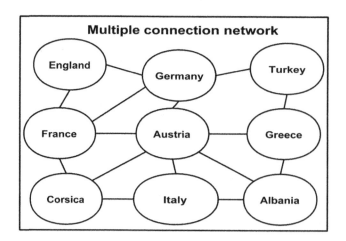

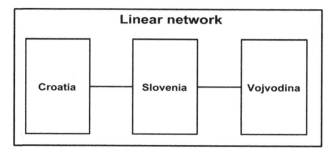

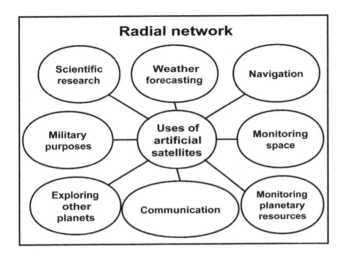

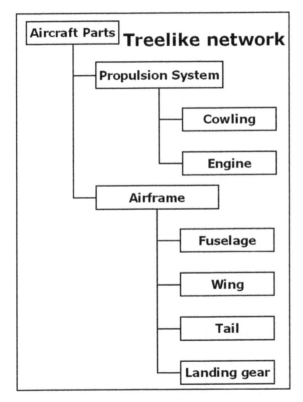

[Last example adapted from Horn's Visual Language]

Now I've shoe-horned information into some of these formats; I hope the clumsiness of the fit in some cases makes it clear that there is no single diagram format that will fit any information. Sometimes the information you have simply will not fit into a particular type of diagram; other times the fit is possible, but not the best. To get the most of your diagram, you should make an effort to match the information with the most appropriate diagram.

Let's go quickly through the examples.

As you can see, in the examples given, the level diagram represents the same information as the concentric diagram. However, this is not invariably the case. Information represented in a concentric diagram can always be represented in a level diagram, but the reverse is not necessarily true. In the concentric diagram, smaller circles are clearly contained in larger circles. Thus, an individual is contained within a family, and both within a culture, and all are part of the human species. However, this doesn't have to be true for information contained in a level diagram. Note, too, that there are no links between the boxes. Gestalt principles lead us to assume they are related, but the lack of connection between them indicates the relationship is not a strong one — certainly not a causative one. A drop-down menu could be thought of as an example of a level diagram.

The next pair are also largely substitutable for each other: proximity grouping and boundary. Using different Gestalt principles, both indicate that some items in the diagram have a stronger connection with each other than with other items — but the implication is of some sort of shared similarity, not a causative link as would be suggested by actual links.

The network diagrams are where we find causative and other strong connections. Causative connections and those of influence and flow (as in the simple food chain represented in the directional linear network) are indicated by arrows. Single-headed arrows represent a one-way process, while double-headed arrows indicate an interaction that goes both ways — where each influences the other equally. If one side of the arrow exerts greater influence than the other side, you should use two arrows of different thicknesses. For example:

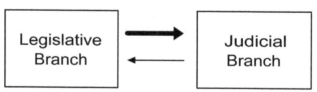

Horn gives three basic classes of directional networks (networks that use arrows rather than lines; networks representing items that affect each other in some way): loop networks, linear networks, and those that are neither. Concept maps, as we will see, fit into this last category.

Networks can also use lines instead of arrows, to represent information that is related in some way, but not through causation or influence or flow. A tree network can represent information that is related hierarchically. A linear network can represent information that can also be represented in a proximity grouping or boundary diagram. Radial networks are used where the items all stand in equal relationship, while multiple connection networks can be used for items that are connected in a more complex fashion. Mind maps, as we shall see, can come in both these forms.

Like arrows, there are certain conventions with lines that connect items. Most particularly, a solid line indicates a degree of certainty that isn't present in a broken line, which can be used to indicate an uncertain relationship.

When deciding which type of diagram is most helpful, it may help to first identify the type of information you are dealing with.

Information classes

Horn names seven basic types of information:

- **Procedure**: involves sequential steps for accomplishing a task

- **Process**: involves sequential events leading to a specific end

- **Structure**: defines the parts of something

- **Classification**: involves dividing things into classes

- **Concept**: defines a group of things

- **Fact**: bare information that states something without providing any evidence

- **Principle**: such as rules and guidelines

Unsurprisingly, these types are reminiscent of our different types of text structure, since the information contained in text has a strong effect on the way the text is structured.

Procedures and processes are clearly directional, and both would seem most appropriately represented by one of the directional networks. Whether a loop or linear or neither depends on the nature of the specific process/procedure, but it is probably fair to say a procedure is most commonly a linear activity, while a process is equally (if not more) likely to be a loop.

Structures and classifications are both analytic in a way that usually is hierarchical. Such information is usually best represented by a treelike network.

Principles are probably best represented in a level diagram.

Concepts and facts are different from these other types in that they are building blocks, and in themselves say little about how they might be used. The decision rests on the nature of the concepts/facts in the specific context you're looking at, most particularly on the relationships between concepts/facts.

Returning to our organizational signal example, the information clearly doesn't involve processes or procedures; there's some classification, but only in the sense usually involved when we're defining concepts. There's no real structural analysis, as there would be if it concerned a taxonomy, for example. Basically, you would class this information in the concept category.

That leaves the field wide open, so our next question is: are our information blocks connected by strong, causative or influential, links, or merely by a similarity of association? If we look at our labels, we see "Implications" and "Benefits"; these words certainly suggest causative or influential links.

Next question: do these links involve directional flow?

This is a tricky question, and emphasizes the fact that, although Horn's taxonomy is a useful guide to the possibilities open to us, not all information falls readily into one particular category. In this case, some of the links are directional, but not all. But that's fine, visual language is not about forcing information into a rigid format. If we scan the directional and non-directional networks, both non-loop network and multiple connection network, and perhaps even treelike network, should occur to us as possible formats for at least some of the information.

We don't, and shouldn't, make a hard and fast decision about format before we start trying to put the information into the format — we won't really know if it works until we try it. So at this stage, all you're looking for is a starting place. Now we have it, let's try putting our information blocks into a network (next page).

You'll notice that this diagram includes both lines and arrows, and there's no clear shape as there is in the models of diagram types exemplified here. It's important to remember that the models are just that — ideal examples of pure types. In the real world, information is often messy, and can't be shoehorned into such pure formats.

If you compare the diagram with the original information blocks, you'll also notice a few changes — which is exactly what should happen. This is at least half the value of drawing a visual representation — the process of formatting

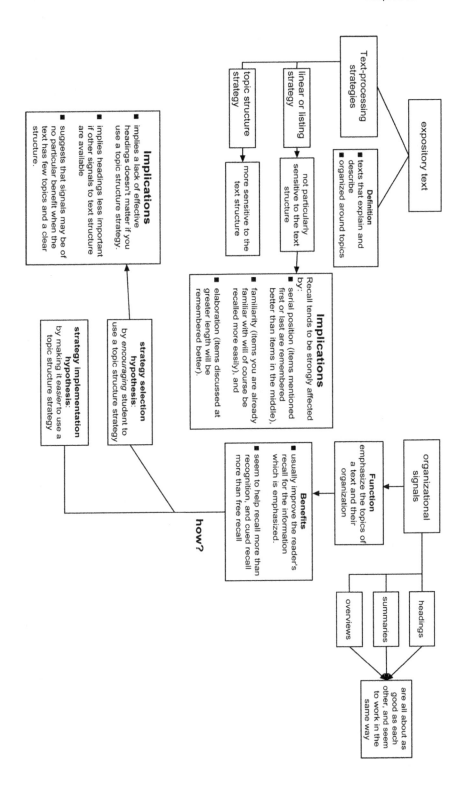

the information in this way should reveal different relationships and connections between information blocks, causing you to arrange them in different ways, and even to break up some.

The diagram also doesn't use any images. Remember that visual language includes shapes, so this is perfectly acceptable as an example of visual language; it's not necessary to use images. In this case, the subject matter is fairly abstract, and also, I personally am very text-oriented rather than image-oriented. How much, and whether or not, you use images, should depend on the subject matter and your own preferences. Don't use them just for the sake of it.

> ## Formats for arranging your information blocks:
>
> - Matrix
> - Network
>   - directional
>   - loop networks (often appropriate for processes)
>   - directional linear networks (often appropriate for procedures and processes)
>   - other
>   - non-directional
>   - linear networks
>   - tree-like networks (often appropriate for structures and classifications)
>   - radial networks
>   - multiple connection networks
> - Level (often appropriate for principles)
> - Proximity grouping
> - Concentric
> - Boundary

Exercise 6.2

Use information from the example texts to construct your own simple examples of each format.

> ## To construct information blocks
>
> - Chunk information
>
> - Keep chunks relevant
>
> - Be consistent
>
> - Label your chunks
>   - Clearly
>   - Briefly
>   - Consistently
>   - Appropriately
>   - Using familiar words
>   - With independent labels
>
> - Organize related chunks into a hierarchy
>
> - Choose an appropriate format to organize your information
>
> - Use the six Gestalt principles to more effectively arrange your information

Exercise 6.3

Apply this strategy to the Benjamin Franklin text.

Individual differences

Okay, I've suggested that some people are intimidated by drawing; some people are more verbal-oriented and others more visual. These are clearly differences that have implications for how likely you are to use visual strategies. Do they affect how likely you are to *benefit* from such strategies?

There hasn't been a lot of research into this question, but the inconsistency in research findings[24] suggests that, indeed, individual differences are important.

Of course part of the problem is simply the difficulty in designing a good study. Requiring people to draw, in whatever format, whether diagrammatic or illustrative, usually results in them spending much more time with the material to be learned, which in itself is going to improve recall.

We also need to distinguish between illustrative and diagrammatic drawing — the first may or may not require you to think more deeply about the material; the second always does.

For practical purposes, however, we might say that drawing illustrations yourself is helpful, if only because it forces you to spend considerable time and attention on the material.

But it does seem that the wide differences in the quality of drawings may affect recall. This is, however, a learnable skill! The main problem with drawing, I believe (and I have one son who's very artistic, and one whom you might describe as drawing-phobic), is that it appears to be like mathematics — children can develop an intense anxiety about the whole subject (I say children because that's when it begins; the problem, of course, extends throughout the lifetime).

More innate, perhaps, is another personal attribute that may affect the usefulness of illustrations in enhancing memory — the ability to visualize. Since good visualizers can recall illustrations more accurately than poor visualizers[25], it may be that illustrations are of greater usefulness to good visualizers. On the other hand, one could argue that poor visualizers are in greater need of physical illustrations (because they are less able to visualize from text).

To a certain extent, visualizing is a matter of cognitive style. According to one analysis, people fall into two types: visualizers and verbalizers. Of course, this is a continuum not a dichotomy; we all visualize, and we all verbalize. "Visualizers" are defined as people who rely mainly on imagery processes when performing cognitive tasks, while "verbalizers" are those who prefer to process information verbally.

One study found that cognitive style interacted with the degree of background knowledge the person had. Visualizers with little knowledge actually benefited most from seeing text only, while verbalizers, regardless of their amount of knowledge, benefited more from seeing graphics as well as the text. Those who had a fair amount of background knowledge, regardless of whether they were verbalizers or visualizers, benefited the most from seeing text plus graphics[26].

It's worth noting that the distinction between visualizers and verbalizers doesn't necessarily equate to imagery ability. Visualizers are not necessarily people with high imagery ability, and verbalizers are not necessarily people with low imagery ability. The distinction refers to cognitive style — that is, a person's preference for how they process information — not a person's ability to create vivid images.

This seems counter-intuitive, but researchers have suggested a distinction that may make sense of it. They suggest that there are two types of visualizer:

- iconic: these construct detailed images
- spatial: these create images that represent spatial relations

Their study found that verbalizers tended to be of intermediate spatial ability, while visualizers either had high spatial ability (the spatial type) or low spatial ability (the iconic type)[27].

Another recent study, however, makes a distinction between cognitive style (which is regarded as a general attribute) and learning preference (which is modified by context). It may be that learning preference is of more importance than cognitive style[28].

Whether it is or not, it is worth noting the salient point, which is that your approach to information processing is flexible — to say you are a visualizer is not to say that you will approach all situations as a visualizer.

Another very relevant finding of that study was that, in general, people had a good idea of their learning style and their spatial ability — they didn't need complicated tests. You can probably reasonably accurately rate your spatial ability, and know whether you prefer to process information verbally or visually, and if visually, whether you tend to draw detailed, iconic pictures or sketch maps and diagrams that give a sense of the spatial relations that exist.

Partly, of course, this will be reflected in your subject matter, but it seems likely that your choice of subject matter will reflect these abilities and preferences. To take an obvious example, you wouldn't be attracted to architecture or engineering without a strong tendency to see things in terms of spatial relationships; a literature student, on the other hand, probably has a preference for the written word.

So where does that leave you?

The first thing to note is that actually drawing graphic summaries is a very different matter from studying graphics provided for you. Why this research is important for us in this context is that it suggests that developing some skill in this area is even more important for those who are *not* inclined to attend to visuals.

But there will be a learning curve — if you really have difficulty with the whole concept of drawing graphic summaries, do expect it to take some effort to get to the point where the benefit is clear. But the benefits to you will probably be all the greater, because you haven't been utilizing this tool at all.

Hopefully the breakdown I've given of the principles of visual language (which may have seemed obvious to those already comfortable in this area) will assist you in gaining mastery. But after studying those, there really is no other way than practice! Don't be discouraged by initial difficulties; it really will come with perseverance. But don't bite off more than you can chew — if this isn't your particular area of competence, take small steps.

On the other hand, if you already use graphic summaries, I hope this discussion has extended your knowledge of them.

Drawing helps comprehension and free recall rather than recognition[29]. There's evidence that drawing helps you construct an integrated mental model, while simply looking at illustrations with text may produce a verbal and a visual mental representation, but not an integrated one. Integration (which helps both memory and comprehension) doesn't seem to happen naturally, but requires some active task that forces you to integrate the two[30]. Drawing is one good means of doing this.

Main points

Illustrations provided for you

Your ability to visualize may affect how useful illustrations are to you, but this depends on how much knowledge you have of the subject.

Text only (no illustrations) is better for visualizers with little knowledge.

Illustrations benefit verbalizers, regardless of amount of knowledge.

Illustrations benefit those with a fair amount of background knowledge, regardless of whether they were verbalizers or visualizers.

Drawing your own illustrations

Drawing is a useful tool if only because it forces you to spend time and attention on the material.

Differences in the quality of drawings may affect recall.

Drawing helps comprehension and free recall rather than recognition.

Drawing may help you construct an integrated mental model, which helps both memory and comprehension.

Review questions

1. Graphic summaries

    a.   are pictures of topical summaries

    b.   re-organize the text

    c.   always show hierarchical relationships

    d.   make it easier to see relationships between topics

    e.   are summaries that use graphs

2. Graphic organizers

    a.   are always more effective than topical summaries

    b.   help you make better memory codes

    c.   are most useful when you don't have much time to study

    d.   are easier to create than outlines

    e.   can be created as a complete substitute for verbal notes

3. Outlines

    a.   are better than graphic organizers for difficult texts

    b.   are quicker to create and to process, compared to graphic organizers

    c.   are useful for showing hierarchical information

    d.   are most useful for simplifying complicated concepts

    e.   are useful for lots of different types of information

4. Scientific cause-&-effect relationships are best shown by

    a.   outlines

    b.   graphic organizers

    c.   multimedia summaries

    d.   overviews

    e.   maps

5. Multimedia summaries are most effective when

    a. they're mainly text

    b. they have a lot of different pictures

    c. they contain only the minimal required text

    d. images and text are closely coordinated

    e. there's a clear sequence

6. The principles of visual language will help you create good graphic summaries   T / F

7. The principles of visual language are also known as Gestalt principles   T / F

8. Information blocks are

    a. diagrams

    b. graphic organizers

    c. graphic summaries

    d. multimedia summaries

    e. expressions of visual language

9. Creating information blocks requires you to

    a. sort important information into small, tightly focused chunks

    b. work out concise, meaningful labels for each chunk

    c. use lots of colors

    d. draw well

    e. know lots of visual icons

10. Each type of information block is uniquely associated with a specific text structure   T / F

PART II

Connection strategies

I said at the beginning that a crucial part of effective note-taking is about selecting what information is important, and we have looked at those various tools that can help us do so. But selection is not the whole story. I also said that note-taking is a strategy for making information meaningful, and *connection*, not selection, is the heart of what makes information meaningful.

Of course, when we come to strategies, we cannot completely separate selection from connection. The selection strategies we've been discussing have for the most part also been to some degree connection strategies, especially the visual strategies. But in this section we're going to delve more deeply into what connection means, how it helps you understand and remember, and the strategies that emphasize connection.

In particular, it's about those strategies that help you make connections that foster understanding.

These strategies include:

- asking questions
- making comparisons
- looking for similarities and differences
- making analogies

- drawing concept maps

- drawing mind maps

Some readers may think I've forgotten an obvious class of connection strategies! I touch on mnemonics, but only very briefly, because mnemonics don't make connections that help you build your understanding. They make connections that help you memorize details, which is a very different thing.

If you're interested in that (and it is another valuable tool in your study strategy tool-box), I have written a book on the subject.

Understanding connection

I said the most important study skill was learning how to create good summaries. This is the next most important! You can't understand your material if you don't make connections between the concepts you're learning, and with the knowledge you already have in your head. In this short chapter, we work through an example showing how to ask the right questions to make those vital connections. I also discuss the importance of anchor facts.

Let's start with a demonstration of how connection leads to understanding.

An example

Here are some facts:

> Arteries are thick and elastic and carry blood from the heart. With the exception of the pulmonary artery, that blood is rich in oxygen.

> Veins are thinner, less elastic, and carry blood to the heart. With the exception of the pulmonary veins, that blood is rich in carbon dioxide.

Now if you know nothing else about veins and arteries and the circulation of blood, this is a set of facts with little meaning. You can learn this information by rote (through simple repetition) or by using a mnemonic aid (for example, you could make up a sentence such as "*Art* (ery) was *thick* around the middle so he wore trousers with an *elastic* waistband").

But you will remember the information much better for longer if you *understand the connections* between the facts.

One of the best ways of making connections is by asking questions. Thus, you might ask *why* arteries need to be thicker than veins and *why* arteries need to be elastic and veins don't.

Let's look at some of the questions we might ask, and where they would lead us.

1. **Why** do arteries need to be more elastic than veins?

2. **Why** do arteries need to be thicker than veins?

3. **Why** do arteries carry blood away from the heart?

4. **Why** do arteries usually carry the blood that is rich in oxygen?

5. **Why** is the pulmonary artery an exception?

These five questions lead directly from the facts as they are given. But we can also reinterpret these questions in a way that integrates the facts at a deeper level.

When we ask: *Why do arteries carry blood away from the heart?* It may be that the right question really is: *Why do the vessels carrying blood from the heart need to be thicker and more elastic?*

When we ask: *Why do arteries carry the blood that's rich in oxygen?* It may be that the right question actually is: *Why do the vessels carrying oxygen-rich blood need to be thicker and more elastic?*

Or it may be that the right question is: *Why do the vessels carrying blood from the heart need to be rich in oxygen?*

That question takes us another step: *Why should blood be rich in oxygen? Why is blood sometimes rich in oxygen and sometimes rich in carbon dioxide?*

Why do the pulmonary artery and veins reverse the normal rules?

1. **Why** do arteries need to be more elastic than veins?

2. **Why** do arteries need to be thicker than veins?

3. **Why** do arteries carry blood away from the heart?

   = **Why** do the vessels carrying blood from the heart need to be thicker and more elastic?

4. **Why** do arteries carry the blood that is rich in oxygen?

= **Why** do the vessels carrying blood rich in oxygen need to be thicker and more elastic?

or = **Why** do the vessels carrying blood from the heart need to be rich in oxygen?

⇨ **Why** should blood be rich in oxygen?

⇨ **Why** is blood sometimes rich in oxygen and sometimes rich in carbon dioxide?

5. **Why** is the pulmonary artery an exception?

= **Why** do the pulmonary artery and veins reverse the normal rules?

Asking the right questions

Asking questions is fundamental to developing understanding (and thus helping you remember), but they have to be the *right* questions.

To understand what types of question are effective, let's look at the answers to the questions we have posed.

Q: Why are arteries thicker and more elastic than veins?

A: The arteries carry blood from the heart. The heart is a pump. Because the heart is a pump, blood comes out in spurts, causing the outflow to vary in volume and speed. This means that blood flow can occur at a high pressure, which is why the arteries need to have thick walls. It also means that the arteries need to be able to expand and contract to accommodate the changes in pressure, which is why the arteries need to be elastic.

Veins, on the other hand, carry blood to the heart, in a continuous, even flow. Therefore they are thinner, and less elastic.

This information can be expressed graphically (next page).

We've now answered three of our five main questions:

1. **Why** do arteries need to be more elastic than veins?

2. **Why** do arteries need to be thicker than veins?

3. **Why** do arteries carry blood away from the heart?

= **Why** do the vessels carrying blood from the heart need to be thicker and more elastic?

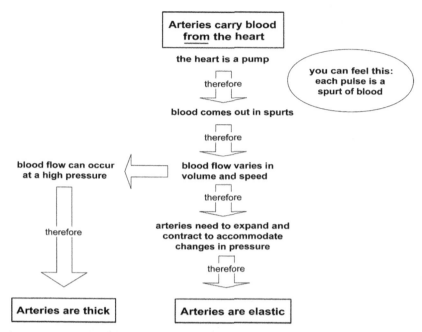

We've not only answered these questions, we've *connected* them.

What about our fourth question (*Why* do arteries carry the blood that is rich in oxygen)? Can we tie it in to what we know?

What do we know? We know that arteries carry blood *from* the heart. To understand why the blood in the arteries is oxygen-rich, we need to know that oxygen, which we breathe in, binds itself to the blood. This blood passes from the lungs to the heart, and then moves on, carrying the oxygen to the tissues. Thus, the blood that passes from the heart is rich in oxygen.

Blood is not only the conduit for oxygen to reach our tissues, it also removes carbon dioxide from the cells. The blood going *to* the heart is therefore rich in carbon dioxide. This blood carries the CO_2 waste product from the heart to the lungs, from where it is released and breathed out. Hence, the fact that the veins carry the blood *to* the heart means that veins carry blood rich in carbon dioxide.

This also explains why the pulmonary artery and veins are the exception to the general order of things. The pulmonary artery carries the blood from the heart to the lungs, and the pulmonary veins carry the blood from the lungs to the heart. Blood coming from the heart must be carried by arteries, because of the pumping action. Therefore one particular artery — the one sending the blood from heart to lungs — must carry "dirty" blood. And because blood flowing into the heart must be carried by veins, some veins — those bringing the "clean" blood back to the heart — must carry "clean", oxygen-rich blood.

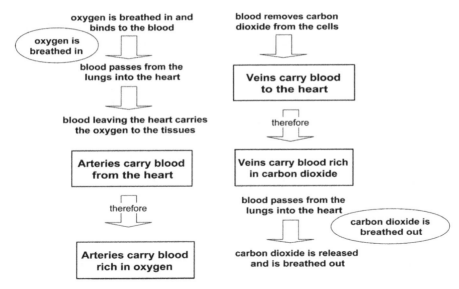

(This illustrates the general principles, ignoring the exception of the pulmonary artery and veins).

So the fact that arteries carry oxygen-rich blood is connected to the fact that arteries carry blood *from* the heart; and veins carry carbon dioxide-rich blood because they carry blood *to* the heart — and all of these are connected to the well-known fact that we breathe in oxygen and breathe out carbon dioxide. Just as our earlier cluster of facts — that arteries are thick and elastic and carry blood *from* the heart — was connected to the well-known fact that the heart is a pump (which we can feel when we feel our pulse).

Facts that you already know very well and have no trouble remembering act as anchor points.

The more anchor points you can connect to, the more meaningful the new information becomes, and the more easily you will remember it.

The value of anchor points

Think about it for a moment. When you are told something new, you only understand it to the extent that you can relate it to something you already know.

Here's a quote from *The complete idiot's guide to Microsoft Office*:

After you select the data source to use, the Mail Merge Helper displays the Label Options dialog box, asking you to specify the type and size of the mailing labels on which you intend to print.

Now if you don't know anything about computers this will be complete gibberish and there's no way you're going to remember it. If you have some experience with Microsoft Office, but have no experience of Mail Merging, then you will sort of understand what's going on, but not have enough anchor points to really understand it — and you're not going to remember it either. But if you are already *au fait* with Mail Merging, and merely want to know how to do the labels, then you will have a well-organized, strong cluster of facts already recorded in memory, and the new fact will slot in easily. You'll understand it, and you'll remember it — to the extent that your existing cluster of information about Mail Merging is strong and well-connected.

It's like learning a new word. *Pediment*, for example. If you were told this was a triangular part crowning the front of a building in the Grecian style — assuming you don't already know the word, and assuming you have no particular knowledge of architecture — you're not likely to remember it without repeatedly coming across it. You might make the connection *pediment — impediment*, but since there is no meaningful connection between these words, this won't help you remember the meaning of *pediment*. It might help you remember the word itself, but to remember the meaning of the word, you need a meaningful connection. That might be provided by the suggestion that *pediment* is derived from a corruption of *pyramid*, which as we all know, is triangular, and is also a building.

The more connections to existing anchor points, the more meaningful the fact becomes; the more easily remembered it is.

Exercise 8.1

Look again at the ozone layer text, and try to pick out any anchor points.

Framing effective questions

Questions — especially *why* questions — help us make connections to existing anchor points (facts we know well). But as I've already pointed out, some questions are better than others.

Let's look at our facts about blood again:

> Arteries are thick. Arteries are elastic. Arteries usually carry blood rich in oxygen. Arteries carry blood from the heart.

> Veins are thinner. Veins are less elastic. Veins usually carry blood rich in carbon dioxide. Veins carry blood to the heart.

Now, we could have simply turned these into *why* questions:

Why are arteries elastic?

Why are arteries thick?

Why do arteries carry blood away from the heart?

Why do arteries carry blood that is rich in oxygen?

Why are veins less elastic?

Why are veins less thick?

Why do veins carry blood to the heart?

Why do veins carry blood that is rich in carbon dioxide?

And we could answer these on the basis of the connections we've already made:

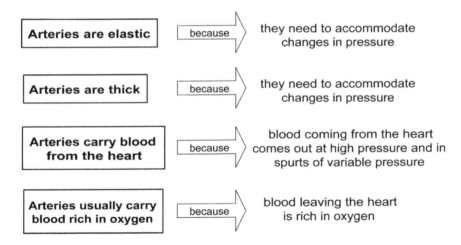

But is this enough? No. Something's missing. Connections between these facts. Although the facts have become more meaningful, to be really understood you need to make the connections between the facts explicit.

Let's look again at our original questions.

1. **Why** do arteries need to be more elastic than veins?

2. **Why** do arteries need to be thicker than veins?

3. **Why** do arteries carry blood away from the heart?

= **Why** do the vessels carrying blood from the heart need to be thicker and more elastic?

4. **Why** do arteries carry the blood that is rich in oxygen?

= **Why** do the vessels carrying blood rich in oxygen need to be thicker and more elastic?

or = **Why** do the vessels carrying blood from the heart need to be rich in oxygen?

⇨ **Why** should blood be rich in oxygen?

⇨ **Why** is blood sometimes rich in oxygen and sometimes rich in carbon dioxide?

5. **Why** is the pulmonary artery an exception?

= **Why** do the pulmonary artery and veins reverse the normal order?

Do you see how these questions relate the facts to each other? We don't ask: Why are arteries elastic? But: Why do arteries need to be more elastic than veins? Not: Why do arteries carry blood that is rich in oxygen? But: Why do vessels carrying blood from the heart need to be rich in oxygen?

By asking and answering these questions, we have built up an understanding of the facts that ties them together in a multi-connected cluster:

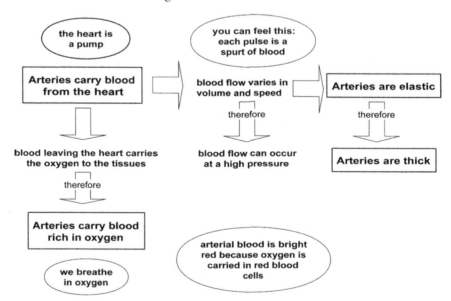

(For simplicity, I've just focused on the arteries.)

See how the four facts about arteries are connected together. *Meaningfully* connected. In a perfect world we'd be able to close the circle with a direct connection between the facts "Arteries carry blood rich in oxygen" and "Arteries are thick", but as far as I know, the only connection between them is indirect, through the fact that "Arteries carry blood from the heart".

So ... the world isn't perfect, and information doesn't come in neatly wrapped bundles where every fact connects directly to every other fact. But the more connections you can make between related facts — the stronger a cluster you can make — the more deeply you will understand the information, and the more accessible it will be. That is, you will remember it more easily and for longer. Indeed, if it's well enough connected, you will remember it forever. *If* it's connected to strong anchor points.

You're never going to forget that you breathe in oxygen and that your heart pumps out blood. These are strong anchor points. If the facts about arteries are strongly connected to these anchor points, you'll never forget *them* either.

What this means for note-taking

We take notes to remember information. An important part of remembering is understanding. If we don't understand something, it's much more difficult to remember. Accordingly, effective note-taking not only involves selecting the important information, it also involves making it meaningful to you.

Making information meaningful is about connecting new information to existing knowledge. The more connections you make, the better you will understand the information. Moreover, the more connections you have, the more entry points you have to the information, therefore the easier it will be to find in your memory.

This then, is how you can judge the value of a particular note-taking strategy in a particular situation — ask yourself:

- Does it help me connect the facts together?
- Does it help me connect the new information with information I already have?
- Does it make any connection with facts I already know very well, and am unlikely to forget?

Review questions

1. Anchor points

    a. are the most important facts

    b. are the facts that are critical to a concept

    c. are facts you already know well, that connect to the new concept

    d. help make new information more meaningful

2. Effective questions

    a. always ask why

    b. help you make connections

    c. use what, where, how, why, who, or when

    d. have to be very simple

3. You understand a concept or topic when

    a. you know all the relevant facts

    b. you know how the facts are connected

    c. you have a memory network of strongly connected facts

    d. you have a memory network of strongly connected facts that is also strongly connected to other established networks

Elaboration strategies

This brief chapter describes some other ways of making connections. Making comparisons, and asking questions, are ways of creating meaningful connections — these help you understand the material better. I also touch on mnemonics, which are a way of creating connections that don't help you understand, but can help you memorize specific details.

What I've been discussing are examples of elaboration. Elaboration is what enables you to connect new information to the information already in your mental database. Elaboration involves going beyond the information presented.

I touched on that in the brief discussion of advance organizers, but we didn't at that time explore *how* you make those connections, how you elaborate. There are a number of strategies that help you do this. I've divided them into three broad categories: making comparisons, asking questions, and mnemonics.

Making comparisons

Comparisons help learning, but why? It's suggested that comparison acts by focusing our attention on common elements in the deeper structure[1], beyond the surface attributes. For example, when the brain is compared to a computer, we are forced to look beyond surface attributes (clearly a lump of wet, greyish spongy stuff is completely unlike the PC on your desk) to something more abstract (an ability to process information).

Simply reading about multiple cases is not enough though[2] — you need to make direct comparisons[3]. How do we do that?

Well, the obvious way is to look for similarities. But it's not the only way. Looking for differences is also an effective way of making useful comparisons.

Similarities and differences are closely related. There are two kinds of differences: ones that are alignable, and those that are not[4]. Alignable differences are related to a common structure. For example, to say that a dog has four legs but a human two, is to point to an alignable difference — one that belongs on a common dimension (number of legs). However, to say that a dog has four legs but humans can talk, is to point to a nonalignable difference — there is no connection between the two facts. People usually see more alignable differences between things that are highly similar, and more nonalignable differences between things that are dissimilar.

Although it may seem counterintuitive, people actually find it easier to list differences for things that are very similar, compared to things that are very dissimilar[5]. Similarity and difference are two sides of the same coin.

Indeed, listing differences between similar objects *increases* their perceived similarity. Comparing differences also seems to lead to an understanding of common structure — perhaps not quite as effectively as comparing similarities6, but depending on the situation, perhaps more easily.

One quite specific way of making comparisons is through the use of analogies.

Exercise 8.2

List the similarities between veins and arteries, then the differences. Consider which was easier, and which gave you a better understanding of blood vessels.

Now, using the text on brain cells, do the same for neurons and glia.

Analogies

Rutherford's comparison of the atom to the solar system gave us a means to understand the atom. The story goes that Newton 'discovered' gravity when an apple fell on his head — because of the comparison he made, realizing that the motion of an apple falling from a tree was in some sense like the motion of the planets. These are comparisons called analogies, and analogy has been shown to be a powerful tool for learning[7].

But the problem with analogies is that we have trouble coming up with them.

Generally, when we make analogies, we use an example we know well to help us understand something we don't understand very well. This means that we need to retrieve from memory an appropriate example. But this is clearly a difficult task; people frequently fail to make appropriate connections[8] — even, surprisingly, when an appropriate connection has recently come their way. In a study where people were given a problem to solve after reading a story in which an analogous problem was solved, 80% didn't think of using the story to solve the problem until the analogy was pointed out to them[9].

It's thought that retrieving an appropriate analogy is so difficult because of the way we file information in memory[10]. Certainly similarity is an important attribute in our filed memories, but it's not the same sort of similarity that governs analogies. The similarity that helps us retrieve memories is a surface similarity — a similarity of features and context. But analogies run on a deeper similarity — a similarity of structure, of relations between objects. This will only be encoded if you have multiple examples (at least more than one) and make an explicit effort to note such relations.

The problem goes deeper than memory retrieval difficulties. Memory and reasoning are after all working with the same material, using cognitive processes that are based on this same way of linking information. Think of the study I mentioned earlier. Clearly those who had just read an analogous story weren't hampered by memory failure. But "seeing" an analogy requires you to look beyond the surface details to the structure beneath; you need to see what your new situation has in common with another.

We think of making analogies as a comparison between an unfamiliar instance and a familiar one, but this isn't the only way to do it, and especially for the novice, an easier strategy may be to compare two partly understood situations, searching for the common structure. This has been called analogical encoding[11] or mutual alignment[12], and research suggests that the most effective strategy for making this type of analogy is to:

1. view two examples side-by-side

2. assign specific correspondences between the elements of each example (correspondence list)

3. describe them as a unit, by comparing one to the other (joint interpretation)

Note that making a correspondence list is not sufficient on its own; to be truly effective, you need to follow through to the final step.

For example, in a study[13] that had students compare two situations — (1) A pancake being cooked on a griddle on a gas stove; (2) A mug of hot coffee with a metal bar in it that has an ice cube at the end — the correspondences were:

Situation 1	Situation 2
batter	ice cube
griddle/frypan	metal bar
gas stove/flame	coffee
pancake	drops of water

And the joint interpretation was: Heat is transferred through the griddle (metal bar), causing the batter (ice cube) to become pancakes (drops of water).

It's also worth noting that just being given the underlying principles or structure involved isn't nearly as effective as working it out from specific examples. We need the examples. Indeed, even if we are unable to clearly articulate the principle, an understanding of how the examples are related gets encoded and leads to a better memory code — one that not only helps retrieval of those examples, but also makes it easier to retrieve appropriate examples you have previously stored in memory[14].

In other words, digging into examples to see their structure not only means that the material you are currently working on is more effectively encoded, but that relevant examples in memory become better encoded (memory is not simply a matter of construction but of re-construction; there is nothing final about a memory code, you tweak it every time you retrieve it).

Mutual alignment, rather than the more traditional way of making analogies, appears to be particularly helpful for novices, but it does require some minimal level of understanding — it's not a strategy for complete beginners to a subject.

What's the difference between similarity and analogy? Analogy is a very specialized type of similarity — a similarity solely of relations. A computer screen and a keyboard may be considered analogous to paper and pen, but they are not similar. A pen and a pencil, on the other hand, are similar. A useful way of thinking of it is that similarity is more a function of nouns (a cat is like a dog), and analogies largely involve verbs (a computer is like a brain — because they both process information).

Analogies are worth seeking out, because they are a very effective means of developing understanding. But they are difficult to come up with on your own, so don't worry too much if you can't. Do ask your teacher if they can think of any, but the most important lesson I want you to take from this is that, if the writer or your teacher has provided analogies or case examples, do spend time on them. Compare them, feature by feature. Work out what they have in common. Describe them as a unit. And by doing that, you will come to an understanding of the structure, of the underlying principles.

However, it needs to be remembered that analogies are primarily a comprehension strategy, not, directly, a memory strategy. Yes, understanding helps you remember, and, yes, developing expertise requires you to understand, not simply remember facts. However, analogies may actually hinder your recall of the facts themselves — the principles and concepts that the analogies are demonstrating[15]. If you are using analogies to develop your understanding, therefore, you should also use memory strategies to remember the facts you need to learn.

Exercise 8.3

Work out the correspondences between the following problems and provide a joint interpretation statement.

Problem 1:

You're at war. You need to capture a fortress. It's right in the middle of the hostile country, and there are many roads radiating out from it, all of which are mined. Small groups of men can pass over them safely, but a large force will detonate them, so a largescale attack is out of the question. You decide to divide your soldiers into small groups, sent them each to different roads, and have them converge simultaneously on the fortress.

Problem 2:

You're a doctor, and you have a patient with a malignant tumor in his stomach. You need to destroy the tumor, but you can't operate. There is a type of ray that can destroy it, but at high intensity it may destroy not only the tumor, but the healthy tissue around it. But if you use a lower intensity so that the healthy tissue isn't damaged, the tumor won't be destroyed. What do you do?   *[problems taken from a study by Gick and Holyoak 1980[16]]*

Asking questions

I said earlier that asking questions is one of the best ways of making connections, but like any strategy, it depends. Bad questions can be worse than no questions at all. Rote questions that direct your attention to unimportant details are better not asked.

Effective questions *prepare* you to pay attention to the important details in the text. The best questions not only direct your attention appropriately, but also require you to *integrate* the details in the text.

Elaborative interrogation

Elaborative interrogation involves asking questions — in fact, it's the strategy I discussed in the previous chapter. The idea behind elaborative interrogation is that relevant prior knowledge doesn't always readily come to mind when you are trying to learn new information, and sometimes you need help to make the right connections. To help you do that, elaborative interrogation guides you to construct reasons for the relationships between bits of information, taking you beyond the information given to you.

Elaborative interrogation, though it sounds somewhat intimidating, basically means something very simple: asking *why* questions.

So how does elaborative interrogation work? It's a simple strategy to explain, although carrying it out is not always so simple! Elaborative interrogation involves taking a fact, asking yourself why it's true, and attempting to answer your question.

The technique has been shown to improve recall of facts, and improve comprehension, even in children[17]. But clearly it depends on the ability of the individual to answer the questions — thus the level of relevant prior knowledge is crucial.

However, the answer doesn't have to be correct — although it does need to be reasonable! The important point to using this strategy is to make connections with your existing knowledge.

Asking the right questions

Why questions, like any questions, are only effective to the extent that they direct attention to *appropriate* information.

For example, in one study where students studied information about Canadian provinces, it was found that trying to confirm why a particular fact *made sense* for the province was more effective than trying to answer why the fact was *unexpected* for the province[18].

Essentially, it seems that to be effective, elaborative interrogation requires you to attend to information that is *consistent* with the information to be learned. In many cases your background knowledge may include information that is consistent with the new information, and information that is inconsistent. By asking "Why is this true?" you focus on the consistent information.

For example, the question "Why are arteries thicker and more elastic than veins?" is more helpful than the question "Why is it surprising that arteries are thicker and more elastic than veins?" The latter question would have led you to focus on reasons why veins and arteries should be the same, rather than concentrating on the differences.

Promoting distinctiveness

Several studies have found that creating interactive images is just as effective as elaborative interrogation[19]. Imagery, through the creation of interactive images, makes connections, and also promotes distinctiveness[20].

Both of these are important for memory. Elaborative interrogation, while it makes connections, doesn't promote distinctiveness. Studies that have manipulated concept familiarity have found that imagery is a better strategy when concepts are unfamiliar.

This is in keeping with the evidence that elaborative interrogation, to be effective, requires a certain level of understanding and knowledge on the part of the student. When students have a rich knowledge base, elaborative interrogation promotes the creation of associations (connections) and memory benefits. Those with a more limited knowledge base, however, are more likely to access general information, leading to a lack of distinctiveness.

This is confirmed in a finding that elaborative interrogation was most effective when the students were able to draw on a rich knowledge base, but that when their knowledge base was low, imagery-based strategies were more effective[21].

So, the bottom line is that elaborative interrogation is an effective strategy when you have enough background knowledge to ask good questions. However, if you don't know enough to ask good questions, you're probably better choosing another strategy.

Research also indicates that while elaborative interrogation can significantly help with cued recall (remembering in response to specific questions, as in multi-choice and short answer questions), it isn't of any particular benefit to free recall (as is required in writing an essay)[22].

Exercise 8.4

Go through the ozone text and see how many "why?" questions you can come up with.

Self-explanation

Self-explanation is a strategy that involves you explaining the meaning of information to yourself while you read. It's a strategy that is probably only effective when the text is demanding[23] — which varies of course with the knowledge and abilities of the student. However, when the material is appropriate, self-explanation may be more effective than elaborative interrogation.

In a study involving university students learning facts about the cardiovascular system, those who were required to explain what the facts meant to them and how they related to their prior knowledge (self-explanation) remembered more than those who explained why the facts made sense (elaborative interrogation). Indeed, those in the elaborative interrogation group did no better than those who simply repeated the facts aloud[24].

Self-explanation is seen as a more flexible strategy than elaborative interrogation. Elaborative interrogation requires you to ask why something is so, and that is not always an appropriate question. Self-explanation has no such constraints. Self-explanation, because its emphasis is on clearly describing the material presented, is also thought to rely less on prior knowledge than elaborative interrogation. This makes it the better strategy for a novice.

To use this strategy, you simply ask yourself what the fact (question or paragraph) means to you. What new information does it provide? How does it relate to what you already know? Does it help you understand something better? Does it raise questions in your mind?

The students in this study found self-explanation very easy to learn, and were much more likely to think they would continue to use it than those taught elaborative interrogation.

This should not be taken as indicating that self-explanation is always superior to elaborative interrogation, and thus is the only strategy you need learn. Remember, all the strategies described in this book have their uses! Elaborative interrogation is probably the more effective strategy in situations in which you already have a good background knowledge of the topic.

Exercise 8.5

Take the text on how blood flows, and ask yourself what you already knew before reading that passage, and what was new. Explain how the new information connects to what you already knew. Are there any questions in your mind about how it all works?

Mnemonics

Mnemonic strategies are "artificial" memory aids such as stories, rhymes, acronyms, and more complex strategies involving verbal mediators or visual imagery.

Unlike everything else I've discussed in this book, mnemonics do *not* help you understand your material. They do not help you make meaningful connections.

The purpose of mnemonics is simply to help you remember something — not by understanding it, not by incorporating it into your developing "expert database", but simply in the manner of a parrot. They are used to enable you to regurgitate information.

That sounds terribly contemptuous, but the ability to regurgitate information on demand is undeniably a useful one — indeed, in the context of examinations, often a vital one!

Even in the context of material you need to understand, there are often details that must simply be memorized. Sometimes, too, it helps to remember certain details before you can reach the understanding you seek. Moreover, mnemonics can help you retrieve clusters of meaningful information by facilitating your memory of the tags or labels that are access points to those clusters.

The subject of mnemonics is, however, too big to encompass in this book. I discuss effective mnemonic strategies for learning in my book *Mnemonics for Study*.

Main points

Elaboration connects new information to information you already know. Elaboration strategies include:

- Making comparisons
- Asking questions
    - Elaborative interrogation
    - Self-explanation
- Mnemonic associations

Comparisons help by focusing attention on common relational structure. Looking for differences is usually more effective than looking for similarities.

An effective strategy when given more than one example is mutual alignment.

Asking questions is an effective elaboration strategy, as long as the questions are good ones. Bad questions direct your attention to unimportant details. Good questions direct your attention to important details and force you to integrate them with other details in the text and in your existing knowledge.

Elaborative interrogation requires a sufficient level of prior knowledge.

Without relevant background knowledge, creating interactive images may be a more effective memory strategy.

Elaborative interrogation may be of more benefit to cued recall than free recall.

Self-explanation is an effective strategy when the text is demanding.

Self-explanation is a more flexible strategy than elaborative interrogation, and requires less prior knowledge.

Review questions

1. Elaborative interrogation

    a. makes comparisons that focus on similarities

    b. is a fancy way of saying "asking *why* questions"

    c. is a way of coming up with analogies

    d. is a strategy for asking questions that direct your attention to appropriate information

    e. involves you explaining the meaning of the text to yourself as you read

2. Mutual alignment

    a. is a way of coming up with analogies

    b. involves identifying specific correspondences between elements of different examples

    c. helps you make connections to knowledge you already have

    d. refers to differences that share the same dimension

3. Alignable differences

    a. share the same dimension (e.g., size)

    b. don't share the same dimension (e.g., comparing a size attribute to an ability attribute)

    c. are specific correspondences between elements of different examples

    d. are differences that are really very similar

4. The best questions

    a. focus on similarities

    b. focus on differences

    c. direct your attention to important information

    d. help you see connections between the details in the text

5. The best strategy for making comparisons is

   a. using analogies

   b. elaborative interrogation

   c. self-explanation

   d. mutual alignment

   e. the strategy that is best suited to the specific situation

6. Mnemonics help you

   a. understand complex material

   b. make meaningful connections

   c. make arbitrary connections

   d. memorize simple details

   e. connect new information to knowledge you already have

Concept maps

This is another important and lengthy chapter, in which I work through how to create a concept map, step-by-step. Don't let your opinion of mind maps affect your attitude to concept maps! I'm a big fan of concept maps for building and testing your understanding of a subject. In this chapter, I discuss both concept and mind maps, and the pros and cons of each.

In our discussion of graphic summaries and visual language, I mentioned concept maps and mind maps. I held back discussion of these till now because these are examples of visual language strategies that particularly emphasize connection. Having said that, I should note that the essence of graphic summaries is that they promote connection. My distinction between selection and connection strategies is designed to emphasize these two components of the note-taking process, but let's not forget that they can't be completely separated from each other.

Concept maps were developed by Joseph D. Novak in 1972. The technique is based on the idea that meaningful learning requires you to connect new concepts to existing knowledge[1]. Broadly speaking, a concept map is a graphic display that attempts to show how concepts are connected to each other. More specifically, a concept map is a diagram in which labeled nodes represent concepts, and lines connecting them show the relationships between concepts.

One type of concept map you're probably aware of is mind maps. Mind maps are a specialized form of concept map popularized very successfully by Tony

Buzan. There are important differences between mind maps and concept maps, which I'll discuss shortly.

But first, let's look at concept maps. Here's a concept map:

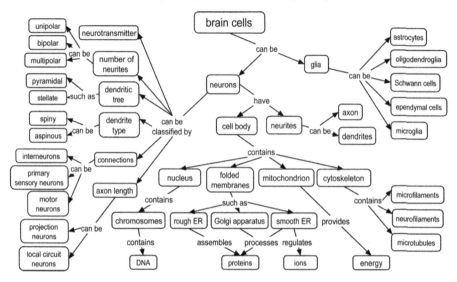

(This was constructed using a software program called Cmap, by the way; it's very easy to use and you can download it from the internet — it was created by academics for an academic environment.)

The first thing to note is that a "concept" can be just about anything. In this example, they are all nouns, mostly single nouns, but not always. However, they could have been single verbs, or even adjectives or adverbs (although these are rarer, and less recommended), or descriptive phrases. Here's one that incorporates all of those for Vivaldi:

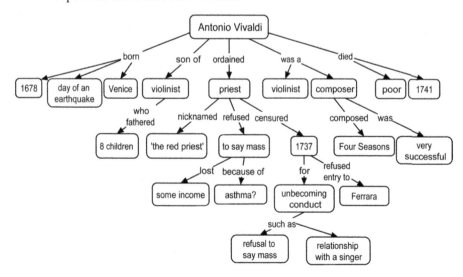

There aren't any formal rules about what is a concept and what isn't, or what is an appropriate level of concept in a particular map and what isn't. You have to make a judgment depending on the context of your concept map.

The second thing to note is that all the links are labeled. This is a crucial factor in what makes concept maps such an effective tool for developing understanding, as you'll see when you construct your own maps. It's one thing to realize that two concepts are connected; it's quite another to be able to articulate the nature of that connection.

When concept maps are useful

There are three stages in the study process when concept maps are useful. The first is at the very beginning. Remember when we looked at advance organizers and pre-questions? Priming your mind for what you are about to learn is a very important stage in studying. Constructing a concept map is a good way of doing that.

For example, say you were about to read (or listen to a lecture) about Vivaldi. You could have sketched a map outlining what you already knew about him beforehand, like this:

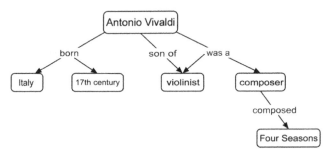

This is a quick way of getting down what you know, and at the same time providing an initial structure to sort out your thoughts. How good a structure it will be depends on the extent of your background knowledge — obviously the more you know about a topic, the better your structure (your framework for understanding) will be. But even if you are a complete novice, the action of constructing even a very simple map will help organize and prepare your thoughts.

In the same way, concept maps are useful at the end stage, as a means of reviewing what you have learned. Again, this involves you sketching out what you know.

Using them in these ways — as a priming or a testing mechanism — is reasonably straightforward. So let's look in detail at the tricky middle stage: constructing a concept map as a way of taking notes.

Building concept maps: a case study

Now this is a learning process — we're not going to get it right first time — so read through the whole section before deciding what is really needed.

Let's start where a lot of novices start, by selecting key concepts. We'll use our familiar text about the gene that affects event memory.

Here are the summary sentences again:

1. People with a particular variant of the gene controlling the brain factor BDNF have reduced hippocampal function.

2. BDNF plays a key role in memory.

3. Two variants: "Met" variant linked to poorer episodic memory; "Val" variant more common.

4. "Met" variant might increase risk of Alzheimer's and other disorders involving the hippocampus.

5. Study finds those with two copies of "met" perform dramatically worse on tests of episodic memory but not on other memory tests.

6. Two copies of "met" worse than one, but any "met" variant is associated with hippocampal dysfunction.

7. "Met" variant less successful in distributing BDNF proteins to the synapses.

8. Possible connection with memory problems in old age.

From these, we might come up with the following key concepts:

1. gene

2. BDNF

3. hippocampus

4. "Met" variant

5. "Val" variant

6. episodic memory

7. synapses

8. age-related memory problems

How well do these work as key concepts? The next step should help us decide. Let's try and list the attributes of each of these key concepts:

- gene controls BDNF

- BDNF plays a key role in memory.

- "Met" is a variant of the gene; linked to poorer episodic memory; linked to hippocampal dysfunction; might increase risk of Alzheimer's; less successful in distributing BDNF proteins to the synapses

- "Val" is a variant of the gene; more common.

Okay, that's about all we can get from the summary statements. Let's pull up the summary:

> Brain derived neurotrophic factor (BDNF) plays a key role in neuron growth and survival and, it now appears, memory. We inherit two copies of the BDNF gene - one from each parent - in either of two versions. Slightly more than a third inherit at least one copy of a version nicknamed "met," which the researchers have now linked to poorer memory. Those who inherit the "met" gene appear significantly worse at remembering events that have happened to them, probably as a result of the gene's effect on hippocampal function. Most notably, those who had two copies of the "met" gene scored only 40% on a test of episodic (event) memory, while those who had two copies of the other version scored 70%. Other types of memory did not appear to be affected. It is speculated that having the "met" gene might also increase the risk of disorders such as Alzheimer's and Parkinson's.

Now we can add:

- BDNF: short for Brain derived neurotrophic factor; affects function of hippocampus

- "met": contains the amino acid methionine in the location where the other version contains valine; slightly more than a third inherit at least one copy; only affects episodic memory

- "val": contains the amino acid valine in the location where the other version contains methionine

- "val" BDNF spreads throughout the cell and into the branch-like dendrites that form synapses

- "met" BDNF mostly clumps inside the cell body without being transported to the synapses

"Age-related memory problems" hasn't really made it into our attribute list; maybe we should drop it. But there is mention that the 'met' variant "might increase risk of Alzheimer's" — Alzheimer's might be a better key concept.

Now we start the connection process. How do the key concepts relate to each other?

- "Met" and "Val" are variants of a gene

- the gene controls BDNF

- BDNF is expressed in the hippocampus

- the hippocampus is critical for episodic memory

Okay, we're missing a connection here, to do with the synapses. If we look at the full text, we find this sentence: 'To regulate memory function, BDNF must be secreted near the synapses.' This provides the necessary relationship:

- BDNF must be secreted near the synapses

Let's try diagramming it.

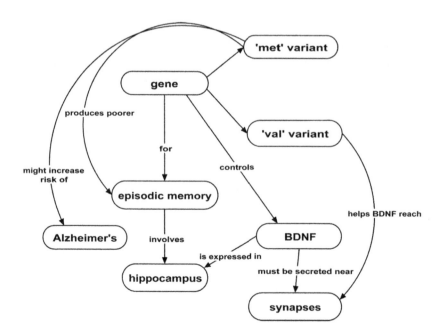

(These concept maps are constructed using graphics software called SmartDraw.)

Now this is just a first quick stab; we expect to have to play with it more before it will be satisfactory. What does this first attempt tell us?

There are several aspects that are not very satisfactory:

- there are three arc connections (as opposed to the preferred straight-line connections), which suggest we need to rearrange the concepts better;

- the connection between 'val' variant and synapses is labeled helps BDNF reach, but there is no direct connection between 'val' variant and BDNF;

- Alzheimer's is connected only to 'met' variant;

- the connections between 'met' and 'val' variants and gene aren't labeled.

Let's check whether everything we want is here by adding all the attribute information that isn't represented in the links:

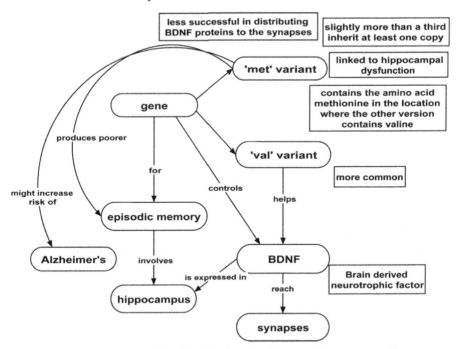

These comments suggest that 'met' variant is the crucial concept — because nearly all our notes refer to it — so we should probably make it more central. Two of the comments involve two of our key concepts, indicating links we don't have; again, making *'met' variant* more central will probably help with that. The connection to Alzheimer's seems unrelated to anything else, but if we look back at the full text, we see the comment "other disorders involving hippocampal dysfunction, such as Alzheimer's disease". We also know, from general knowledge, that episodic memory is poor in Alzheimer's. So now we can add a couple of connections.

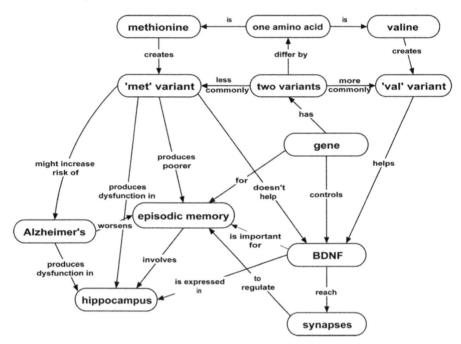

Notice how we now have the new concept *two variants*, which enables us to create that whole subnetwork, incorporating the information about the amino acids, and the relative commonness of the variants. We have two extra connections for the *Alzheimer's* concept, making it now clear why the 'met' variant might be thought to be associated with Alzheimer's. We've added another connection to *synapses*, thus making it clearer why it matters.

One problem with this concept map is that there are several lines that cross. This isn't against the rules, but it does make it harder to read. You do want to try and avoid this — but it's not always possible. Your choice is then whether to live with the crossing, or subdivide your map into more than one. Which approach you choose is up to you.

I hope you noticed that all the connecting lines are actually arrows. If you read the labels, you will see that they generally only make sense in one direction, so it is vital you make them point the right way! Otherwise the meaning will be quite different.

This is quite an informative map, but there is one big problem, and that is that there's no obvious place to start. This is not so bad in itself, although it does make it harder to deal with, particularly for an uncertain learner, but more importantly, it is a symptom of a deeper malaise.

There are two reasons for this problem. The first is that we started by listing the concepts; we should have started by framing a question. Before beginning a concept map, we need to understand exactly what we want the map to describe — not simply think of it as a summary for a section of text.

So what's our question here?

Well, the text was headed up "Human Gene Affects Memory" — can we turn that into a question? Perhaps, "How does a gene affect memory?"

We'll test that out as our focal question, but first, let's look at the other reason our map had no focus. There is another rule in concept mapping, one I haven't mentioned yet, and that is that concepts are represented hierarchically, with most general concepts at the top and most specific ones at the bottom. Not everyone obeys this rule, but doing so will certainly help you, both in constructing and reading the map.

So let's put our concepts in a hierarchy, from most general to most specific. This will be tricky for those that are not part of a hierarchy (e.g., 'met' variant is clearly below gene in a hierarchy, but how do gene and hippocampus relate?). We'll start with the easy stuff: by grouping those concepts that seem to be at the same level, and grouping them with concepts that are clearly related:

1. gene ⇨ two variants; 'met' variant; 'val' variant; one amino acid; methionine; valine

2. BDNF

3. hippocampus

4. episodic memory

5. synapses

6. Alzheimer's

Now there are two things to bear in mind when considering what might appear to be an intractable problem of hierarchically arranging things that aren't obviously part of a hierarchy. The first is that a concept map isn't a tree diagram; the sweep of general to specific is a guide not a rigid hierarchy. The second is that the general-to-specific wave relates to the context, not to some ordained taxonomy. So let's remind ourselves of our focal question: "How does a gene affect memory?" and of our links.

Look at our map and you'll see that all the arrows flow out of *gene*; none flow in. *Alzheimer's* points to *episodic memory* and *hippocampus*; but one of the *gene* subnetwork (*'met' variant*) flows in. *BDNF* points to *synapses* and *episodic memory*, and *synapses* points to *episodic memory*. All of which suggests that *gene* is clearly at the top; that *Alzheimer's* and *BDNF* are below; and *hippocampus*, *episodic memory* and *synapses* are below that again:

1. gene ⇨ two variants; 'met' variant; 'val' variant; one amino acid; methionine; valine

2. Alzheimer's; BDNF

3. hippocampus; episodic memory; synapses

We took these from the map, but if we had performed these steps before drawing our map, then we could have taken this information from the attribute list.

Now we have a focal question and a roughly hierarchical arrangement in mind, let's have another go at our map.

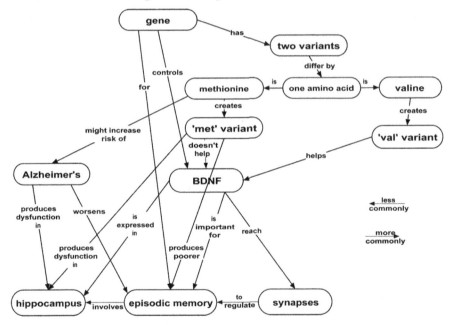

Well, that's pretty horrible! We have a line crossing a concept, several crossing lines, and two floating links that can't fit in anymore. If we examine the map, we can see that the problem lies in the fact that *'met' variant* and *gene* are both linking to the same concepts. Let's subdivide the map to get a bit of clarity:

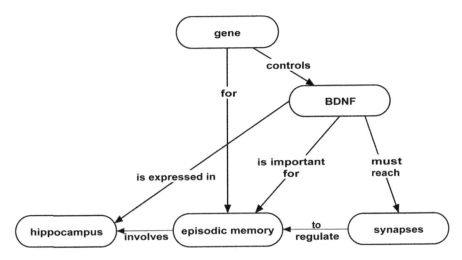

See how even when we restrict ourselves to the links that don't involve the gene variant subnetwork, we still get a crossed line.

Here's another rule: we don't have to include all possible connections; in fact, we shouldn't. What we need to do is select what's important **in the context of our focal question**. Which is "How does a gene affect memory?"

The operative word is *how*. And the link between gene and episodic memory is in fact an indirect one: the gene affects memory through its action on BDNF. So let's confine ourselves to this issue:

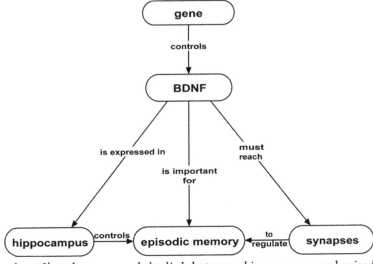

Notice how I've also reversed the link between *hippocampus* and *episodic memory* and altered the label to reflect that change. And now, I hope, the answer to our question is clear. Which, since we have entirely left out our section about the gene variants, makes it clear that the question wasn't the right one — or at least, was only part of the question. What we really want to know is why some people's genes mean they have a poorer memory.

Which brings us to our gene variant subnetwork:

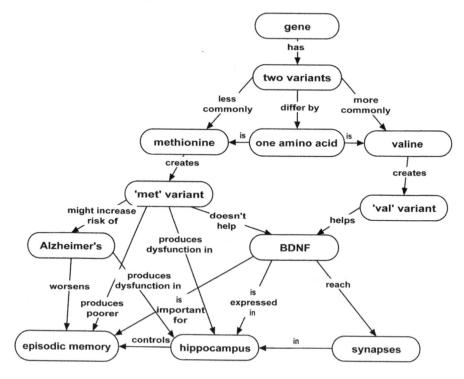

Still a little messy in the bottom-left corner; one last tweak, I think:

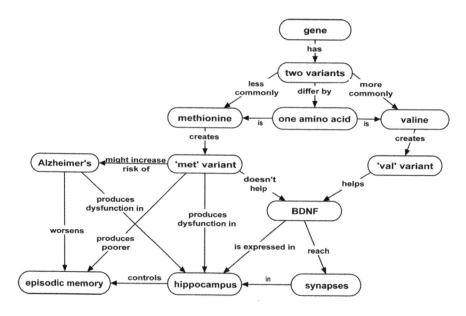

By bringing *Alzheimer's* up to the same level as *'met' variant*, and removing the direct connection between *BDNF* and *episodic memory*, we've removed a lot of the confusion of the crossing lines, and indeed the symmetry of the remaining crossed lines underlies the reason why the 'met' variant is suspected of involvement in some Alzheimer's cases.

When to use concept maps for taking notes

I hope this step-by-step analysis has revealed to you the strengths and weaknesses of this approach. As far as note-taking is concerned, concept maps are most useful for organizing your knowledge. They help you sort out the big picture; they show you where everything fits. They're not so good for detail. For example, the map doesn't explain what BDNF is, or the hippocampus, or synapses, or amino acids ... There's a lot it doesn't explain!

You could add concept maps, nesting them as it were. Thus there could be a small map for each of the concepts in the gene map. But you may prefer to use concept maps simply to overview topics that you have detailed using other note-taking strategies. Remember, it's not about finding 'the' right strategy for you; it's about finding several, from which you can choose the most appropriate for the task.

Creating concept maps, as we have seen, tends to take a lot of time (although the time will become much less with practice), so it's not a preferred strategy for note-taking (as opposed to preparing and reviewing). However, as I hope this example has shown you, they're great for showing you what you don't properly understand. For that reason, I recommend them for topics that are complex.

And as I said, they're good for the big picture, so if there's lots of different bits of information and you're not sure how it all fits together, concept maps can be a good tool. However, it's easy to overload a concept map with too many interlinking concepts — too many concepts; too much interconnection — so it's a good idea not to try and portray too much in a single concept map[2]. Which is where the idea of nested concept maps is useful.

But not all information lends itself to concept mapping. Sequential information, for example, is more appropriately represented in a linear structure.

How to concept map

Concept maps can be drawn on paper, but they can also be drawn on a computer, and this has a big advantage over paper. As we've seen, constructing a concept map is a process of revision and refinement —changing it is a lot easier on a computer!

If you want to use a computer, there are several concept mapping programs available, and I list some of them at www.mempowered.com/books/resources/effective-notetaking.

Building a concept map, step-by-step

1. Articulate your focal question

2. List the key concepts

3. Describe the attributes of these concepts

4. Articulate the relationships between the concepts

5. Order the concepts in a rough hierarchy from most general to most specific, in this context

6. Draw your first map

7. Evaluate it: Are all the links clearly labeled?

   a. Are concepts as short as possible? (short phrases are fine; if they're full sentences, it's a sign you're overloading the concept — it needs to be broken up)

   b. Are there good cross-links (ones from one section of the map to another), but not so many it's confusing? (remember, almost everything can be seen to be connected; you have to be selective)

   c. Does the map cover the material?

   d. Does it answer the focal question? (novices are prone to wandering from the point; a good map is a focused map)

Common problems and their solutions

Novices, or indeed more experienced users, usually start by trying to cover too much. That's okay. Start big — that gives you your overview, your big picture. Now break it up. And again, and again. When it comes down to it, we can't deal with too much information at one time. Remember working memory capacity is severely limited.

Concept maps provide a concrete demonstration of a process that should be going on during any studying. Start big; keep breaking it down into smaller and smaller bits, until you are down to small, approximately 4-item chunks.

Once you've got to that point, you can start building them up again.

The point about getting down to that point is that now you have integrated, well-understood chunks that are your building blocks. As you use them to build, you can make the connections.

But while you're breaking down and building up, there's something else that's important to do, and that's keeping a hold on your main idea.

This is trickier than you might think. Reflecting, perhaps, the associative nature of the human mind, we are all inclined to digress, to wander from the point, led by new information or new thoughts.

That's why your focal question is so important. It isn't cast in stone; you can change it. You may well find, as you come to a better understanding of the topic, as you craft your map, that your first question wasn't exactly right. That's fine — getting your question right is part of the process of revision and refinement — just make sure you always have a question to guide the process.

Here's some specific problems you may observe in your draft concept map, and what you should do about them:

- **Too many concepts**: break your map down into smaller maps, with one 'overview' map that shows how each map fits together

- **Too many links**: again, you need to create separate maps for some of the subtopics

- **Descriptions on the links too long**: probably a sign that you're loading too much on a single concept — think about whether the concept can be divided into smaller concepts; or it may be that you don't clearly understand the relationship between the concepts — think about it a little more

- **Concept descriptions too wordy**: again, you map be loading too much on the concept — think about whether it should be divided into smaller concepts

- **Too many maps**: there is a happy medium! If some of your smaller maps are too small (only contain 3 or 4 concepts), think about merging them with another

- **Not enough detail**: consider adding more concepts

- **Doesn't cover the material**: probably a sign that you haven't clearly and accurately articulated what the concept map is about — try and formulate the question you want the concept map to deal with; if you've got that right, that question should include as its subject the concept that will be the starting point for your map. If that doesn't work out, reformulate your question.

You may want to add specific examples to help you clarify a concept. If you do that, don't enclose the examples in ovals or boxes, because you don't want them mistaken for concepts.

Exercise 9.1

Draw a concept map for each of the example texts.

Mind maps

Here's a mind map of the brain cell information we saw in the concept map:

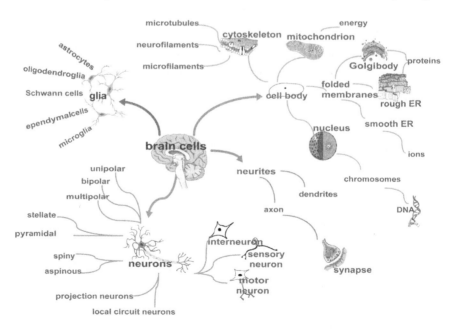

You'll notice some obvious differences. The most obvious is artistic — a mind map, as envisaged by Tony Buzan, is much more colorful and pictorial than a concept map. In fact, if I hadn't been constrained by the clip art available in SmartDraw (and let me say I was greatly impressed by what was available!), if I had been drawing by hand (and felt my artistic skills were up to it), all the words would have accompanying images, and the map would be essentially a solid block of color. Indeed, Buzan is quite happy to do without words at all, but I think that would be tricky with this particular content.

I'm not going to go into great detail about the principles of mind mapping and how to create them; all that information is available in Buzan's books. What I want to do here is talk about how mind maps differ from concept maps, the tasks mind maps are most appropriate for, and the problems you might have with them.

How mind maps differ from concept maps

A mind map has four essential characteristics:

- the subject is crystallized in a central image
- main themes radiate from it as branches
- the branches comprise a key image or key word
- the branches form a connected nodal structure

Keywords — what Buzan calls BOIs (Basic Ordering Ideas) —are basically concepts, as we've used them in concept maps. Basically, what mind maps do is display keywords in a memorable format. So, again, like concept maps, they're about the big picture, not the detail.

The essential difference between a mind map and the more general concept map is that in a mind map the main themes are connected only to this single central image — not to each other. In a concept map, there are no restrictions on the links between concepts.

Also, the connections between concepts in a concept map are labeled — they have meaning; they're a particular kind of connection. In a mind map, connections are simply links; they could mean anything.

Mind maps are also supposed to be very pictorial. In Buzan's own words: "The full power of the Mind Map is realised by having a central image instead of a central word, and by using images wherever appropriate rather than words."

Concepts in a concept map, on the other hand, can be (and usually are) entirely verbal. But the degree to which you use words or pictures is entirely up to the user.

In fact, this insistence on images is one of the things I don't like about mind maps (I hasten to add that there are many things I do like about mind maps). While images are certainly powerful memory aids, they are not for everyone, nor for all circumstances.

Images are also far more ambiguous than words. If you use a keyword often, or if you have an association that is already strong and will spring to your mind, then certainly you can use an iconic symbol instead of a word, but you do need to be sure its meaning is the one you immediately think of.

Buzan greatly emphasizes the creative aspect of mind maps. Along with the pictures, he wants lots of color. Basically, he sees a mind map as a work of art, and talks about the noncreative, stultifying nature of linear notes.

From this, you can see that mind maps and concept maps are really aimed at different purposes, and, perhaps, different personalities.

When to use mind maps

Mind maps are good for:

- generating ideas
- getting your head in the right space preparatory to listening to a lecture or reading a text
- doing a quick review — checking that you have all the main points down before a test.

But they're less useful as a means of taking notes.

The chief usefulness of mind mapping, I believe, is when you're still trying to come to grips with an idea. Mindmapping is good for brainstorming, for outlining a problem or topic, for helping you sort out the main ideas.

Concept maps, by comparison, are particularly useful further down the track, when you're ready to work out the details, to help you work out or demonstrate all the multitudinous ways in which different concepts are connected.

Concept maps, being more formal than mind maps, are better suited to situations where the concept is to be shared with others. Mind maps are very personal; they don't tend to be easy to share, because they so much reflect the individual mind that created them. In fact, they can revealingly demonstrate how we ourselves are not the same person we were a month ago — when we look back at a mind map we created earlier and no longer understand why we structured the information that way!

That is not a reason to despair; the change in the way you would do a particular mind map over time is a demonstration of the changes in your understanding. However, it does underline how personal mind maps are, which is why they're best as a thinking aid rather than a note-taking strategy.

Both mind maps and concept maps are good at clarifying your thoughts, but because of the greater formality of the concept map — the need to be more precise in your connections — concept maps are better at showing you exactly what you don't understand properly.

Mind maps don't suit everyone. In fact, more than any other technique, mind maps tend to engender strong feelings for and against — people who think they're the greatest thing since sliced bread; people who think they're seriously over-hyped.

This is evidenced in a study involving 50 medical students that compared their own study methods with the mind map technique for a 600-word text. Although both groups did well on the immediate test, when tested a week later only the mind map group seemed to have held onto any of it. Despite this, the students in the mind map group were not enthused by the technique — it seems unlikely that they would use the strategy when left to their own devices[3]. This fits in with anecdotal evidence suggesting few of the people who attend seminars or read books on mind mapping end up using it.

However, mind mapping can be a very useful tool for certain people, and in certain circumstances.

I don't want to suggest that those people who don't immediately respond well to mind maps should give up. Mind maps are deceptively tricky to come to grips with, particularly for people whose minds are not used to thinking this way. But for that very reason, they can be of particular benefit to such individuals. So it's worth persevering a little, before you decide whether or not they're for you.

Problems people often have

Many people have problems staying 'on track' when creating a mind map.

This is understandable — the method encourages free association, and it's very hard to be disciplined when free-associating! But there's a difference between a 'brainstorming' mind map and a 'summarizing' one. You do need to be more focused when summarizing.

If you are having this sort of problem in a summarizing mind map, it probably means your Central Image — the main idea in the center of your map — isn't properly focused, or that you haven't got your BOIs quite right. This isn't a sign of failure; you will rarely get these right first time. That's why creating a good mind map, like creating a concept map, is all about re-creating until you get it right. Which is one reason why mind maps are memorable; they encourage you to think deeply about the material.

The relative disorganization of a mind map also makes it harder to know if you've covered everything. The only answer to that is to check it against a more structured outline.

If there are too many connections between nodes, then a mind map is probably not the best way to represent the topic. A concept map would be better. Remember that in a mind map, the subtopics (the BOIs) are only connected to the main topic (the Central Image), not to each other. Of course this means the mind map is generally a gross simplification of a topic, since subtopics rarely only connect to each other through the main idea.

Being a simplification in this way isn't necessarily a bad thing — learning is all about simplification; bringing things down to a level we can understand before complicating the subject with details that might confuse — the trick is to make sure the degree of simplification is appropriate. In this case, you need to make sure the links between subtopics aren't something you need to consider at this point in your understanding. If you do, then you should use a concept map rather than a mind map.

Coming up with your BOIs is often difficult. If you're trying to summarize a textbook, or a significant portion of one, then chapter titles are a good place to start, with sub-headings being used for branches.

But you can only go so far studying the 'rules'. The best way to come to grips with mind maps is to study examples, and to work on your own. (Buzan suggests you need to create 100 mind maps before you can really understand them well enough to do them right!). There's a lot of examples on the internet; I provide some places to start in my list of resources.

Although Buzan encourages color merely for the sake of it — to make things prettier and more interesting, and hopefully more memorable — I'm inclined to think the indiscriminate use of color can be distracting. Better to develop some consistent habits, so that particular colors mean something. Moreover, while mind maps are inherently memorable, that doesn't mean you will remember them without effort. If you use a standard order of colors (perhaps reflecting the colors of the rainbow, which is a standard mnemonic everyone knows), then you could use this as a framework for remembering. Perhaps you could also link your BOIs to their color somehow — such as, making *power* yellow; *plants* green; *weather* blue; *happiness* yellow; *money* green (your color associations don't have to be the same as mine; what's important is that the association works for you).

Do remember that none of the strategies I've discussed in this book should be used to the exclusion of the others. What you should be aiming to develop is a number of preferred strategies (note the plural!) that cover the various tasks and situations you'll come across. For example, one student I heard of used mind maps extensively, but she also printed out her mind maps in outline format, which she could use for all the details she needed.

It's important to remember that mind maps are not only a subset of concept maps, but both are subsets of that much more expansive concept: visual language. Although I have discussed the 'rules' of concept and mind maps, I don't think you should be constrained by these. Certainly you should follow them initially — as with a recipe, you need to know how something works before you can modify it — but once you have achieved a certain level of expertise, you should start to adapt the strategy to suit your own cognitive style.

Exercise 9.2

Draw a mind map of this book.

Main points

Concept maps and mind maps are visual language strategies that particularly emphasize connection.

A concept map is a diagram in which labeled nodes represent concepts, and lines connecting them show the relationships between concepts.

Mind maps are a specialized form of concept map.

Concept maps are useful as priming tools.

Concept maps are particularly useful as a means of reviewing what you have learned.

Concept maps are most useful for showing you the big picture.

Concept maps are great for showing you what you don't properly understand.

A mind map differs from a concept map in that the main themes are connected only to a single central image, not to each other, and the connections between concepts are not labeled.

Mind maps are usually more visual, and concept maps more verbal.

Mind maps are good for generating ideas, and for doing a quick review.

Both mind maps and concept maps are good at clarifying your thoughts, but in different ways.

Review questions

1. Concept maps are another name for mind maps   T / F

2. Concept maps are useful for
   a. preparing for study
   b. revising
   c. building an understanding of complex or difficult material
   d. getting down all the details
   e. brainstorming

3. The first step in building a concept map is
   a. to break the material into a lot of small chunks
   b. to work out your focal question
   c. to sort out the concepts from most general to most specific
   d. to work out all the connections

4. Concept maps differ from mind maps in
   a. labeling the connections between concepts
   b. being able to make connections between any concepts
   c. using more colors and icons
   d. using visual language

5. Mind maps are useful for
   a. preparing for study
   b. revising
   c. brainstorming
   d. building an understanding of complex or difficult material
   e. getting down all the details

PART III

Applying your strategies

We've covered selection and connection strategies — both critical for learning, for developing understanding, and for remembering — but these will only get you so far if you don't know how, and when, to use them.

In this final section, we'll look at

- the very different situation of taking notes during lectures
- ways of using your notes
- ways your own learning styles and preferences can affect your choice of strategies
- how to evaluate the text and the task before you, in order to choose the right strategy.

Don't neglect these aspects, even if you think it's just icing on the cake! If you don't use your strategies appropriately, you're less likely to see the benefits, and less likely to continue to use them.

Taking notes in lectures 10

In this brief chapter, I discuss the challenges of taking notes in lectures, and ways in which you can improve your lecture note-taking. Lecturers might also like to take note!

How taking notes in a lecture is different from taking notes from text

So far, I have talked almost exclusively about notetaking from text. That is partly because far more research has been done on this topic than on notetaking from lectures, and partly because it's much easier to teach, and learn, to take effective notes from text.

However, the time has come to talk about how different the lecture situation is.

For a start, you have no control over the rate of presentation. With a textbook, you can go as fast or slow as you want; in a lecture, you must keep up with the lecturer.

Secondly, and of equal importance, you have no great ability to go back over information you don't understand or didn't catch (apart from asking the presenter to repeat themselves or explain more fully — something many students are shy of doing).

Why lecture notetaking is more difficult

The research that has been done on lecture notetaking has had very mixed results, and the main reason seems to be rate of presentation[1]. Studies where the rate has been 100 words per minute or slower have shown an encoding benefit for notetaking, but studies where the rate has been faster than that tend to show a disadvantage. The normal rate of speech is around 150 words per minute, so you can see the acceptable rate is decidedly slow.

Note that I said an *encoding* benefit. Notetaking, whether from text or lecture, is assumed to be potentially beneficial in two ways — by deepening your processing of the material (the encoding advantage) and by giving you material to review. This second advantage is particularly important for lecture material, because if you don't take notes, you presumably won't have a record to review.

Most of the research has looked at the encoding aspect, although most students take notes for review.

But how good are these notes for review purposes?

A survey of notetaking[1] across 12 different courses found that the average student recorded 60% of the information recorded in a set of ideal notes, with a great deal of variability across courses (from 39% for American Literature to 76% for Textiles — presumably there is not only a subject effect, but also a very strong lecturer effect, so don't take this to mean American Literature is a difficult subject to record, and Textiles easy). Other studies have put the typical amount as low as 20-40% of the important ideas[2].

In the survey, information that was written on the board was, unsurprisingly, much more likely to be recorded (88% on average, compared to only 52% of information that wasn't recorded on the board). This is particularly important because the study also found a direct linear correlation with grades, with course grades being higher for students who recorded more of the information units *not* written on the board.

In other words, students who were better at recognizing the important information in the absence of the giant prompt, got higher grades.

An experiment with some of the students in the study also suggests that students greatly overestimate the adequacy of their notes. When they were told to self-score their own notes, the average student claimed to have noted 77% of the information not written on the board (compared to the actual amount of 52%).

It's also worth noting the marked fatigue effect. Normal college lectures are, after all, lengthy affairs, but the amount of information recorded in the second twenty minute period was significantly less than that recorded in the first twenty minutes, and that recorded after the first forty minutes less still.

One of the problems with lecture notetaking is that some of your attention is spent on your own hand-movements and the writing you're producing. It's been found that notetaking is best (produces the greatest benefit) when you're taking notes from a purely audio source (a tape recording or a podcast, say), and worst when the source is audio-visual (as in a lecture)[3].

Are there special strategies for taking notes in lectures?

The notetaking skills you've learned need to be well practiced to deal successfully with information that is coming at you at a rate you can't control. Attention is also far more critical — because of the rate of presentation, and because you don't have the luxury of multiple readings.

When you have a book open in front of you, you have the time to reflect on the text and rephrase pertinent details in your own words. In a lecture situation, this is much more difficult. If you are very familiar with the topic, and have a high working memory capacity, and the lecturer doesn't talk too fast, then you may well be able to paraphrase and commentate as you go (or to be more precise, as the lecturer goes). Otherwise, your best strategy is, unfortunately, to leave the thinking for later.

But there is some evidence[4] that typing (rather than writing by hand) may partially overcome this problem. Remember that I said that part of the difficulty in lectures is the attention you're giving to your own hand-movements (of course this is always true, but remember that the lecture situation is putting more demands on working memory than the more leisurely textbook situation). For many people, typing is a less demanding activity. Because typing allows you to produce more, it helps reduce the cognitive load (one comparison found that the average typist can produce 33 words per minute compared to 19 WPM for the average hand writer).

It may be, then, that this strategy would particularly help students with a low working memory capacity, and also (we may speculate) students with low background knowledge (because they need to take much fuller notes).

Having said that, if you're typing on a device that you're also using to do other things (keeping your eye on email, facebook, etc), then the additional distraction may reduce the effectiveness of the strategy. Remember that it's all about cognitive load and your working memory capacity! The more you use your very limited WMC for other tasks, the less capacity will be available to take good notes.

Keeping pace means you want to use as many abbreviations as you can. Oddly, most students don't tend to make much use of abbreviations and diagrams in their notes. One study[5], for example, found that only 40% of students showed any sort of abbreviations, and for the most part these were limited to 'e.g.' and arrows (for 'therefore' or 'leads to'). Another study[6], analyzing 25 sets of lecture notes, found that only 20% used abbreviations and only 12% included diagrams.

Remember that typing helps because it enables you to produce more words more easily; abbreviations and quickly sketched diagrams do likewise (a picture is worth 1000 words!).

By the way, abbreviations are not limited to handwriting. The beauty of typing using word-processing software is that you can instruct it to rewrite your common abbreviations as the full word (using auto-correct options).

I have quite a number included in my auto-correct options. Some of these are quite general: for example, # (number), gen (generally), incl (including), situ (situation), circs (circumstances), orgn (organization), envt (environment). Others are more specific to my field of study: for example, wmc (working memory capacity), recogn (recognition), mem (memory), rem (remember), cog (cognitive), cogn (cognition).

You want to develop a good repertoire. Remember, the abbreviations only need to have meaning for you, so they can be quite idiosyncratic. On the other hand, don't use any you're going to have trouble interpreting later.

If you're still having trouble keeping up with your notes, consider whether you're being sufficiently selective in what you're recording. Because your time is so limited, it's more important than it is with text that you don't record information you already know, or details that are interesting rather than important (chances are you'll remember such details anyway).

Because successful notetaking in lectures requires you to be as selective as possible, it's also vital that you come to the lecture with a reasonable knowledge of the material being covered — so you need to do the reading!

It's worth emphasizing that unwritten information may be at least as important as written information. Discussions, in particular, tend to be ignored by note-takers. But this is precisely where valuable ideas may come up, that don't appear in any lecture handouts or other written texts.

Notwithstanding this, you shouldn't feel obliged to take notes if you sincerely think the information isn't worth recording. Research has shown[7] that forcing students to take notes only benefits those students with low prior knowledge of the topic; those with greater knowledge show no benefit.

In other words, don't take notes just because you feel you're expected to! Remember, thoughtful selection is the key to good notes.

All of this means that you should not approach lecture note-taking in the same way as you do note-taking from written text. However, after the lecture, you can now apply your text note-taking strategies to the material you have produced. The time constraints on your ability to re-work the material at the time of hearing it mean that it's vital that you work on your notes after the lecture, paraphrasing and organizing them in the ways I have discussed.

This reworking stage is best done as soon as possible after the lecture, so that the information is fresh enough that you can expand on the notes. Indeed, one study[8] found that note-taking was even better if students were given three five-minute pauses during the lecture to add to and revise their notes.

While this isn't under a student's control (teachers might like to take note!), there may well be opportunities during the lecture when, for one reason or another, you don't need to pay attention (for example, the lecturer might be setting up something, or having a private discussion with a TA). Instead of using these periods to talk to your friends, or check your phone, why not use them to add bits to your notes?

When teachers provide support

If you're fortunate enough to have a teacher that provides an outline before the lecture, this can be very useful. Do use it. Remember that anything that reduces your cognitive load will help you take better notes.

Some teachers even provide a full set of notes. If that's the case, you can relax. Rather than trying to get everything down, you have the luxury of sitting back and actually listening to the lecture. This doesn't mean you shouldn't take any notes! But you can be more selective. Rather than trying to take down everything that seems important, you can note down thoughts that come to you, and items of more personal relevance.

It *is* important to make your notes 'your own'; you don't want to solely rely on teacher handouts. Teacher handouts are written texts — treat them as such. In other words, you need to make your own notes from the handouts — and your more personal notes from the lecture will help with this.

Failing all this, many teachers will at least provide verbal cues to what they consider important — words like *always, remember, main, important, principal, chief*, etc. Unfortunately, these cues are not always as obvious to the student as the teachers think! Perhaps the reason is that the students aren't listening for the cues. I suggest you do so.

Best of all are cues to the organization of the lecture. If your teacher (in the absence of a handout providing a written outline) begins the lecture by outlining what is going to be discussed, you should record this outline, and use it to organize your notes.

The best support that a teacher can offer is a recording of the lecture. If you can replay a lecture, either as an audio or video recording, then you have the opportunity to end up with excellent notes. One study[9], for example, found a marked improvement in the quality of notes when the students had the opportunity to repeat the recordings more than once.

This was particularly true for 'lower-level' ideas. It seems that students first focus on top-level information. When they reached a certain level of coverage (about 70-80% of the information covered in their notes), they shifted their attention to the next level of information, and so on. To get the details, therefore, you need to take several bites!

I would urge you in such circumstances to repeat the lecture one more time after you have completed your notetaking. Listen to it once without taking any notes. The experience of simply listening, rather than listening in order to take notes, is quite different, and you may be surprised how much more you get out of it.

If you do, however, have only one presentation of the lecture, then you do need to focus on those 'top-level' ideas. Indeed, what distinguishes better note-takers from less successful ones is the ability to capture more of the important ideas. One study[10] found that poor note-takers recorded an equal number of important and unimportant ideas, while more successful students recorded about the same number of unimportant ideas (showing that even the better students have much to learn about notetaking!), but many more important ideas.

Different approaches to lecture notetaking

Students have different ideas about lectures[11]. Some think the right idea is to record everything, as if they're a tape recorder or a stenographer. Others think it's more like cracking a code — they have to uncover the mysterious signals the lecturer sends out, that tells what bits of information are important. Other students think the idea is to sit there and simply try and soak up everything. And some see the lecture as one source among many, a source they must integrate with all their other references, or as a guide, helping them find their path through all the information.

The idea you have about lectures will influence the strategies you use — before, during, and after class. But it's not as if there's a single correct idea. Each of these metaphors encompasses some truth.

Part of the challenge is that lecturers are different, and subject areas are different. The lectures, and the appropriate strategies, are different for mathematics and history, for physics and political science. Some lectures are dense with vital information, while others are filled with interactive activities and entertaining stories.

There is no single 'best' strategy, just as there isn't for taking notes from text. You need to adapt to your different teachers.

Which strategies are most useful for lecture notetaking depends on the lecturer's organization. The more formally organized lecturers will tend to follow a structure that is probably best captured in a topical outline or a matrix; more disorganized or informal lectures are probably best recorded with some sort of loose concept map.

Don't overlook the benefits of collaboration! Because students are, by and large, such poor note-takers in lectures, collaboration can be very useful, especially in the early days. Comparing your notes with others in the class can enable you both to fill out your notes with important information you've missed, and to learn from each other's different styles and strategies.

Reworking not recopying

I mentioned the importance of reworkng your notes after, or even during, the lecture. I want to emphasize this aspect. Many students recopy their lecture notes. This is a complete waste of time. Really. You're not doing anything useful.

But my notes won't make any sense to me later, when I use them to revise, I hear you wail. *I probably won't even be able to read them, they're such a mess.*

I'm not saying you shouldn't do anything with your notes! But simply recopying, to make them neater, easier to read, is not using your time wisely. What you need to do is *rework* them. Ideally, you'll be using any moments during the lecture to expand on your notes — if stolen moments are all you have (as opposed to teacher-provided pauses), keep these additions to the barest minimum, just enough to remind you after the lecture, when you can expand on them properly. Later in the day, or no later than the next day, rework your notes properly, using the strategies we've discussed for text.

This is when you re-organize the material in a way that makes sense to you, when you re-write verbatim material into your own words (with the obvious exception of any quotes you want), when you build concept maps or other graphic organizers, when you add any new thoughts you've had or connections you've seen. Add a quick summary of the main points of importance to you.

Preparation is key

Because you have limited time to think and write during the lecture, preparation is absolutely crucial to taking good notes. As I said, the more you know about the subject, the fewer notes you need to take, and this is particularly important for those with a lower working memory capacity. If you can hold more in working memory, you have an advantage in being able to get more information down. If you have a more limited capacity to remember what was said, then it is even more critical that you prepare for the lecture.

What does it mean, to prepare? First, if the teacher has assigned reading, make sure you do it! And do it properly — that means using the strategies we've discussed, to make sure you have as good a grasp of the material as you can get.

Some of you will be saying now, *why bother? why not wait for the teacher to explain it?*

Here we come back to your beliefs about the purpose of lectures. If you think the purpose of lectures is to be your sole, or at the very least main, source of information, then you'll be sceptical of this advice. But if you see lectures more as guides, then you'll realize that the better you understand the topic, the more you reduce the amount of notes you need to take. This means your mind is free to actually engage with what the teacher is saying, and will be better able to determine what is really important.

If you do the reading, and take / make notes of it, and assuming your teacher has told you what the next lecture will be about, you'll be able to construct a skeleton for your notes. This might be an outline or something more graphic. Hopefully, too, you'll have developed questions. Make sure you include those in your skeleton.

Your aim for your skeleton should be to have enough headings and questions to reduce the things you need to write down during the lecture, without putting down so much that it hampers you when you're taking notes during the lecture (you don't want to spend time searching for the right place to note something down!).

Mindwandering is your enemy

Why does notetaking get worse as the lecture goes on? Noone who has sat through an hour-long lecture needs research to tell them the answer to this! Of course it gets harder to concentrate, of course your mind wanders off more and more. What can you as a student do about it? (Most of the power to prevent mindwandering is of course with the lecturer — carefully spaced moments of interaction provide one obvious strategy, and one particularly effective activity is getting students to answer questions on the material from the preceding part of the lecture.)

One study[12], which found that there was significantly more mindwandering in the second half (52% vs 35%), and that students got significantly more questions right on a post-lecture test if the questions came from the first half (71% vs 57%), showed that the simple act of asking whether or not the student's mind had been wandering, was enough to bring their attention back to the lecture (when some questions were taken from just before the mindwandering probes and just after, it was found that the first half vs second half difference wasn't there for post-probe questions). Perhaps you could use your laptop or phone to periodically ask the question.

Another study[13] interspersed a 21-minute video lecture with three 3-minute breaks, during which students either did arithmetic problems, or did a few problems followed by a quick test on the material covered in the previous lecture segment. Those who were tested showed less mindwandering, took more notes, and did much better on the test at the end of the lecture (84% vs 59%). A follow-up experiment added a group who studied the test answers, but were not actually tested. The performance of this group was not significantly different, on any of these measures, from the other non-tested group. Scores on the final test were: 89% vs 70% vs 65% (tested, nontested, restudy groups, respectively).

A fascinating finding was that, despite all this, the students in the tested group actually found the lecture less mentally taxing than those in the other two groups.

Another possible strategy for reducing mindwandering is meditation. There's some evidence[14] that a brief (6 minutes) period of focused meditation before the lecture reduces mindwandering. The focused meditation simply involved closing one's eyes and counting breaths.

Main points

Most students overestimate how well they've recorded the important information in a lecture.

You're more likely to omit important information the later it's presented.

You need to use strategies that help you maintain attention.

To reduce the cognitive load, you need to:

- be well-practiced at the particular note-taking strategies you use (make sure you practice both an outline strategy suitable for a well-organized lecture, and a looser mapping strategy suitable for a disorganized lecture).

- have an established vocabulary of useful abbreviations

- read up on the topic beforehand

Reducing cognitive load is particularly important when the lecturer is disorganized and/or a fast speaker, or you have a low working memory capacity (permanently or temporarily).

In the lecture, your priority is to select the important information. After the lecture, you need to re-work your notes using the strategies we have discussed.

Remember that you shouldn't try to fit a single strategy to every subject or teacher.

Review questions

1. How well you take notes in lectures depends on

   a. how far through the lecture it is

   b. how good you are at recognizing when something is
       important *even when it's not written on the board*

   c. how quickly you can write

   d. how quickly the lecturer talks

   e. your beliefs about the purpose of lectures

2. The best way to take lecture notes is by using

   a. the Cornell note-taking system

   b. a visual organizer like a mind map

   c. shorthand, so you can get down every word

   d. any format, as long as it's well-organized and you use it all the
       time (so you get expert)

   e. an appropriate format for the subject and lecturer style

3. The main problem with taking notes in lectures is

   a. cognitive load

   b. disorganized lecturers

   c. maintaining concentration

   d. lecturers that mumble

   e. not being able to write/type quickly

Using your notes 11

This very brief chapter looks again at the various purposes
of note-taking, discussed at the beginning of the book —
this time exploring what that means in terms of how that
affects how you use your notes.

I said at the beginning that note-taking, although students tend to think it's
all about keeping a record, is primarily important through its effect on how
you encode information in your brain (although this is less true of the lecture
situation, unless notes are provided and you are augmenting them rather
than trying to cover everything).

It has this effect in a number of different ways. Here's a list of the various
functions taking notes can have:

- to provide a record
- to focus attention
- to reduce cognitive load
- to organize information
- to help you select what's important
- to help you make connections
- to help you review

Let's look at each of these in turn.

Providing a record

Note-taking to provide a record is important only in a lecture situation, or where you have only temporary usage of a text (for example, a library book). In such cases, of course, you will usually want fuller notes than in the circumstances where the source material is permanently available.

However, as we have discussed, in many cases you will be forced to be more selective in a lecture. Where taking full notes is a problem (by reason perhaps of the lecturer's speed of presentation), and the lecturer doesn't provide written material, it is particularly important that you prepare before the lecture, by reading relevant material, and perhaps sketching a mind map or concept map. Remember, the more knowledge you have beforehand, the more selective you will be able to be in your note-taking.

Treat the lecture not so much as your major source of information, but rather as an opportunity to find out what the lecturer thinks is important (vital if you're to do well in exams and essays), to clarify areas you didn't understand fully, and to gain motivation.

Focusing attention

Don't underestimate the role of note-taking in focusing attention. This is particularly important when the lecture or text is boring! Sometimes just listening or reading can be the best thing to do, but when the material is dull or difficult, only the activity of note-taking (even if it's only mental) will keep the material from 'going in one ear and out the other'.

It's particularly important in such cases for you to have a specific and clearly articulated goal, preferably written down. Notetaking can become an automatic process. To get the most benefit from its function of focusing attention, you need to be an active note-taker, alert to your goal of selecting only that information that is relevant to your goal.

Helping you select what's important

As I've said before, selecting what's important is the first essential step in successful learning. note-taking is only a tool to help you do this. This function is closely related to the function of focusing attention, and like that, rests heavily on first specifying your goal.

However, specifying your goal is less important in the lecture situation, where your goal is usually defined by the lecturer. You want to record what the lecturer thinks is important, so all you need do is be alert to the cues she provides. She might also make a preliminary statement telling you what your goal should be (e.g., "You should come away from this lecture with a clear understanding of why Caesar returned to Rome, and the significance of the act of crossing the Rubicon"). Write that goal at the top of your notes, and use it throughout the lecture to guide you in selecting what information is important — remembering that cues from the lecturer always take precedence, even if the emphasized information appears unrelated to the stated goal.

The text situation is less clear. The problem here is that the goals and interests of the writer are not likely to perfectly match your goals or the goals of your instructor (which may be the same, if your only motive is to do well, or may be different, if you have a personal interest in the topic).

If you don't first specify your goal, you'll be at the mercy of the writer's goals. Remember that cues to what is important, whether they are signal words or phrases (such as "It's important to note", "chiefly", "the most important"), headings, or highlighted text, are only useful to the extent that the one providing the cues has the same goals as you. So while you should certainly pay attention to these cues, you shouldn't take heed of them blindly. Always use your own specified goal as your yardstick in judging whether information is important to you.

A priming strategy, such as an advance organizer or a priming mind map or concept map, is very useful here.

Organizing information / Helping you make connections

Your memory is not a junk-heap (though it might seem like it sometimes!). Memory is a database. If you don't understand how you've organized it, that's because you haven't taken conscious control of the process. If you just toss information into it, hoping it will find its right place and that you will be able to find it again, it's going to be a lot harder to find than if you had thought carefully about how the new information fits in with the information you already have in there. And if you cram the new information in as a lot of different unrelated facts, why should they stick together (and thus later be found all in one place)?

The more organized you are when encoding information, the more likely it is to stay together, which means it will be found much more easily. The more connections it has with information you already know well, the more easily you will find it. (For more about how information is organized in memory and how to encode information effectively, see my book *The Memory Key* or *Perfect Memory Training*.)

Helping you review

Although taking effective notes is a great deal more than half the battle, it's not necessarily going to produce an improvement in your exam scores. note-taking is not only about encoding the information to be learned; it's also about reviewing. You can't expect to remember everything on one reading, however well-organized your notes are! To benefit fully from your note-taking activities, you need to review your notes, and more than once.

The best way to review your notes is *not* simply to re-read them. Reviewing should be an active process. This is where concept maps and mind maps are particularly useful. But the essence of review, whatever strategy you use, is to condense.

How many times you do this will depend on how full your original notes are (which will depend on how much relevant knowledge you already possess), but basically the process of review involves a repeated selection of important information until you are left with one single brief sentence or keyword for each coherent unit of information, and a repeated reorganization of that information to achieve those tight clusters of information.

In other words, where the material is difficult and complex, you might use several note-taking strategies on the same material — say, starting with heading construction, building to a topical summary, then reorganizing in a graphical format (graphic organizer; multimedia summary; map; diagram), reorganizing it again (and again and again) as you refine your graphic summary, and finally reviewing it in a series of concept maps.

It should be clear from this that there is no clear boundary between review and construction of notes. Effective note-taking is a process of reconstruction, of working the information until you get it right. However, you do reach a point (and it may be on the first attempt if the material is undemanding) where you are happy with your notes. Once you do that, you reach the review stage. But even if you no longer need to condense or reorganize the material, it is still not enough to re-read them for your review.

There are two main principles you need to bear in mind:

- Effective review involves retrieval.
- Review should occur at increasingly spaced intervals.

The first principle means that you review by recalling as much as you can — by constructing a summary (outline, graphic organizer, mind or concept map, ...) *without* reference to your notes. It is repeated retrieval that really matters when it comes to providing the repetition necessary to improve memory. Retrieval attempts are also necessary to check your learning.

And such review should occur at intervals that become progressively far apart with each successful review (if your review shows gaps in your memory or your understanding, obviously you have to return to your notes and work on them some more).

You should also note that if you review the material right after reading it, you're going to have a lot of information in your short-term memory — information that isn't necessarily properly understood, or effectively encoded in long-term memory. Accordingly, you may get a quite erroneous feeling that you understand the material. Reviewing after a delay will give you a much better sense of how well you really understand the material.

It's also useful to vary the manner of review. If you simply try to recreate the exact same words in the same format every time, you will not only fix the information into one particular, inflexible form, reducing the number of situations in which it can be easily retrieved, but you may also get an inaccurate idea of how well you know the material. In a not uncommon story, one researcher[1] describes a statistics student who could solve all the problems in his study sheet and consequently felt prepared for his exam. However, when a friend cut out all the problems and shuffled them, he failed miserably. Without realizing it, he was relying on chapter cues to tell him which formulas and principles were applicable; he didn't know which were applicable without those cues. Most of us have at some time had a similar experience.

Remember that note-taking, in itself, is more about understanding than memory. Accordingly, on its own, it is of more help in tests of understanding, such as solving problems, and drawing inferences[2]. It's the repeated retrieval that you undertake during review that will ensure the material is properly learned.

Reducing cognitive load

Notes can be helpful in reducing cognitive load by providing an external representation — that is, by having information written down in front of you, you don't have to hold it in memory.

Remember, working memory is about holding in mind all the information you're working on. The more you have written down in front of you, the less you have to hold in your mind. But because you have to be able to see all the information you need in one sweep, you need to limit the information you have in front of you to the information you need at that time — and so we come back to selection, and also to organization. As I mentioned in the discussion of graphic organizers, the way in which the information is organized affects how easily you can see it all, and the connections between information.

Note-taking also helps with reducing cognitive load less directly, by encoding the information in a coherent whole, and providing a means for review. Frequent revision makes information in long-term memory much easier to find and retrieve, which reduces the need to hold so much in working memory.

Note-taking strategies, like any strategies, can also *add* to your cognitive load, in the initial stages, when you are still unskilled at using the strategies. This is why less successful learners so often use less effective strategies — because they are less demanding. And why are they less demanding? Not because of any inherent demands of the strategy — successful learners are using them without any trouble — but because any skill is more demanding when you are learning it, and becomes less and less demanding of your working memory resources as you practice. I don't mean to deny that some note-taking strategies are more demanding than others, but this simply means that they require more practice to reach the same level.

It's worth noting at this point the crucial difference between practicing a skill and *deliberately* practicing it. First of all, let's start by reiterating a point made at the beginning of this book: it's not about the time you spend. How much time you spend studying doesn't have much relationship to how well you do academically[3]. Part of the reason for that is that students have differing degrees of prior knowledge and skills. The other part — the less appreciated part — is that the quality of that study time varies[4].

Research into expertise has provided convincing evidence that experts, be they musicians or chess masters or top sportspeople, achieve their expertise by engaging in a considerable amount of deliberate practice — a term coined by the foremost researcher in the field to refer to high quality, focused practice[5].

What distinguishes deliberate practice from less productive practice? Ericsson suggests several factors are of importance:

- The acquisition of expert performance needs to be broken down into a sequence of attainable training tasks.

- Each of these tasks requires a well-defined goal.

- Feedback for each step must be provided.

- Repetition is needed — but that repetition is not simple; rather the student should be provided with opportunities that gradually refine his performance.

- Attention is absolutely necessary — it is not enough to simply mechanically "go through the motions".

- The aspiring expert must constantly and attentively monitor her progress, adjusting and correcting her performance as required.

In line with this emphasis on concentrated attention, it's been found that the habit of studying alone in a quiet environment is associated with better academic performance[6].

The expertise research also suggests that the best way to become skilled at the various strategies described in this book is not simply to use them, but to deliberately practice them, with careful attention to each specific step in the strategy, and directed effort at those parts you find most difficult.

It's worth remembering that students often prefer strategies that require less effort, but the strategies that benefit them most are those that they (initially at least) find less enjoyable.

Main points

Note-taking provides a selective record, not a complete one.

Note-taking can be useful in helping you maintain attention when you are having trouble doing that.

Articulating a specific goal helps you keep focused, and helps you select what is most important.

A priming strategy can help you articulate your goal.

The more organized you are when encoding information, the more easily it will be remembered. An effective note-taking strategy helps you organize information.

To get the most out of your notes, you need to actively review them.

Notes can help reduce cognitive load:

- by providing an external representation

- by organizing information to make connections clearer

- by involving visual as well as verbal forms of representation.

Note-taking strategies can add to your cognitive load until you have practiced them sufficiently.

Less preferred strategies are often the most effective.

Review questions

1. The best notes

    a. contain everything you need to know

    b. are neatly written, so you can easily reread them

    c. contain all your thoughts and questions, as well as everything you need to know

    d. provide sufficient details to help you remember what you need to know

    e. make sense of the material

2. Notes are

    a. mainly for later review

    b. to help you keep your thoughts on track

    c. in case you need to look up something later

    d. to help you clarify and organize your thoughts

    e. to help you 'select & connect'

Learning style and individual differences

There's a lot of misinformation out there about learning styles. We do, as students, have characteristics that impact on the way we learn, and how well we learn. However, they may not be the ones you're thinking of. The important thing about individual differences is not that they are inborn, and doom (or reward) us. The important thing is to know yourself, so that you can learn what attributes and skills to strengthen or to compensate for.

How individual differences affect your strategy

'Individual differences' is a term I keep tossing about. It's a term much used in psychology, which is largely the study of individual sameness (that is, what we all have in common; what it means to be human), and basically it means that we're all different in a lot of different ways, and these differences mean we don't all perform the same way or get the same score. 'Individual differences' covers a lot of territory.

In this discussion of note-taking strategies, it means that a strategy that is effective in a particular context will not be effective, or will not be *as* effective, for some people, as it is for others.

There are a number of reasons for this:

- Differences in cognitive style
- Differences in learning preferences

- Differences in ability

  - Differences in skills (particularly reading skill, in this context)

  - Differences in knowledge

  - Differences in working memory capacity

- Differences in motivation and interest level

Notice that differences in ability is only one of several important differences, and notice too, that differences in ability encompass three areas of difference, only one of which is in any way innate. Differences in skill and knowledge are clearly something that change with time and application.

Differences in working memory capacity are more problematic. Although training programs to increase working memory capacity have had some measure of success, it is very specific to the particular tasks being targeted. This doesn't mean that there's no value to such programs, but it does suggest that adult working memory capacity is less malleable than we hoped (working memory capacity does increase during childhood, as the brain develops — unfortunately, it also may shrink in old age).

Nevertheless, a low working memory capacity is something that can be accommodated, once you are aware of the problem and become attuned to situations when it is a problem. Thus, those with low working memory capacity should make every effort to work in a distraction-free environment, clear their minds of distracting thoughts, focus on only one goal at a time, and reduce the amount of information they're processing at one time as much as possible.

Moreover, the limited success of training programs does also point to the most useful way in which we can 'improve' our working memory capacity —by becoming sufficiently skilled at particular tasks that they take up less of our working memory (see the discussion of what constitutes deliberate practice in *Using your notes*).

Remember, too, that, even if you have a 'natural' high working memory capacity, at any particular time you may effectively be low — for example, because you're worried, in pain, surrounded by noise, or you're a novice in the topic or in the skill you're applying to the topic.

Notice too, that interest and motivation are linked together. Interest is of course also connected to knowledge — the more you know, the more interested you'll be, and as your interest in a subject grows, so does the ease with which you acquire more knowledge (contrariwise, one assumes that the more your interest diminishes, the less you learn!).

The link between knowledge and interest does depend on the subject though. For example, knowledge and interest have been found to have a reasonably high degree of correlation in statistics, but only a small degree of correlation in psychology[1] — very believably: most people have a high degree of interest in psychology, regardless of how much knowledge they have, and it is not surprising that an increase in knowledge doesn't affect level of interest much, since interest level already starts off high; on the other hand, most people probably begin to study statistics because it is a necessary tool, but increasing knowledge of statistics might well lead to an increased interest in the subject for some people.

I don't suppose it surprises you to learn that it's easier to acquire knowledge when you're interested, but it's worth thinking about why this might be so. Interest may be an indirect measure of another critical factor: your inclination for effortful processing — that is, the pleasure you take in engaging your mind. Which brings us to motivation.

It's thought that a student's motive is important in determining whether he'll process information deeply or superficially. Students' motives have been categorized as belonging to one of three categories:

- A pure interest in the subject for its own sake

- The need to do well (perhaps to gain a qualification, or to look good in front of other people)

- The need to avoid looking a fool

It's not surprising that these last two are associated with a tendency to only process information superficially. In other words, what we may term 'intrinsic' motivation — an interest in something for its own sake — tends to make you more inclined to put effort into processing. Of course, if you're very competitive, or have a compelling need to do well, you will also be more likely to put the effort in.

So the distinction between extrinsic and intrinsic motives doesn't necessarily distinguish between deep and surface processing. Another way of looking at motivation is in terms of three approaches to learning[2]:

- Surface

- Achieving

- Deep

197

What does it mean, to take a surface approach? Surface learners are more inclined to simply rote-learn details, but the approach is more than that. The essence of the approach is that the student uses a low-level strategy that gets them by, but doesn't lead to any understanding.

Surface learners also tend to focus on the words rather than the writer's meaning. Surface learners are more likely to be found among less skilled readers, who need to consciously process words. The more automatic these lower levels of processing, the easier it is to concentrate on the higher levels of meaning and inference.

However, students who haven't reached this level of reading skill shouldn't give up! As with low working memory capacity (an attribute which is not unrelated), it's a matter of learning how to deal with the problem. What you need to do is take things level by level:

1. first tackle the words;

2. when you have read them comfortably, go back and look for larger chunks of meaning, such as propositions (the smallest unit of meaning that can stand alone as a statement);

3. then go back again and look for the macropropositions (the main ideas; macropropositions include several propositions and most importantly, the relationships between them).

The trick is to only be focusing on one level at a time, having mastered the level below.

Students with an achieving approach are, like those with a surface approach, focused on the product, but because they focus on what will be rewarded, they are more likely to allocate their time and effort optimally, on the basis of importance. An achieving approach is nearly as effective as a deep approach.

A deep approach, of course, involves the sort of search for understanding that we have been talking about throughout the section on connection strategies.

Cognitive style

Whether you take a surface, achieving, or deep approach to learning, you will do it in your own way. Cognitive style is your general tendency to process information in a particular way.

Although researchers have come up with several different ways of classifying and assessing cognitive style, it's been argued that all these labels can basically be accommodated within two fundamental dimensions[3]:

- **Wholist-Analytic**: whether you tend to organize information in wholes or parts
- **Verbal-Imagery**: whether you tend to represent information in your thoughts verbally or in pictures

Now these are dimensions, not either/or dichotomies! That means that few of us will be at the extremes, one or the other. The extent to which we approach a topic will have as much to do with the topic, and how it is presented, as on our personal tendencies. But personal tendency is certainly of importance, and it is helpful to be consciously aware of your own tendencies in this regard.

It's also important to note that there is nothing good or bad about these different approaches. They all have their strengths and weaknesses (although it has to be said that our education system tends to favor an analytical approach).

Wholists, for example, are good at seeing things in context, but may miss important details and are more likely to have trouble selecting what's important. Analytics are good at detail and good at seeing similarities and differences, but may focus on one or two aspects to the exclusion of other, equally important, aspects. Analytics like a step-by-step approach, while wholists can get confused by such an approach, particularly when the steps are large. Analytics may find overviews confusing; wholists may be confused without an overview. Interestingly, analytics tend to prefer to take control of their learning, but wholists don't care.

In general, imagers prefer and learn best from pictorial presentations, while verbalizers prefer and learn best from text. Imagers remember visually descriptive text better than acoustically complex and unfamiliar text; verbalizers remember complex and unfamiliar text better than visually descriptive text.

The two dimensions also pair off. Wholist and imager styles go together; analytic and verbalizer styles are similarly compatible. But that doesn't mean that if you're a wholist you're also an imager, or if an analytic, a verbalizer. Those who do fit this pattern are said to have a unitary style; those who fit the opposite pattern are said to have a complementary style.

- unitary style: analytic-verbalizer; wholist-imager

- complementary style: wholist-verbalizer; analytic-imager

Those with complementary styles can better compensate for weaknesses —
thus, an analytic-imager might gain an idea of the overall context by studying
a picture; a wholist-verbalizer might be able to compensate for her less
analytical approach through her facility for words.

There's also an interaction with gender. One study[4] found that headings and
overviews seem to help male analytics and female wholists most. For the
complementary groups (wholist-verbalizer and analytic-imager), males do
better on multimedia presentations of picture and speech but females do
better with picture and text. For unitary groups (analytic-verbalizer; wholist-
imager), it's the other way around (males do better with picture and text and
females do better with picture and speech).

Interestingly, the same study found that working memory capacity seems to
be of much less importance to wholists than analytics. Analytic processing
probably requires much more capacity than wholist processing. Similarly,
although not to the same extent, verbalizers are more affected by working
memory capacity than imagers. This implies that reducing cognitive load is
much more important for low working memory analytic-verbalizers than
anyone else.

It has been argued that cognitive style develops from wholist to analytic
(probably as a result of our education system), but that in the most skilled
students, the two styles eventually integrate. In other words, what you should
be aiming for is to develop the style that *opposes* your existing style. If you're
analytic, work on wholist strategies; if you're wholist, practice analytic
strategies. But remember your aim is to be able to easily apply both, in
appropriate situations.

Whether you use a strategy that matches your style (for example, drawing a
mind map if you're an imager), or a strategy that makes up for the
weaknesses of your style (for example, drawing a concept map if you're an
analytic) depends also on the time you have available, the difficulty of the
material, and the amount of effort the material justifies. For example, in a
lecture situation, where you are at the mercy of the lecturer's speed of
presentation, you should go with what is easiest for you — that is, a strategy
that fits in with your 'natural' style. Again, if the material is difficult, you will
probably come to grips with it better if you go with your natural style (but
later on, when you've grasped the essentials, it's a good idea to review it
using an opposing strategy).

This also points to the way you should initially approach new material. When the text is analytical, going through points one by one, wholists should look first for something to give them the big picture, like a summary at the end, if no overview or advance organizer is provided, or illustrations. Analytics, on the other hand, are often best to leave any 'big picture' information, such as an overview or advance organizer or illustrations, until they have worked through the text.

Wholists:

- good at seeing things in context
- may miss important details
- have more trouble selecting what's important
- may get confused by a step-by-step approach, particularly when the steps are large.
- need an overview
- less affected by working memory capacity

Analytics:

- good at detail
- good at seeing similarities and differences
- may focus on one or two aspects to the exclusion of other, equally important, aspects
- need help with big picture
- like a step-by-step approach,
- may find overviews confusing
- more affected by working memory capacity

Imagers

- learn best from pictorial presentations
- remember visually descriptive text better than acoustically complex and unfamiliar text
- recall illustrations more accurately
- with little knowledge benefit most from seeing text only
- less affected by working memory capacity

Verbalizers

- learn best from text
- remember complex and unfamiliar text better than visually descriptive text.
- regardless of their amount of knowledge, benefit more from seeing graphics as well as the text
- more affected by working memory capacity

Learning preferences

Learning style is a term that is no doubt far more familiar to you than cognitive style. I have chosen in this discussion to use the terms cognitive style and learning preferences because the term 'learning style' has been used by different researchers in a variety of ways.

Learning preferences encompass personal properties that affect the best conditions for cognitive processing to take place.

There is considerable evidence that matching a student's learning preferences and cognitive style (as measured by the Dunn & Dunn Learning Style Model) with appropriate instruction significantly improves academic achievement and attitude to learning. The effect appears strongest for average students, students with strong preferences, students from public schools, and students in rural areas[5].

According to Dunn and Dunn[6], "Many people can learn things that are easy for them without using their learning styles, but all people can learn new and difficult information better when they capitalize on their learning styles."

The Dunn & Dunn Learning Style Model distinguishes five classes of elements, of which one is cognitive style (termed global vs analytic processing style). The other four (which I am calling learning preferences) are:

- environmental elements:
  - a preference for
    - sound vs quiet
    - low vs bright light
    - warm vs cool temperature
    - formal vs informal setting
- emotional elements:
  - persistence vs needing breaks
  - high vs low academic motivation
  - conformity vs nonconformity
  - need for internal vs externally-imposed structure
- sociological preferences:
  - working alone or in pairs or with a team or with an authoritative or collegial adult
  - working in a routine vs learning in a variety of ways
- physiological elements:
- perceptual preferences (auditory or visual or tactual (handling manipulative instructional materials) or kinesthetic (actively learning while standing or moving))
- time-of-day preferences
- need for intake (snacking)
- mobility while learning

Of these, Dunn and Dunn suggest perceptual preferences (whether you're auditory or visual or tactual or kinesthetic) may be the most important element.

Not all of these elements will be important to you, of course. Dunn and Dunn suggest that most people are affected by 6 to 14 of the 15 elements (I imagine cognitive style and perceptual preferences are always in the mix though).

If you think about all the different combinations of elements that are possible, you'll see why no single instructional or learning method can work for everyone.

I have to say I was surprised by some of these elements; several of them would never have occurred to me to consider in this way! Which is why I've listed them for you. You don't need a special test to tell you which of these are important to you; all you need to do is consider each one. It's worth doing so, and it's worth actually writing down your own profile. Here's a worksheet for you to do so.

Although there is an element of genetics in your learning preferences, other factors are also important in determining them. Age, for example, and academic achievement, and culture[7]. This means that they are able to be changed (some elements more than others) — although I don't recommend it unless some element is a particular problem, for it does take time and effort.

The main message here is simply that, to optimize your learning, particularly when the material is difficult, you should try and set up your learning environment to fit in with your preferences (particularly if they are strong ones).

Personal preferences and strategy choice

So how do all these personal attributes affect your choice of note-taking strategies? Most of the learning preferences don't — they're worth noting only in terms of setting up your learning environment. Motivation and interest are worth considering only in terms of choosing strategies that you find more enjoyable, especially if your interest in the topic is low. The attributes that are important for strategy choice are:

- level of skill (reading skill; note-taking skills)
- level of relevant knowledge
- inclination to engage in effortful processing
- working memory capacity
- cognitive style

- perceptual preferences

- working in a routine vs learning in a variety of ways

- need for internal vs externally-imposed structure

As you can see, not only does the number of personal variables indicate why you can't simply say, *this strategy is best for this task and this type of information*, or even, *this strategy is best for this task and this type of information for verbal wholists*, but why the strategy used will vary for the specific information (because it depends on your level of knowledge in that particular area). So choosing a strategy is not a matter simply of following the 'rules', and this is why you need to understand how the strategies work, so that you can make an informed decision in each context.

However, I can supply a number of guidelines, which is what I do in the next chapter.

Review questions

1. Which notetaking strategy is best for you depends on

    a. how deeply you want to process the information

    b. how smart you are

    c. whether you're verbal or visual

    d. how well you can draw

    e. the subject and your goals

2. Being a surface learner means

    a. that you're not very smart

    b. that you don't care about the subject

    c. that you don't understand the subject

    d. that you just want to learn enough to get by

3. Wholists

    a. like to take a step-by-step approach

    b. see the big picture

    c. like pictures

    d. often miss the details

    e. are good at details

4. Analytics

    a. like to take a step-by-step approach

    b. see the big picture

    c. like pictures

    d. often miss the details

    e. are good at details

5. Pick the true statements:

    a. Students are either wholist or analytic learners

    b. Wholists are imagers, and analytics are verbalizers

    c. Women are wholists, and men are analytics

    d. Wholist and imager styles are compatible, while wholist and verbalizer styles are complementary

    e. Having a unitary style is better than having a complementary style

    f. The style you have is fixed at birth

Choosing the right strategy 13

> We've looked at lots of different note-taking strategies, and you might be feeling a bit overwhelmed by it all. Here's the last step: knowing when to use which strategy. This is about being able to assess not only the learning situation (which includes the type of text), but also your very specific needs.

Assessing the text and the task

The first step in choosing the right strategy for a task is to accurately analyze the problem — indeed, to identify that there *is* a problem. By which I mean, a situation that needs a deliberate strategy. One of the reasons less successful learners are less successful is because they are often unaware that they haven't understood something, or that they won't remember something without deliberate effort.

So, first you need to be able to recognize when simply reading or listening to the material isn't enough. Then you need to accurately define the problem so that you know which note-taking strategy to use. Defining the problem involves three actions:

- evaluating the text
- articulating your goal
- defining the retrieval context

Let's look at each of these in turn.

Evaluating the text

We can classify text at one of three different levels, according to its structure and density:

1. **simple** (straightforward text with clear connections)

2. **complex** (characterized by many changes of topic and more than one level of information)

3. **difficult** (dense text with many topic changes, often unclear, inconsistent and/or abstract)

These different types of text require progressively more sophisticated strategies.

Within each level of course, there are gradations of complexity / difficulty, which also affect your choice of strategy and the number of different strategies you require.

To assess the difficulty of text:

- assess density:
  How many different ideas are there in each paragraph? How many on a page?

- assess the effectiveness of the structure:
  Is it divided into logical sections? Do the headings encapsulate the themes of the sections? Are changes of theme signaled by headings?

- look for the presence of effective cues:
  Are key points signaled in some way (by headings; some form of highlighting; use of clear signal words)?

- assess connectivity:
  Is the information in each section meaningfully connected? How many changes of topic are there?

- assess complexity:
  Can important concepts be easily conveyed in single words or brief phrases?

- assess style:
  Is it formal or informal? A text written in a casual, chatty style is more easily read and understood than a dry, academic one.

Here's a simplified assessment structure to help you sum it all up:

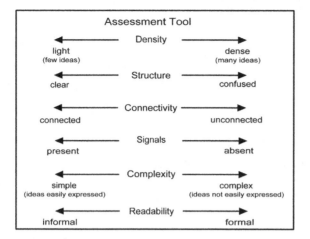

Let's see how we can use this tool to assess a text as simple, complex, or difficult.

Here's a profile of the Benjamin Franklin text:

From this we would conclude that the text is simple.

Here's a profile of the original gene-for-memory text:

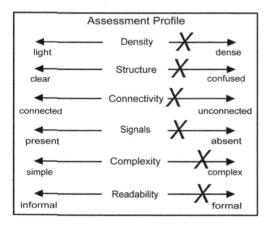

This profile suggests a difficult text. Notice, however, how the density is actually a little less than that of the Benjamin Franklin text. Any one of these characteristics is not in itself a marker of text difficulty — it's the complete profile that paints the picture.

Note, too, the difference to the profile if we used the final gene-for-memory text (the one with the detailed headings):

See how structure, connectivity, and signals, have all improved, although the text would still be classified as reasonably difficult.

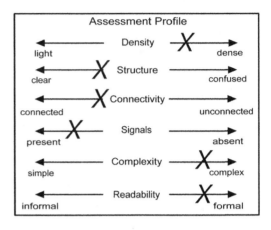

Exercise 13.1

Construct profiles for the remainder of the example texts, and classify them as simple, complex or difficult.

Strategies that are particularly appropriate for the different levels of text difficulty

Simple	highlighting; outline; topical summary
Complex	headings; graphic organizer; multimedia summary; map; elaborative interrogation; mind map; concept map
Difficult	self-explanation; concept map

I don't want to suggest that these are the only strategies appropriate when texts are at these levels of difficulty, or that they will always be appropriate. This table is merely a guide to suggest a place to start

Of course, it's not just about text difficulty; it's also about text structure. Remember our six main types of text structure? Here are strategies that are particularly appropriate for these different structures:

Description	topical summary; concept map; mind map
Collection	level diagram; topical summary; mnemonics
Classification	outline; graphic organizer; treelike network diagram
Sequence	multimedia summary; directional network diagram
Comparison	analogies; elaborative interrogation; self-explanation
Problem	elaborative interrogation; self-explanation; mind map; concept map

Again, I don't want to suggest that these are the only strategies appropriate for these structures, or that they will always be appropriate for that structure.

Articulating your goal

I talked about the importance of specifying your goal in *Using your notes*, and I hope you've seen this portrayed in the examples and exercises throughout this book. So here I want to simply remind you that a clearly articulated and specific goal greatly increases the likelihood that your notes will be effective — that you will have selected the right information, chosen an appropriate format for it, and reviewed it to an appropriate depth.

But there's another part of your goal that has a more direct effect on strategy choice, and that is the retrieval context.

Defining the retrieval context

Here are possible contexts in which you might need to retrieve information stored in your notes:

- Preparing for an exam:
  - For multichoice questions
  - For short answers
  - For essay answers
- Writing an essay

- Writing a summary

- Preparing for group discussion

- Preparing for class

These are all different situations with different requirements. Having to write essays in an exam situation will generally be the most demanding on your memory; writing an essay may be the most demanding on your understanding. Preparing for class will in most cases simply require a priming strategy.

Here's a table indicating the different memory tasks involved in these different situations:

Situation	Tasks
Preparing for an exam:	
For multi-choice questions	Recognition
For short answers	Cued recall
For essay answers	Free recall
Writing an essay	Organization; Comprehension
Writing a summary	Selection
Preparing for group discussion	Priming; Cued recall
Preparing for class	Priming

Of course, how much trouble you go to also depends on personal factors. One study[8] found that, among students reading for the purpose of discussing it in class, those with good topic knowledge were much more likely to report using memorization and organization strategies to prime their minds beforehand. This may be because students with little knowledge anticipated not participating in class.

From this, you'll realize that your goal has two parts to it: a broad one that specifies the memory task, and a much more specific one, that has to do with the content. For example, you might want to:

- organize information to help you understand why Benjamin Franklin is considered a great American

- prime your mind before a lesson on Benjamin Franklin and his inventions

- review information before a multichoice test on Benjamin Franklin's life

The specific content (why Benjamin Franklin is considered a great American; Benjamin Franklin and his inventions; Benjamin Franklin's life) is vital in your selection of the right information, but it is the broad memory task, indicated by retrieval context, that points to the appropriate strategy.

Here's a table that indicates the strategies that are particularly appropriate for various memory tasks:

Priming	advance organizers; mind maps; concept maps
Selection	highlighting; headings; topic structure strategy; overviews; topical summaries
Organization	outlines; graphic organizers; multimedia summaries; maps
Comprehension	advance organizers; making comparisons; elaborative interrogation; self-explanation; concept maps
Review for:	
Recognition	elaborative interrogation
Cued recall	elaborative interrogation; mind map; concept map
Free recall	headings; mind map; concept map

Again, this shouldn't be taken as a rulebook, merely as a guide to suggest a place to start.

Choosing the right strategy

To choose the right strategy for a task, you need to know:

- The difficulty of the text

- The structure of the text
- Your goal
- Your personal style

And you must be able to match this information with the appropriate strategy.

So here are the various strategy guides all together. Do remember that your choice is very much a personal one and depends on so many personal variables that no rules can be laid down, these are merely provided to help you. Don't worry if your chosen strategy doesn't appear as one recommended for a particular task.

Text Difficulty

Simple	highlighting; outline; topical summary
Complex	headings; graphic organizer; multimedia summary; map; elaborative interrogation; mind map; concept map
Difficult	self-explanation; concept map

Text structure

Description	topical summary; concept map; mind map
Collection	level diagram; topical summary; mnemonics
Classification	outline; graphic organizer; treelike network diagram
Sequence	multimedia summary; directional network diagram
Comparison	analogies; elaborative interrogation; self-explanation
Problem	elaborative interrogation; self-explanation; mind map; concept map

Goal

Priming	advance organizers; mind maps; concept maps
Selection	highlighting; headings; topic structure strategy; overviews; topical summaries
Organization	outlines; graphic organizers; multimedia summaries; maps
Comprehension	advance organizers; making comparisons; elaborative interrogation; self-explanation; concept maps
Review for:	
Recognition	elaborative interrogation
Cued recall	elaborative interrogation; mind map; concept map
Free recall	headings; mind map; concept map

Personal style

Wholist strategies (ones easily used by wholists, that reduce cognitive load)	overviews; advance organizers; maps; mind maps; concept maps
Analytic strategies (ones easily used by analytics, that reduce cognitive load)	highlighting; elaborative interrogation; self-explanation; analogies
Imager strategies (ones easily used by imagers, that reduce cognitive load)	maps; multimedia summaries; diagrams; mind maps; concept maps
Verbalizer strategies (ones easily used by verbalizers, that reduce cognitive load)	highlighting; headings; topical summaries; elaborative interrogation; self-explanation; analogies

A reminder: Just because you prefer a particular strategy, at least at first blush, that should not be taken as evidence that it's 'compatible' with your personal style. We're inclined to prefer what's easiest, but what's easiest is very often not what is best for us! If you want to become a truly successful learner, endeavor to master those strategies that counteract your weaknesses.

Remember that wholist strategies are ones that analytics should use to counteract their weaknesses, and similarly, analytic strategies should be used by wholists to counteract their weaknesses. The same applies to imagers and verbalizers.

Summary of note-taking strategies

Finally, here in one place, is a summary of the main points of each of the strategies I have discussed in this book.

Highlighting

Highlighting is an aid to focus your attention.

Don't use highlighting when the text is brief or familiar, or is dense — that is, has too many important points, or the ideas are too complex to be conveyed in a brief phrase.

Don't use highlighting when your time is severely limited.

Use highlighting when the text is relatively simple and reasonably long.

In information-dense text, or where the text is difficult, highlighting can be used in addition to other strategies.

Headings

When the text has many topics or is not clearly organized, and headings are not provided, create headings that succinctly capture the main idea of the passage.

When the text has many topics or is not clearly organized, and headings are provided but are uninformative, re-write the headings to succinctly capture the main idea of the passage.

Where you've used headings to organize information, use the headings as retrieval cues.

Headings used in this way are most useful when you're going to be tested by writing essay-type answers in an examination (free recall).

Overviews

If an overview is provided, use it to provide a structure for you as you listen to a lecture or work your way through a text.

Wholists benefit from overviews; analytics may be best to read them as end-summaries

Organizational signals (headings, overviews, topical summaries)

- are of greatest benefit to those whose reading skills are of intermediate degree — that is, not so poor that signals won't help them develop an understanding of the text's structure; not so good that signals aren't needed (although even experienced readers usually benefit from assistance).

- are of greater benefit (in recall, though not recognition) to those students who are not inclined to engage in effortful processing — presumably because students engaging in effortful processing are already doing the necessary work.

- are of greatest benefit to male analytics and female wholists.

When the text has many topics or is not clearly organized, use a topic structure strategy.

Advance organizers

Use advance organizers to give you an idea of the 'big picture'.

Advance organizers may be of greater benefit to able readers.

Advance organizers may be better read at the end if you're an analytic.

Outlines

Outlines are used for hierarchical information.

Outlines are used for surface processing.

Outlines are useful where the text is short (1000 words or less).

Outlines are easier to produce than graphic organizers.

Graphic organizers

Graphic organizers are used for hierarchical information.

Graphic organizers are generally more effective than outlines.

Graphic organizers are useful where the text is longer and more complex.

Graphic organizers require more time to produce and to interpret than outlines.

Multimedia summaries

Use multimedia summaries for information that involves cause-&-effect relationships.

Maps

If you're provided with a map:

- attend to the relationships *between* the features, rather than the features themselves

- use as an advance organizer.

Maps are helpful for spatial information, where there are only a limited number of features (optimally 12—16).

Diagrams

Use directional networks to portray sequential procedures and processes.

Use treelike networks for structural and categorical information.

Use level diagrams for principles.

Concept maps

Use concept maps to prime your mind before study, when you have a reasonable amount of relevant background knowledge.

Use concept maps to review what you have learned.

Use concept maps to take notes when the topic is complex, to give you an idea of the big picture.

Use concept maps as aids to understanding rather than memory

Use concept maps when you need to work out or demonstrate all the multitudinous ways in which different concepts are connected.

Don't use concept maps for sequential information.

Don't use concept maps when your time is limited, or when you need detail.

Mind maps

Use mind maps to prime your mind before study, when you have little relevant background knowledge.

Use mind maps to review what you have learned.

Use mind maps for brainstorming, for outlining a problem or topic, for helping you sort out the main ideas.

Don't use mind maps for sequential information.

Don't use mind maps if you're working with other people.

Elaborative interrogation

Only use elaborative interrogation when you have enough background knowledge to ask good questions.

Elaborative interrogation is more effective when you're going to be tested by answering multi-choice and short-answer questions, rather than writing essay-type answers.

Self-explanation

Use self-explanation when the text is demanding.

Self-explanation doesn't require as much prior knowledge as elaborative interrogation.

Mnemonics

Create interactive images to help you remember when you lack the knowledge and understanding to use elaborative interrogation or self-explanation.

Use mnemonics to memorize arbitrary details.

Use mnemonics to memorize keywords / labels for information units.

Every learning situation is different. Every piece of text is different. Every lecture is different. It's not enough to have a stock way of organizing your notes, and to try and push all the information that comes your way into that format. Sometimes a matrix structure might be best; sometimes a multimedia summary, sometimes a map, sometimes standard old linear notes. It depends on the information and it depends on how it is packaged.

The only way to know *which* strategy to use *when*, is to understand exactly how they work.

If you understand that the main value of note-taking is to select out the important information and connect it to other pieces of information … if you understand that the information is best understood and remembered when it is part of a tightly connected cluster, and when it is anchored to well-remembered information … then you can judge for yourself whether particular strategies are helpful to you in a particular situation.

Good luck on your journey!

Personal profile

Circle those that apply to you (you can download and print out a pdf document of this on my website). Remember, you won't find every learning preference important for you.

Cognitive style	wholist	analytic
	verbalizer	imager
	unitary	complementary
Learning preferences		
environmental	sound	quiet
	dim	bright
	warm	cool
	formal setting	informal
emotional	persistence	needing breaks
	highly motivated	low motivation
	conforming	nonconforming
	needs external structure	doesn't need external structure
sociological	likes to work alone	likes to work with others
	likes routine	likes variety

Physiological				
perceptual	auditory	visual	tactual	kinesthetic
time of day	morning		afternoon	evening
need for intake	needs snacks		doesn't need snacks	
mobility while learning	needs to move		can sit still	
Ability				
reading skill	poor		high	
knowledge	low		moderate	high
working memory	low		high	
motivation & interest	low extrinsic		high extrinsic	intrinsic

Glossary of terms

advance organizer: information that appears before the text it refers to, with the purpose of putting the information in a broader context. Advance organizers are written at a higher level of abstraction than the text, and may be written in a graphical format.

alignable differences: differences on the same dimension or that share a common structure

analogy: a type of comparison that helps you understand something; uses similarity of structure, of relations between objects

anchor points: facts that you already know very well, that connect to information you're trying to learn. By tying new information to information you already know, anchor points help make the new information meaningful and more memorable.

boundary: a way of arranging elements, one of Horn's 6 major visual topologies, *see* visual language

cognitive load: refers to the burden on your working memory system made by information-processing tasks.

cognitive style: your general tendency to process information in a particular way. Although there have been a number of attempts to classify types of cognitive style, two dimensions seem fundamental: your tendency to process information as a whole or in parts, and your tendency to think in pictures or words.

concentric: a way of arranging elements, one of Horn's 6 major visual topologies, *see* visual language

concept map: a diagram in which labeled nodes represent concepts, and lines connecting them show the relationships between concepts; developed by Joseph D. Novak in 1972.

correspondence list: a list of specific correspondences between the elements of two analogical examples that are being compared — a step in the mutual alignment strategy.

cued recall: remembering in response to prompts, such as specific questions.

directional networks: a subset of Horn's network topology, a network with directional flow

elaboration: any strategy that involves expanding on the information presented — the aim usually being to connect new information with familiar information. It does not necessarily involve deepening your understanding of the material; mnemonic strategies can involve elaboration.

elaborative interrogation: a strategy that tries to bring to mind any relevant prior knowledge, by asking yourself why the new information is true.

encode: transform information into a memory code, and place it in your long-term memory

expository text: text whose main purpose is to provide information, in contrast to narrative text.

free recall: remembering without prompts. For example, when you're asked to write an essay on a topic.

Gestalt principles: principles formulated to describe how we are predisposed to perceive certain arrangements of lines and shapes in particular ways.

graphic organizer: a type of graphic summary appropriate for material that can be expressed hierarchically, that allows the comparison of between-cluster relations. Common examples are tree diagrams and matrix diagrams.

graphic summary: a summary that re-organizes the information in a more visual format. Examples are graphic organizers, outlines, multimedia summaries, maps.

hierarchy principle: similar to, but not one of, the Gestalt principles; we naturally organize related information into a hierarchy

implementation intentions: if-then plans that connect what would be good opportunities to fulfill an intention with the action required to achieve that intention. They differ from simple intentions in that they specify the context in which the intentions can occur.

information blocks: another of Horn's terms, the visual language equivalent of a paragraph

information map: another of Horn's terms, an information map is made up of information blocks

joint interpretation strategy: a statement describing two analogical examples as a unit — a step in the mutual alignment strategy.

learning preferences: personal properties that affect the best conditions for cognitive processing to take place

learning style: a term that is more familiar, but one that has been used in so many different ways that I have instead used the more technical terms (and thus less misused!) cognitive style and learning preferences.

level: a way of arranging elements, one of Horn's 6 major visual topologies, *see* visual language

linear networks: a type of nondirectional network, an example of Horn's network topology

listing strategy: a strategy for processing text that involves simply listing each point as it appears in the text. The strategy is contrasted with the topic structure strategy.

loop network: a type of directional network, an example of Horn's network topology

matrix: a way of arranging elements, one of Horn's 6 major visual topologies, *see* visual language

mental model: in the context of reading or studying, a mental model is a retrieval structure you construct from a text, integrating the information in the text with your existing knowledge. Your understanding of a text depends on its coherence; it's generally agreed that for a text to be coherent it must be possible for a single mental model to be constructed from it

mind map: a type of concept map made famous in a number of books by Tony Buzan

mnemonic aid: aids to memory such as acronyms, acrostics, and techniques that link information by creating visual images or making up a story. They are most suitable for information that is not inherently meaningful.

multimedia summary: a graphic summary that combine pictures and text in an integrated manner. Especially appropriate for demonstrating scientific explanations.

mutual alignment: A way to find analogies, by comparing two partly understood situations, searching for the common structure. This compares to the more familiar strategy of comparing an unfamiliar situation with a familiar one (which requires you to be familiar with a situation that is analogous).

narrative text: text whose main purpose is to tell a story

network: a way of arranging elements, what Horn calls a visual topology, *see* visual language

nonalignable difference: a difference that is unrelated, that doesn't exist within the same structure or dimension

nondirectional network: a subset of Horn's network topology, a network without directional flow

organizational signals: are devices that highlight the topic structure of a text, such as headings, overviews and topical summaries.

outline: a type of graphic summary that systematically lists concepts with their subordinate concepts and their attributes.

overview: a topical summary that appears before the text it is summarizing.

priming: refers to the process of preparing a system for functioning — in this context, preparing the brain for learning by activating relevant prior knowledge and directing attention appropriately.

proximity grouping: a way of arranging elements, one of Horn's 6 major visual topologies, *see* visual language

radial network: a type of nondirectional network, an example of Horn's network topology

recall: the retrieval of information from long-term memory.

recognition: the awareness that you have seen or learned this information before.

retrieval context: the situation in which you attempt to remember the information. In the study situation, examples include an exam, multi-choice test, classroom discussion, writing an essay, or a brainstorming session.

self-explanation: a strategy that involves you explaining the meaning of information to yourself while you read.

serial position: the place of an item in a list; when a list of words is presented for later free recall, words at the beginning of the list and those at the end are more likely to be remembered (the primacy and recency effects, respectively)

topic structure strategy: a strategy for processing text that involves reorganizing the information to reflect the presumed hierarchical organization of topics and sub-topics that underlies the passage. The strategy is contrasted with the listing strategy.

topical summary: is a simple factual summary of the main points of a text that doesn't add any new information or offer a new perspective (for example, by re-organizing the information).

tree diagram: the more familiar term for what Horn calls a tree network

tree network: a type of nondirectional network, an example of Horn's network topology

verbal mediator: a word or phrase used in a mnemonic strategy to tie together the information to be learned with information already well-known to you; a "keyword" is an example of a verbal mediator.

verbalizer: an individual who prefers and learns best from text.

visual language: this is a term formalized by Robert E. Horn in his book *Visual Language: Global Communication for the 21st Century*, where he defines visual language as tightly integrated communication units that are composed of works, images, and shapes, and which have the ability to be embedded in each other and within other nonvisual language documents (e.g., text).

visualizer: an individual who relies mainly on imagery processes when performing cognitive tasks

working memory: includes the part of memory of which you are conscious; the "active state" of memory. Information being "put into" memory is held in working memory; memories being remembered are held in working memory. Working memory governs your ability to comprehend what you are reading or hearing, your ability to learn new words, your ability to plan and organize yourself, and much more.

working memory capacity: how much information a person's working memory can hold at one time. Now thought to be 3-5 chunks.

Chapter notes

Chapter 2: Making notetaking an effective strategy

1. Hartley , J. 1983

2. Bretzing & Kulhavy 1979

3. Kiewra & Benton 1988

4. Linderholm & van der Broek 2002

5. Kane & Engle 2003; Kane et al. 2004

6. Ashcraft & Kirk 2001: Those with high math anxiety showed a smaller working memory span, possibly because of a disruption of central executive processes.

7. Carlson, Chandler & Sweller 2003; Ashcraft & Kirk 2001

Chapter 3: Highlighting

1. Wallace 1965; Cashen & Leicht 1970; Crouse & Idstein 1972

2. Hershberger & Terry 1965

3. Crouse & Idstein 1972

4. Rickards & August 1975

Chapter 4: Headings

1. Brooks et al. 1983

2. Brooks et al 1983; Dee-Lucas & DiVesta 1980

3. Hartley et al. 1980

4. Lorch. & Lorch 1995

5. Loman & Mayer 1983; Lorch et al. 1993; Lorch & Lorch 1996b; Mayer, Dyck & Cook 1984; Meyer, Brandt & Bluth 1980; Meyer & Rice 1982; Meyer et al. 1998

6. Lorch et al. 2001; Lorch & Lorch 1996a; Lorch et al 1993; Mayer et al 1984; Loman & Mayer 1983

7. Lorch & Lorch 1995

8. Meyer et al 1980; Marshall & Glock 1978-9

9. Kardash & Noel 2000

10. Wilhite, S.C. 1989. Headings as memory facilitators: The importance of prior knowledge. *Journal of Educational Psychology, 81,* 115-7.

Chapter 5: Summaries

1. Lorch et al. 1985

2. McLaughlin-Cook 1981; Frase 1969; Lorch et al. 1985

3. Barnes & Clawson 1974; Kloster & Winne 1989

4. Glover, Bullock & Dietzer 1990

5. Day 1980; Garner & McCaleb 1985; Hill 1991

6. Brown 1981

7. Brown and Day 1983

8. Thiede & Anderson 2003

Chapter 6: Graphic summaries

1. Robinson & Kiewra 1995

2. Bera & Robinson 2004.

3. Robinson & Molina 2002

4. Kiewra et al. 1991; Benton et al. 1993

5. Dennison & Kiewra 1993

6. Bera & Robinson 2004.

7. Bera & Robinson 2004.

8. Horton & Lovitt 1989

9. Mayer et al. 1996

10. Stalbovs et al 2015

11. Skuballa et al 2018; Cromley et al 2013

12. Abel & Kulhavy 1986; Kulhavy et al. 1992; Kulhavy et al. 1993a; Schwartz & Kulhavy 1981

13. Verdi & Kulhavy 2002

14. Reynolds 1966,1968

15. Kulhavy et al. 1994

16. Verdi et al. 1997

17. Dean & Kulhavy 1981

18. Doran 1993

19. Kulhavy et al 1983

20. Winn & Sutherland 1989

21. Robinson & Molina 2002.

22. Horn 1998

23. Horn 1989

24. Studies that have found drawing enhanced memory of a text: Alesandrini 1981; Dean & Kulhavy 1981; Rasco Tennyson & Boutwell 1975; Snowman & Cunningham 1975.

 Studies that have found no effect: Tirre, Manelis & Leicht 1979, and Peeck 1980

25. Marks 1983

26. McKay 1999

27. Kozhevnikov, Hegarty & Mayer 2002.

28. Mayer & Massa 2003

29. Van Meter 2001

30. Van Meter et al. 2006; Scevak & Moore 1990; Tabachneck-Schiif & Simon 1998

Chapter 8: Elaboration

1. Gentner, 1983; Gentner & Medina 1998; Markman & Gentner 1993

2. Loewenstein et al. 1999

3. Catrambone & Holyoak 1989

4. Kurtz, Mao & Gentner 2001

5. Gentner & Markman 1994

6. Jameson & Gentner 2003

7. Holyoak & Thagard 1995; Kolodner 1993, 1997; Nersessian 1992; Reed

1987; Reeves & Weisberg 1994; Ross 1984, 1986; Thagard 1992

8. Perfetto, Bransford, & Franks 1983; Ross 1989; Weisberg, DiCamillo, & Phillips 1978

9. Gick & Holyoak 1980

10. Gentner, Rattermann, & Forbus 1993; Holyoak & Koh 1987; Ross 1989

11. Gentner, Loewenstein, & Thompson 2004

12. Kurtz, Mao & Gentner 2001

13. Kurtz, Mao & Gentner 2001

14. Gentner, Loewenstein & Thompson 2004

15. McDaniel & Donnelly 1996

16. Gick & Holyoak 1980

17. Pressley et al 1992

18. Martin, V.L. & Pressley, M. 1991

19. For example, Woloshyn et al. 1990; Pressley et al. 1988.

20. Marschark et al 1987

21. Willoughby, Wood & Khan 1994

22. Martin & Pressley 1991

23. McNamara 2004

24. O'Reilly, Symons & MacLatchy-Gaudet 1998

Chapter 9: Concept maps

1. Ausubel 1968

2. Heinze-Fry 2004: Student concerns with concept maps included the amount of time it took to create maps, the "spaghetti-type confusion" of some maps, and the visual overload of maps with too many concepts.

3. Farrand, Hussain & Hennessy 2002

Chapter 10: Lecture note-taking

1. Locke 1977

2. Kiewra at al 1987

3. Kobayashi 2005

4. Schoen 2012

5. Huxham 2010

6. Sutherland et al 2002

7. Peper & Mayer 1986; Shrager & Mayer 1989; Snow & Lohman 1984

8. Luo et al 2016

9. Kiewra et al 1991

10. Einstein et al 1985

11. Ryan 2001

12. Risko et al 2012

13. Szupunar et al 2013

14. Ramsburg & Youmans 2014

Chapter 11: Using your notes

1. Bransford 1979; Bransford et al 1989

2. Peverly et al. 2003; Peper & Mayer 1986

3. Allen, Lerner & Hinrichsen 1972; Beer & Beer 1992; Gortner Lahmers & Zulauf 2000; Hinrichsen 1972; Michaels & Miethe 1989; Schuman, Walsh, Olson & Etheridge 1985; Wagstaff & Mahmoudi 1976

4. Plant et al 2005

5. Ericsson 1996; Ericsson et al 1993

6. Plant et al 2005

Chapter 12: Learning style

1. Lawless & Kulikowich 2006

2. Biggs & Moore 1993

3. Riding & Rayner 1998

4. Riding et al. 2003

5. Lovelace 2005

6. Dunn & Dunn 1998, p3

7. Honigsfeld & Dunn 2003

8. Bråten & Samuelsten 2004

Answers

Answers to review questions

Chapter 2

1. e

2. b, d, e (yes, a and c could be considered factors too — but it's your ability to deal with these challenges that determines your effectiveness)

3. a, b, c, d

4. F

5. b, c, d, e, f

Chapter 3

1. c

2. d

3. c

4. c

5. d

Chapter 4

1. b, c

2. c, d

3. c, e

4. b, c, d

5. F

6. b, c, d

7. F

8. b, d

Chapter 5

1. b, c

2. b, c

3. F

4. b, e

5. T

6. b

7. c

8. b, c, d

9. a, c

10. b (which is not to say other factors aren't important, but this is key)

Chapter 6

1. b

2. b

3. b, c

4. c

5. c, d, e

6. T

7. F

8. a, c, e

9. a, b

10. F

Chapter 7

1. c, d
2. b
3. d

Chapter 8

1. b, d
2. a, b
3. a
4. c, d
5. e
6. c, d

Chapter 9

1. F
2. a, b, c
3. b
4. a, b
5. a, b, c

Chapter 10

1. a, b, c, d
2. e
3. a

Chapter 11

1. d, e
2. d, e

Chapter 12

1. e

2. d

3. b, d

4. a, e

5. d

Answers to exercises

Exercise 4.1

These are the headings supplied in the original texts; you may well have thought of better ones!

Text 1 = Description

The role of consolidation in memory

"Consolidation" is a term that is bandied about a lot in recent memory research. Here's my take on what it means.

How information becomes a memory

Initially, information is thought to be encoded as patterns of neural activity - cells "talking" to each other. Later, the information is coded in more persistent molecular or structural formats (e.g., the formation of new synapses). It has been assumed that once this occurs, the memory is "fixed" — a permanent, unchanging, representation.

With new techniques, it has indeed become possible to observe these changes. Researchers found that the changes to a cell that occurred in response to an initial stimulation lasted some three to five minutes and disappeared within five to 10 minutes. If the cell was stimulated four times over the course of an hour, however, the synapse would actually split and new synapses would form, producing a (presumably) permanent change.

Memory consolidation theory

The hypothesis that new memories consolidate slowly over time was proposed 100 years ago, and continues to guide memory research. In modern consolidation theory, it is assumed that new memories are initially 'labile' and sensitive to disruption before undergoing a series of processes (e.g., glutamate release, protein synthesis, neural growth and rearrangement) that render the memory representations progressively more stable. It is these processes that are generally referred to as "consolidation".

Recently, however, the idea has been gaining support that stable representations can revert to a labile state on reactivation.

Memory as reconstruction

In a way, this is not surprising. We already have ample evidence that retrieval is a dynamic process during which new information merges with and modifies the existing representation — memory is now seen as reconstructive, rather than a simple replaying of stored information

Reconsolidation of memories

Researchers who have found evidence that supposedly stable representations have become labile again after reactivation, have called the process "reconsolidation", and suggest that consolidation, rather than being a one-time event, occurs repeatedly every time the representation is activated.

This raises the question: does reconsolidation involve *replacing* the previously stable representation, or the establishment of a new representation, that coexists with the old?

Whether reconsolidation is the creating of a new representation, or the modifying of an old, is this something other than the reconstruction of memories as they are retrieved? In other words, is this recent research telling us something about consolidation (part of the encoding process), or something about reconstruction (part of the retrieval process)?

Hippocampus involved in memory consolidation

The principal player in memory consolidation research, in terms of brain regions, is the hippocampus. The hippocampus is involved in the recognition of place and the consolidation of contextual memories, and is part of a region called the medial temporal lobe (MTL), that also includes the perirhinal, parahippocampal,and entorhinal cortices. Lesions in the medial temporal lobe typically produce amnesia characterized by the disproportionate loss of recently acquired memories. This has been interpreted as evidence for a memory consolidation process.

Some research suggests that the hippocampus may participate only in consolidation processes lasting a few years. The entorhinal cortex, on the other hand, gives evidence of temporally graded changes extending up to 20 years, suggesting that it is this region that participates in memory consolidation over decades. The entorhinal cortex is damaged in the early stages of Alzheimer's disease.

There is, however, some evidence that the hippocampus can be involved in older memories — perhaps when they are particularly vivid.

A recent idea that has been floated suggests that the entorhinal cortex, through which all information passes on its way to the hippocampus, handles "incremental learning" — learning that requires repeated experiences. "Episodic learning" — memories that are stored after only one occurrence — might be mainly stored in the hippocampus.

This may help explain the persistence of some vivid memories in the hippocampus. Memories of emotionally arousing events tend to be more vivid and to persist longer than do memories of neutral or trivial events, and are, moreover, more likely to require only a single experience.

Whether or not the hippocampus may retain some older memories, the evidence that some memories might be held in the hippocampus for several years, only to move on, as it were, to another region, is another challenge to a simple consolidation theory.

Memory less stable than we thought

So where does all this leave us? What *is* consolidation? *Do* memories reach a fixed state?

My own feeling is that, no, memories don't reach this fabled "cast in stone" state. Memories are subject to change every time they are activated (such activation doesn't have to bring the memory to your conscious awareness). But consolidation traditionally (and logically) refers to encoding processes. It is reasonable, and useful, to distinguish between:

- the initial encoding, the "working memory" state, when new information is held precariously in shifting patterns of neural activity,

- the later encoding processes, when the information is consolidated into a more permanent form with the growth of new connections between nerve cells,

- the (possibly much) later retrieval processes, when the information is retrieved in, most probably, a new context, and is activated anew

I think that "reconsolidation" is a retrieval process rather than part of the encoding processes, but of course, if you admit retrieval as involving a return to the active state and a modification of the original representation in line with new associations, then the differences between retrieval and encoding become less evident.

When you add to this the possibility that memories might "move" from one area of the brain to another after a certain period of time (although it is likely that the triggering factor is not time *per se*), then you cast into disarray the whole concept of memories becoming stable.

Perhaps our best approach is to see memory as a series of processes, and consolidation as an agreed-upon (and possibly arbitrary) subset of those processes.

Text 2 = Sequence

Early America

The First Americans

At the height of the Ice Age, between 34,000 and 30,000 B.C., much of the world's water was locked up in vast continental ice sheets. As a result, the Bering Sea was hundreds of meters below its current level, and a land bridge, known as Beringia, emerged between Asia and North America. At its peak, Beringia is thought to have been some 1,500 kilometers wide. A moist and treeless tundra, it was covered with grasses and plant life, attracting the large animals that early humans hunted for their survival.

The first people to reach North America almost certainly did so without knowing they had crossed into a new continent. They would have been following game, as their ancestors had for thousands of years, along the Siberian coast and then across the land bridge.

Once in Alaska, it would take these first North Americans thousands of years more to work their way through the openings in great glaciers south to what is now the United States. Evidence of early life in North America continues to be found. Little of it, however, can be reliably dated before 12,000 B.C.; a recent discovery of a hunting lookout in northern Alaska, for example, may date from almost that time. So too may the finely crafted spear points and items found near Clovis, New Mexico.

Similar artifacts have been found at sites throughout North and South America, indicating that life was probably already well established in much of the Western Hemisphere by some time prior to 10,000 B.C. Around that time the mammoth began to die out and the bison took its place as a principal source of food and hides for these early North Americans. Over time, as more and more species of large game vanished whether from overhunting or natural causes plants, berries, and seeds became an increasingly important part of the early American diet. Gradually, foraging and the first attempts at primitive agriculture appeared. Native Americans in what is now central Mexico led the way, cultivating corn, squash, and beans, perhaps as early as 8,000 B.C. Slowly, this knowledge spread northward.

By 3,000 B.C., a primitive type of corn was being grown in the river valleys of New Mexico and Arizona. Then the first signs of irrigation began to appear, and, by 300 B.C., signs of early village life.

By the first centuries A.D., the Hohokam were living in settlements near what is now Phoenix, Arizona, where they built ball courts and pyramid like mounds reminiscent of those found in Mexico, as well as a canal and irrigation system.

Mound Builders And Pueblos

The first Native-American group to build mounds in what is now the United States often are called the Adenans. They began constructing earthen burial sites and fortifications around 600 B.C. Some mounds from that era are in the shape of birds or serpents; they probably served religious purposes not yet fully understood.

The Adenans appear to have been absorbed or displaced by various groups collectively known as Hopewellians. One of the most important centers of their culture was found in southern Ohio, where the remains of several thousand of these mounds still can be seen. Believed to be great traders, the Hopewellians used and exchanged tools and materials across a wide region of hundreds of kilometers.

By around 500 A.D., the Hopewellians disappeared, too, gradually giving way to a broad group of tribes generally known as the Mississippians or Temple Mound culture. One city, Cahokia, near Collinsville, Illinois, is thought to have had a population of about 20,000 at its peak in the early 12th century.

At the center of the city stood a huge earthen mound, flattened at the top, that was 30 meters high and 37 hectares at the base. Eighty other mounds have been found nearby.

Cities such as Cahokia depended on a combination of hunting, foraging, trading, and agriculture for their food and supplies. Influenced by the thriving societies to the south, they evolved into complex hierarchical societies that took slaves and practiced human sacrifice.

In what is now the southwest United States, the Anasazi, ancestors of the modern Hopi Indians, began building stone and adobe pueblos around the year 900. These unique and amazing apartment-like structures were often built along cliff faces; the most famous, the "cliff palace" of Mesa Verde, Colorado, had more than 200 rooms. Another site, the Pueblo Bonito ruins along New Mexico's Chaco River, once contained more than 800 rooms.

Perhaps the most affluent of the pre-Columbian Native Americans lived in the Pacific Northwest, where the natural abundance of fish and raw materials made food supplies plentiful and permanent villages possible as early as 1,000 B.C. The opulence of their "potlatch" gatherings remains a standard for extravagance and festivity probably unmatched in early American history.

Native-American Cultures

The America that greeted the first Europeans was, thus, far from an empty wilderness. It is now thought that as many people lived in the Western Hemisphere as in Western Europe at that time -- about 40 million. Estimates of the number of Native Americans living in what is now the United States at the onset of European colonization range from two to 18 million, with most historians tending toward the lower figure. What is certain is the devastating effect that European disease had on the indigenous population practically from the time of initial contact. Smallpox, in particular, ravaged whole communities and is thought to have been a much more direct cause of the precipitous decline in the Indian population in the 1600s than the numerous wars and skirmishes with European settlers.

Indian customs and culture at the time were extraordinarily diverse, as could be expected, given the expanse of the land and the many different environments to which they had adapted. Some generalizations, however, are possible. Most tribes, particularly in the wooded eastern region and the Midwest, combined aspects of hunting, gathering, and the cultivation of maize and other products for their food supplies. In many cases, the women were responsible for farming and the distribution of food, while the men hunted and participated in war.

By all accounts, Native-American society in North America was closely tied to the land. Identification with nature and the elements was integral to religious beliefs. Their life was essentially clan-oriented and communal, with children allowed more freedom and tolerance than was the European custom of the day.

Although some North American tribes developed a type of hieroglyphics to preserve certain texts, Native-American culture was primarily oral, with a high value placed on the recounting of tales and dreams. Clearly, there was a good deal of trade among various groups and strong evidence exists that neighboring tribes maintained extensive and formal relations -- both friendly and hostile.

The First Europeans

The first Europeans to arrive in North America -- at least the first for whom there is solid evidence -- were Norse, traveling west from Greenland, where Erik the Red had founded a settlement around the year 985. In 1001 his son Leif is thought to have explored the northeast coast of what is now Canada and spent at least one winter there.

While Norse sagas suggest that Viking sailors explored the Atlantic coast of North America down as far as the Bahamas, such claims remain unproven. In 1963, however, the ruins of some Norse houses dating from that era were discovered at L'Anse-aux-Meadows in northern Newfoundland, thus supporting at least some of the saga claims.

In 1497, just five years after Christopher Columbus landed in the Caribbean looking for a western route to Asia, a Venetian sailor named John Cabot arrived in Newfoundland on a mission for the British king. Although quickly forgotten, Cabot's journey was later to provide the basis for British claims to North America. It also opened the way to the rich fishing grounds off George's Banks, to which European fishermen, particularly the Portuguese, were soon making regular visits.

Columbus never saw the mainland of the future United States, but the first explorations of it were launched from the Spanish possessions that he helped establish. The first of these took place in 1513 when a group of men under Juan Ponce de León landed on the Florida coast near the present city of St. Augustine.

With the conquest of Mexico in 1522, the Spanish further solidified their position in the Western Hemisphere. The ensuing discoveries added to

Europe's knowledge of what was now named America -- after the Italian Amerigo Vespucci, who wrote a widely popular account of his voyages to a "New World." By 1529 reliable maps of the Atlantic coastline from Labrador to Tierra del Fuego had been drawn up, although it would take more than another century before hope of discovering a "Northwest Passage" to Asia would be completely abandoned.

Among the most significant early Spanish explorations was that of Hernando De Soto, a veteran conquistador who had accompanied Francisco Pizarro in the conquest of Peru. Leaving Havana in 1539, De Soto's expedition landed in Florida and ranged through the southeastern United States as far as the Mississippi River in search of riches.

Another Spaniard, Francisco Vázquez de Coronado, set out from Mexico in 1540 in search of the mythical Seven Cities of Cibola. Coronado's travels took him to the Grand Canyon and Kansas, but failed to reveal the gold or treasure his men sought. However, his party did leave the peoples of the region a remarkable, if unintended, gift: Enough of his horses escaped to transform life on the Great Plains. Within a few generations, the Plains Indians had become masters of horsemanship, greatly expanding the range and scope of their activities.

While the Spanish were pushing up from the south, the northern portion of the presentday United States was slowly being revealed through the journeys of men such as Giovanni da Verrazano. A Florentine who sailed for the French, Verrazano made landfall in North Carolina in 1524, then sailed north along the Atlantic Coast past what is now New York harbor.

A decade later, the Frenchman Jacques Cartier set sail with the hope -- like the other Europeans before him -- of finding a sea passage to Asia. Cartier's expeditions along the St. Lawrence River laid the foundation for the French claims to North America, which were to last until 1763.

Following the collapse of their first Quebec colony in the 1540s, French Huguenots attempted to settle the northern coast of Florida two decades later. The Spanish, viewing the French as a threat to their trade route along the Gulf Stream, destroyed the colony in 1565. Ironically, the leader of the Spanish forces, Pedro Menéndez, would soon establish a town not far away -- St. Augustine. It was the first permanent European settlement in what would become the United States.

Text 3 = Problem

The Relationship Of Ozone And Ultraviolet Radiation: Why Is Ozone So Important?

In this section, we will explore what is ozone and what is ultraviolet radiation. We then will explore the relationship between ozone and ultraviolet radiation from the sun. It is here that ozone plays its essential role in shielding the surface from harmful ultraviolet radiation. By screening out genetically destructive ultraviolet radiation from the Sun, ozone protects life on the surface of Earth. It is for this reason that ozone acquires an enormous importance. It is why we study it so extensively.

2.1 Ozone and the Ozone Layer

About 90% of the ozone in our atmosphere is contained in the stratosphere, the region from about 10 to 50-km (32,000 to 164,000 feet) above Earth's surface. Ten percent of the ozone is contained in the troposphere, the lowest part of our atmosphere where all of our weather takes place. Measurements taken from instruments on the ground, flown on balloons, and operating in space show that ozone concentrations are greatest between about 15 and 30 km.

Although ozone concentrations are very small, typically only a few molecules O_3 per million molecules of air, these ozone molecules are vitally important to life because they absorb the biologically harmful ultraviolet radiation from the Sun. There are three different types of ultraviolet (UV) radiation, based on the wavelength of the radiation. These are referred to as UV-a, UV-b, and UV-c. UV-c (red) is entirely screened out by ozone around 35 km altitude, while most UV-a (blue) reaches the surface, but it is not as genetically damaging, so we don't worry about it too much. It is the UV-b (green) radiation that can cause sunburn and that can also cause genetic damage, resulting in things like skin cancer, if exposure to it is prolonged. Ozone screens out most UV-b, but some reaches the surface. Were the ozone layer to decrease, more UV-b radiation would reach the surface, causing increased genetic damage to living things.

Because most of the ozone in our atmosphere is contained in the stratosphere, we refer to this region as the stratospheric ozone layer. In contrast to beneficial stratospheric ozone, tropospheric ozone is a pollutant found in high concentrations in smog. Though it too absorbs UV radiation, breathing it in high levels is unhealthy, even toxic. The high reactivity of ozone results in damage to the living tissue of plants and animals. This damage by heavy tropospheric ozone pollution is often manifested as eye and lung irritation. Tropospheric ozone is mainly produced during the daytime in polluted regions such as urban areas. Significant government efforts are underway to regulate the gases and emissions that lead to this harmful pollution, and smog alerts are regular occurrences in polluted urban areas.

2.2 Solar Radiation

To appreciate the importance of stratospheric ozone, we need to understand something of the Sun's output and how it impacts living systems. The Sun produces radiation at many different wavelengths. These are part of what is known as the electromagnetic (EM) spectrum. EM radiation includes everything from radio waves (very long wavelengths) to X-rays and gamma rays (very tiny wavelengths). EM radiation is classified by wavelength, which is a measure of how energetic is the radiation. The energy of a tiny piece or "packet" of radiation (which we call a photon) is inversely proportional to its wavelength.

The human eye can detect wavelengths in the region of the spectrum from about 400 nm (nanometers or billionths of a meter) to about 700 nm. Not surprisingly, this is called the visible region of the spectrum. All the colors of light (red, orange, yellow, green, blue, and violet) fall inside a small wavelength band. Whereas radio waves have wavelengths on the order of meters, visible light waves have wavelengths on the order of billionths of a meter. Such a tiny unit is called a nanometer (1 nm= 10^{-9} m). At one end of the visible "color" spectrum is red light. Red light has a wavelength of about 630 nm. Near the opposite end of the color spectrum is blue light, and at the very opposite end is violet light. Blue light has a wavelength of about 430 nm. Violet light has a wavelength of about 410 nm. Therefore, blue light is more energetic than red light because of its shorter wavelength, but it is less energetic than violet light, which has an even shorter wavelength. Radiation with wavelengths shorter than those of violet light is called ultraviolet radiation.

The Sun produces radiation that is mainly in the visible part of the electromagnetic spectrum. However, the Sun also generates radiation in ultraviolet (UV) part of the spectrum. UV wavelengths range from 1 to 400 nm. We are concerned about ultraviolet radiation because these rays are energetic enough to break the bonds of DNA molecules (the molecular carriers of our genetic coding), and thereby damage cells. While most plants and animals are able to either repair or destroy damaged cells, on occasion, these damaged DNA molecules are not repaired, and can replicate, leading to dangerous forms of skin cancer (basal, squamous, and melanoma).

2.3 Solar Fluxes

Solar flux refers to the amount of solar energy in watts falling perpendicularly on a surface one square centimeter, and the units are watts per cm2 per nm. Because of the strong absorption of UV radiation by ozone in the stratosphere, the intensity decreases at lower altitudes in the atmosphere. In addition, while the energy of an individual photon is greater if it has a shorter wavelength, there are fewer photons at the shorter wavelengths, so the Sun's total energy output is less at the shorter wavelengths. Because of ozone, it is virtually impossible for solar ultraviolet to penetrate to Earth's surface. For radiation with a wavelength of 290 nm, the intensity at Earth's surface is 350 million times weaker than at the top of the atmosphere. If our eyes detected light at less than 290 nm instead of in the visible range, the world would be very dark because of the ozone absorption!

2.4 UV Radiation and the Screening Action by Ozone

To appreciate how important this ultraviolet radiation screening is, we can consider a characteristic of radiation damage called an action spectrum. An action spectrum gives us a measure of the relative effectiveness of radiation in generating a certain biological response over a range of wavelengths. This response might be erythema (sunburn), changes in plant growth, or changes in molecular DNA. Fortunately, where DNA is easily damaged (where there is a high probability), ozone strongly absorbs UV. At the longer wavelengths where ozone absorbs weakly, DNA damage is less likely. If there was a 10% decrease in ozone, the amount of DNA damaging UV would increase by about 22%. Considering that DNA damage can lead to maladies like skin cancer, it is clear that this absorption of the Sun's ultraviolet radiation by ozone is critical for our well-being.

While most of the ultraviolet radiation is absorbed by ozone, some does make it to Earth's surface. Typically, we classify ultraviolet radiation into three parts, UV-a (320-400 nm), UV-b (280-320 nm), and UV-c (200-280 nm). Sunscreens have been developed by commercial manufacturers to protect human skin from UV radiation. The labels of these sunscreens usually note that they screen both UV-a and UV-b. Why not also screen for UV-c radiation? When UV-c encounters ozone in the mid-stratosphere, it is quickly absorbed so that none reaches Earth's surface. UV-b is partially absorbed and UV-a is barely absorbed by ozone. Ozone is so effective at absorbing the extremely harmful UV-c that sunscreen manufacturers don't need to worry about UV-c. Manufacturers only need to eliminate skin absorption of damaging UV-b and less damaging UV-a radiation.

The screening of ultraviolet radiation by ozone depends on other factors, such as time of day and season. The angle of the Sun in the sky has a large effect on the UV radiation. When the Sun is directly overhead, the UV radiation comes straight down through our atmosphere and is only absorbed by overhead ozone. When the Sun is just slightly above the horizon at dawn and dusk, the UV radiation must pass through the atmosphere at an angle. Because the UV passes through a longer distance in the atmosphere, it encounters more ozone molecules and there is greater absorption and, consequently, less UV radiation striking the surface.

Exercise 5.1

Main idea: that the flow of blood through the body, though continuous, is a function of three interlocking systems.

Text structure: Classification.

Your summary should contain the following important ideas:

- Circulatory system: pulmonary; coronary; systemic.
- Pulmonary circulation: between heart and lungs
- Coronary circulation: *within* the heart.
- Systemic circulation: rest of the body.
- Aorta --> smaller arteries --> capillaries --> veins
- Arteries carry fresh, oxygenated blood
- Capillaries release the oxygen
- Veins carry the de-oxygenated blood
- The heart powers the system.
- Blood enters the heart via two large veins, and leaves via the main artery.
- Carbon dioxide is removed and replaced with oxygen in the lungs.

Exercise 6.1

You should have come up with several graphic organizers to cover this material. Here are two possible examples:

Brain cells by function		
I.	Neurons	
		A. interneurons
		B. primary sensory neurons
		C. motor neurons
II.	Glia	
		A. astrocytes
		B. oligodendroglia
		C. Schwann cells
		D. ependymal cells
		E. microglia

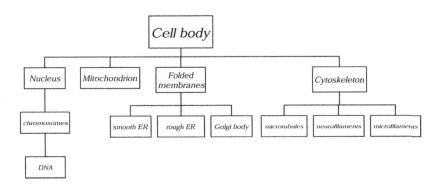

Exercise 6.2

Here are some examples:

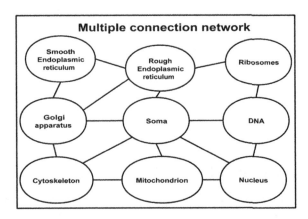

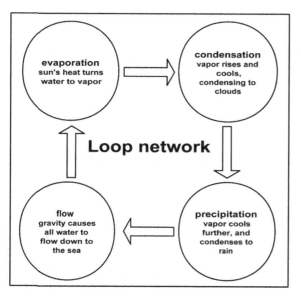

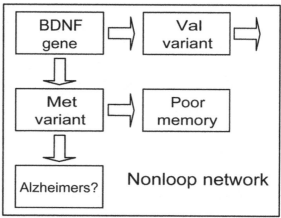

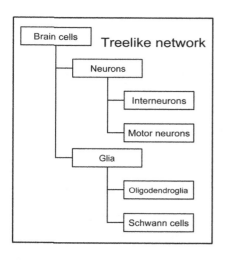

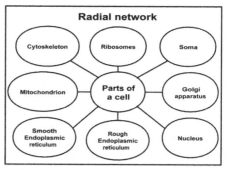

Exercise 6.3

There are no right or wrong answers to this exercise. But a chronological timeline, or a type of directional linear network, would probably be most appropriate.

Exercise 8.1

What constitutes an anchor point is entirely individual, depending as it does on your prior knowledge and what's personally meaningful to you. But here are some possibilities:

- UV rays cause sunburn and can cause skin cancer.

- Ozone at low levels is polluting and can cause smog alerts.

- Radio waves and X-rays are part of the electromagnetic spectrum we can't see.

- We can only see wavelengths in a small part of the spectrum, which is visible light.

- We see different wavelengths in this band as different colors. ROYGBIV is a mnemonic that tells me the order of the colors.

- The sun is most dangerous when it's straight overhead.

Exercise 8.2

veins and arteries

similarities:

- both carry blood

- both are hollow tubes

- both connect to the heart

- both connect to the lungs

differences:

- veins are thinner than arteries

- veins are less elastic than arteries

- veins carry blood to the heart, while arteries carry blood from the heart

- veins carry blood from the lungs, while arteries carry blood to the lungs

- most veins carry de-oxygenated blood, while most arteries carry oxygenated blood

neurons and glia

similarities

- both are brain cells

- both are a broad class of cells, containing different types

differences

- there are many more glia than neurons

- neurons process information; glia provide support functions

Exercise 8.3

Situation 1	Situation 2
fortress	tumor
soldiers	rays
roads	healthy tissue

Joint interpretation: The fortress (tumor) can be captured (destroyed) by having small groups of soldiers (low-intensity rays) converge on it.

Exercise 8.4

Here are some possible "why?" questions you might have come up with:

- Why is ozone important to us?

- Why is most ozone in the stratosphere? Why is so little in the troposphere?

- Why is ozone concentration greatest between about 15 and 30 km?

- Why are some types of ultraviolet (UV) radiation more dangerous than others?

- Why is tropospheric ozone less beneficial than stratospheric ozone?

- Why do governments try to reduce tropospheric ozone?

- Why can't we see radio waves?

- Why is ultraviolet radiation dangerous to us?

- Why don't we worry about UV-c?

- Why is UV radiation more of a concern when the sun is high in the sky?

Exercise 13.1

The role of consolidation in memory: a simple/complex text (by which I mean on the simpler end of complex)

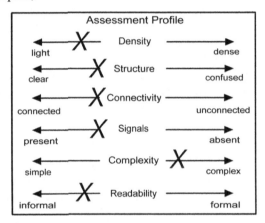

Early America: a simple text

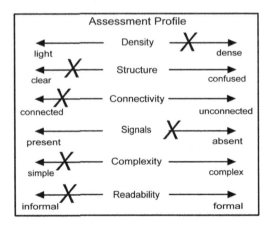

The relationship of ozone and ultraviolet radiation: a complex text

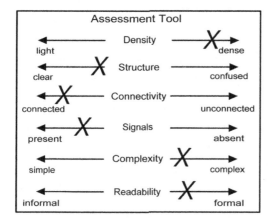

How blood flows: a simple text

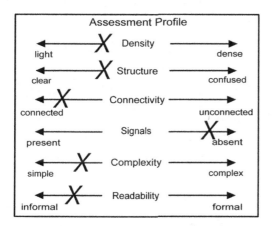

Introducing brain cells: a complex/difficult text (at the difficult end of complex)

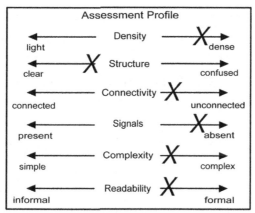

References

Abel, R.R. & Kulhavy, R.W. 1986. Maps, mode of text presentation, and children's prose learning. American Educational Research Journal, 23, 263-74.

Alesandrini, K.L. 1981. Pictorial-verbal and analytic-holistic learning strategies in science learning. Journal of Educational Psychology, 73, 358-68.

Allen, G.J., Lerner, W.M. & Hinrichsen, J.J. 1972. Study behaviors and their relationships to test anxiety and academic performance. Psychological Reports, 30, 407-410.

Anderson, K.C. & Leinhardt, G. 2002. Maps as representations: Expert novice comparison of projection understanding. Cognition and Instruction, 20(3), 283-321.

Ausubel, D. P. 1968. Educational psychology: A cognitive view. New York: Holt, Rinehart & Winston.

Baine, D. 1986. Memory and instruction. Englewood Cliffs, NJ: Educational Technology Publications.

Barnes, B.R. & Clawson, E.V. 1974. Do advance organizers facilitate learning? Recommendations for further research based on an analysis of 32 studies. Review of Educational Research, 45, 637-59.

Barnett, J.E., DiVesta, F.J. & Rogozinski, J.T. 1981. What is learned in note taking. Journal of Educational Psychology, 73, 181-192.

Beer, J. & Beer, J. 1992. Classroom and home study times and grades while at college using a single-subject design. Psychological Reports, 71, 233-234.

Benton, S.L., Kiewra, K.A., Whitfill, J.M. & Dennison, R. 1993. Encoding and external storage effects on writing processes. Journal of Educational Psychology, 85, 267-80.

Bera, S.J. & Robinson, D.H. 2004. Exploring the boundary conditions of the delay hypothesis with adjunct displays. Journal of Educational Psychology, 96(2), 381-388.

Biggs, J.B. & Moore, P.J. 1993. The process of learning. 3rd ed. Sydney: Prentice-Hall.

Bransford, J.D. 1979. Human cognition: Learning, understanding and remembering. Belmont, Calif.: Wadsworth.

254

Bransford, J.D., Vye, N., Adams, L. & Perfetto, G. 1989. Learning skills and the acquisition of knowledge. In A. Lesgold & R. Glaser (Eds.), Foundations for a Psychology of Education (pp. 199-249). Hillsdale, NJ: Lawrence Erlbaum Associates.

Bråten, I. & Samuelsten, M.S. 2004. Does the influence of reading purpose on reports of strategic text processing depend on students' topic knowledge? Journal of Educational Psychology, 96(2), 324-336.

Bretzing, B.H. & Kulhavy, R.W. 1979. note-taking and depth of processing. Contemporary Educational Psychology, 4, 145-153.

Brooks, L.W., Dansereau, D.F., Spurlin, J.E. & Holley, C.D. 1983. Effects of headings on text processing. Journal of Educational Psychology, 75, 292-302.

Brown, A.L. & Day, J.D. 1983. Macrorules for summarizing texts: The development of expertise. Journal of Verbal Learning and Verbal Behavior, 22, 1-14.

Brown, A.L. 1981. Metacognition: The development of selective attention strategies for learning from texts. In M.L. Kamil (ed.), Direction in reading: Research and instruction. Washington: National Reading Conference

Bui, D. C., & McDaniel, M. A. (2015). Enhancing learning during lecture note-taking using outlines and illustrative diagrams. Journal of Applied Research in Memory and Cognition, 4(2), 129–135.

Buzan, T. 1974. Use your head.. London: BBC.

Buzan, T. 1993. The mind map book. London: BBC.

Carlson, R., Chandler, P. & Sweller, J. 2003. Learning and understanding science instructional material. Journal of Educational Psychology, 95(3), 629-640.

Cashen, V.M. & Leicht, K.L. 1970. Role of the isolation effect in a formal educational setting. Journal of Educational Psychology, 61, 484-486.

Catrambone, R. & Holyoak, K.J. 1989. Overcoming contextual limitations on problem-solving transfer. Journal of Experimental Psychology: Learning, Memory, & Cognition, 15, 1147-1156.

Christensen, C.M. & Stordahl, K.E. 1955. The effect of organization aids on comprehension and retention. Journal of Educational Psychology, 46, 65-74.

Cromley, J. G., Bergey, B. W., Fitzhugh, S., Newcombe, N., Wills, T. W., Shipley, T. F., & Tanaka, J. C. (2013). Effects of three diagram instruction methods on transfer of diagram comprehension skills: The critical role of inference while learning. Learning and Instruction, 26, 45–58.

Crouse, J.H. & Idstein, P. 1972. Effects of encoding cues on prose learning. Journal of Educational Psychology, 63, 309-313.

Cummins, D.D. 1992. Role of analogical reasoning in the induction of problem categories. Journal of Experimental Psychology: Learning, Memory, & Cognition, 18, 1103-1124.

Day, J.D. 1980. Teaching summarization skills: A comparison of training methods. Unpublished doctoral dissertation, University of Illinois at Urbana-Champaign.

Dean, R.S. & Kulhavy, R.W. 1981. The influence of spatial organization in prose learning. Journal of Educational Psychology, 73, 57-64.

Dee-Lucas, D. & DiVesta, F.J. 1980. Learner-generated organizational aids: Effects of learning from text. Journal of Educational Psychology, 72, 304-11.

Dennison, R.S., & Kiewra, K.A. 1993. Studying text supplements: Attention focusing and internal connection effects. Paper presented at the American Educational Research Association conference, Atlanta, Georgia.

Doran, J.M. 1993. Map and text: Capacity and charting limitations exhibited by high school students. Master's thesis. Tempe, Arizona State University Press.

Dornisch, M.M. & Sperling, R.A. 2006. Facilitating learning from technology-enhanced text: Effects of prompted elaborative interrogation. The Journal of Educational Research, 99(3), 156-165.

Dunn, R. & Dunn, K. 1998. Practical approaches to individualizing staff development for adults. Westport, CT: Praeger.

Ericsson, K.A. 1996. The acquisition of expert performance: An introduction to some of the issues. In K. Anders Ericsson (ed.), The Road to Excellence: The acquisition of expert performance in the arts and sciences, sports, and games. Mahwah, NJ: Lawrence Erlbaum.

Ericsson, K.A., Krampe, R.T. & Tesch-Romer, C. 1993. The role of deliberate practice in the acquisition of expert performance. Psychological Review, 100, 363-406.

Farrand, P., Hussain, F. & Hennessy, E. 2002. The efficacy of the `mind map' study technique. Medical Education, 36 (5), 426-431.

Ferry, B., Hedberg, J. & Harper, B. 1997. How do Preservice Teachers use Concept Maps to Organize Their Curriculum Content Knowledge?

Presented at the Australian Society for Computers in Learning in Tertiary Education (ASCILITE) annual conference, December 7-10 1997, Perth, Australia.

Frase, L.T. 1969. Paragraph organization of written materials: The influence of conceptual clustering upon the level and organization of recall. Journal of Educational Psychology, 60(5), 394-401.

Friend, R. 2001. Effects of strategy instruction on summary writing of college students. Contemporary Educational Psychology, 26, 3-24.

Garner, R & McCaleb, J.L. 1985. Effects of text manipulations on quality of written summaries. Contemporary Educational Psychology, 10, 139-149.

Gentner, D. & Kurtz, K.J. 2006. Relations, Objects, and the Composition of Analogies. Cognitive Science, 30, 609–642.

Gentner, D. & Markman, A.B. 1994. Structural alignment in comparison: No difference without similarity. Psychological Science, 5, 152-158.

Gentner, D. & Medina, J. 1998. Similarity and the development of rules. Cognition, 65, 263-297.

Gentner, D. 1983. Structure-mapping: A theoretical framework for analogy. Cognitive Science, 7, 155-170.

Gentner, D., Loewenstein, J. & Thompson, L. 2004. Analogical encoding: Facilitating knowledge transfer and integration. Proceedings of the Twenty-sixth Annual Meeting of the Cognitive Science Society.

Gentner, D., Rattermann, M. J., & Forbus, K. D. 1993. The roles of similarity in transfer: Separating retrieval from inferential soundness. Cognitive Psychology, 25, 524-575.

Gick, M.L. & Holyoak, K.J. 1980. Analogical problem solving. Cognitive Psychology, 12, 306-355.

Gick, M.L. & Holyoak, K.J. 1983. Schema induction and analogical transfer. Cognitive Psychology, 15, 1-38.

Glover, J.A., Bullock, R.G. & Dietzer, M.L. 1990. Advance organizers: delay hypotheses. Journal of Educational Psychology, 82, 291-7.

Gortner Lahmers, A. & Zulauf, C.R. 2000. Factors associated with academic time use and academic performance of college students: A recursive approach. Journal of College Student Development, 41, 544-556.

Griffin, M.M. & Robinson, D.H. 2000. Role of mimeticism and spatiality in textual recall. Contemporary Educational Psychology, 25, 125-49.

Hartley , J. 1983. note-taking research: Resetting the scoreboard. Bulletin of British Psychological Society, 36, 13-14.

Hartley, J., Kenely, J., Owen, G. & Trueman, M. 1980. The effect of headings on children's recall from prose text. British Journal of Educational Psychology, 5, 304-7.

Heinze-Fry, J. 2004. Applications of concept mapping to undergraduate general education science courses. In Cañas, A.J., Novak, J.D. & González, F.M. (eds). Concept Maps: Theory, Methodology, Technology. Proceedings of the First International Conference on Concept Mapping, Pamplona, Spain 2004.

Hershberger, W.A. & Terry, D.F. 1965. Typographical cuing in conventional and programmed texts. Journal of Applied Psychology, 49, 55-60.

Hill, M. 1991. Writing summaries promotes thinking and learning across the curriculum — But why are they so difficult to write? Journal of Reading, 34, 536-539.

Hinrichsen, J.J. 1972. Prediction of grade point average from estimated study behaviors. Psychological Reports, 31, 974.

Holyoak, K.J. & Koh, K. 1987. Surface and structural similarity in analogical transfer. Memory and Cognition, 15, 332-340.

Holyoak, K.J. & Thagard, P. 1995. Mental leap: Analogy in creative thought. Cambridge, MA: MIT Press.

Honigsfeld, A. & Dunn, R. 2003. High school male and female learning-style similarities and differences in diverse nations. The Journal of Educational Research, 96 (4), 195-205.

Horn, Robert E. 1989. Mapping hypertext. The Lexington Institute.

Horn, Robert E. 1998. Visual Language. Bainbridge Island, Washington: MacroVU, Inc.

Horton, S.V. & Lovitt, T.C. 1989. Construction and implementation of graphic organizers for academically handicapped and regular secondary students. Academic Therapy, 24(5), 625-640.

Hyona, J. 1995. An eye movement analysis of topic-shift effect during repeated reading. Journal of Experimental Psychology: Learning, Memory & Cognition, 21, 1365-73.

Jameson, J. & Gentner, D. 2003. Mundane comparisons can facilitate relational understanding. In R. Alterman & D. Kirsh (Eds.), Proceedings of the Twenty-Fifth Annual Meeting of the Cognitive Science Society (pp. 611-615). Mahwah, NJ: Erlbaum.

Kane, M.J. & Engle, R.W. 2003. Working-memory capacity and the control of attention: The contributions of goal neglect, response competition, and task set to Stroop interference. Journal of Experimental Psychology: General, 132 (1), 47-70.

Kane, M.J., Hambrick, D.Z., Tuholski, S.W., Wilhelm, O., Payne, T.W. & Engle, R.W. 2004. The generality of working memory capacity: A latent-variable approach to verbal and visuospatial memory span and reasoning. Journal of Experimental Psychology: General, 133(2), 189-217.

Kardash, C.M. & Noel, L.K. 2000. How organizational signals, need for cognition, and verbal ability affect text recall and recognition. Contemporary Educational Psychology, 25, 317-331.

Kiewra, K.A. & Benton, S.L. 1988. The relationship between information-processing ability and note-taking. Contemporary Educational Psychology, 13, 33-44.

Kiewra, K.A., Dubois, N.F., Christian, D., McShane, A., Meyerhoffer, M. & Roskelley, D. 1991. Note-taking functions and techniques. Journal of Educational Psychology, 83, 240-5.

Kloster, A.M. & Winne, P.H. 1989. The effects of different types of organizers on students' learning from text. Journal of Educational Psychology, 81, 9-15.

Kobayashi, K. 2005. What limits the encoding effect of note-taking? A meta-analytic examination. Contemporary Educational Psychology, 30 (2), 242-262.

Kolodner, J. 1993. Case-based reasoning. San Mateo, CA: Morgan Kaufmann.

Kolodner, J.L. 1997. Educational implications of analogy: A view from case-based reasoning. American Psychologist, 52, 57-66.

Kotovsky, L. & Gentner, D. 1996. Comparison and categorization in the development of relational similarity. Child Development, 67, 2797-2822.

Kozhevnikov, M., Hegarty, M. & Mayer, R.E. 2002. Revising the Visualizer-Verbalizer Dimension: Evidence for Two Types of Visualizers. Cognition and Instruction, 20(1)77.

Kulhavy, R.W., Schwartz, N.H. & Shaha, S.H. 1983. Spatial representation of maps. American Journal of Psychology, 96, 337-51.

Kulhavy, R.W., Stock, W.A. & Caterino, L.C. 1994. Reference maps as a framework for remembering text. In Schnotz, W. & Kulhavy, R.W. (eds). Comprehension of graphics. Elsevier Science B.V. Amsterdam: North-Holland. (Advances in psychology 108), pp153-162.

Kulhavy, R.W., Stock, W.A., Peterson, S.E., Pridemore, D.R. & Klein, J.D. 1992. Using maps to retrieve text: A test of conjoint retention. Contemporary Educational Psychology, 17, 56-70.

Kulhavy, R.W., Stock, W.A., Verdi, M.P., Rittschof, K.A. & Savenye, W. 1993. Why maps improve memory for text: The influence of structural information on working memory operations. European Journal of Cognitive Psychology, 5, 375-92.

Kurtz, K.J., Mao, C-H. & Gentner, D. 2001. Learning by Analogical Bootstrapping. The Journal Of The Learning Sciences, 10(4), 417-446.

Lawless, K.A. & Kulikowich, J.M. 2006. Domain knowledge and individual interest: The effects of academic level and specialization in statistics and psychology. Contemporary Educational Psychology, 31, 30–43.

Linderholm, T. & van der Broek, P. 2002. The effects of reading purpose and working memory capacity on the processing of expository text. Journal of Educational Psychology, 94(4), 778-784.

Locke, E.A. 1977. An empirical study of lecture note taking among college students. The Journal of Educational Research, 77, 93-99.

Loewenstein, J., Thompson, L. & Gentner, D. 1999. Analogical encoding facilitates knowledge transfer in negotiation. Psychonomic Bulletin & Review, 6, 586-597.

Loman, N.L. & Mayer, R.E. 1983. Signaling techniques that increase the understandability of expository prose. Journal of Educational Psychology, 75, 402-12.

Lorch, R.F. Jr. & Lorch, E.P. 1995. Effects of organizational signals on text-processing strategies. Journal of Educational Psychology, 87, 537-44.

Lorch, R.F. Jr. & Lorch, E.P. 1996a. Effects of headings on text recall and summarization. Contemporary Educational Psychology, 21, 261-78.

Lorch, R.F. Jr. & Lorch, E.P. 1996b. Effects of organizational signals on free recall of expository text. Journal of Educational Psychology, 88, 38-48.

Lorch, R.F. Jr., Lorch, E.P. & Matthews, P.D. 1985. On-line processing of the topic structure of a text. Journal of Memory and Language, 24, 350-62.

Lorch, R.F. Jr., Lorch, E.P. & Mogan, A.M. 1987. Task effects and individual differences in on-line processing of the topic structure of a text. Discourse Processes, 10, 63-80.

Lorch, R.F. Jr., Lorch, E.P., Ritchey, K., McGovern, L. & Coleman, D. 2001. Effect of headings on text summarization. Contemporary Educational Psychology, 26, 171-91.

Lorch, R.F., Lorch, E.P. & Inman, W.E. 1993. Effects of signaling topic structure on text recall. Journal of Educational Psychology, 85, 281-90.

Lovelace, M.K. 2005. Meta-analysis of experimental research based on the Dunn and Dunn model. The Journal of Educational Research, 98 (3), 176-83.

Luo, L., Kiewra, K. A., & Samuelson, L. (2016). Revising lecture notes: how revision, pauses, and partners affect note taking and achievement. Instructional Science, 44(1), 45–67.

Markman, A.B. & Gentner, D. 1993. Structural alignment during similarity comparisons. Cognitive Psychology, 25, 431-467.

Marks, D.F. 1983. Mental imagery and consciousness: A theoretical review. In A.A. Sheikh (ed.), Imagery. (pp 96-130). New York: Wiley.

Marschark, M., Richman, C.L., Yuille, J.C. & Hunt, R.R. 1987. The role of imagery in memory: On shared and distinctive information. Psychological Bulletin, 102, 28-41.

Marshall, N. & Glock, M.D. 1978-9. Comprehension of connected discourse: A study into the relationships between the structure of text and information recalled. Reading Research Quarterly, 14, 10-56.

Martin, V.L. & Pressley, M. 1991. Elaborative-interrogation effects depend on the nature of the question. Journal of Educational Psychology, 83, 113-9.

Mayer, R.E. & Gallini, J. 1990. When is an illustration worth ten thousand words? Journal of Educational Psychology, 83, 715-726.

Mayer, R.E. & Massa, L.J. 2003. Three Facets of Visual and Verbal Learners: Cognitive Ability, Cognitive Style, and Learning Preference. Journal of Educational Psychology, 95(4), 833-846.

Mayer, R.E. & Moreno, R. 1998. A split-attention effect in multimedia learning: Evidence for dual processing systems in working memory. Journal of Educational Psychology, 90, 312-320.

Mayer, R.E. & Sims, V.K. 1994. For whom is a picture worth a thousand words? Extensions of a dual-coding theory of multimedia learning. Journal of Educational Psychology, 86, 389-401.

Mayer, R.E. 2001. Multimedia learning. New York: Cambridge University Press.

Mayer, R.E., Bove, W., Bryman, A., Mars, R. & Tapangco, L. 1996. When less is more: meaningful learning from visual and verbal summaries of science textbook lessons. Journal of Educational Psychology, 88, 64-73.

Mayer, R.E., Dyck, J.L. & Cook, L.K. 1984. Techniques that help readers build mental models from scientific text: Definitions pretraining and signaling. Journal of Educational Psychology, 76, 1089-1105.

McDaniel, M.A. & Donnelly, C.M. 1996. Learning with analogy and elaborative interrogation. Journal of Educational Psychology, 88(3), 508-519.

McKay, E. 1999. An investigation of text-based instructional materials enhanced with graphics. Educational Psychology, 19, 323-35.

McLaughlin-Cook. N. 1981. Summaries: further issues and data. Educational Review, 33 (3), 215-222.

McNamara, D.S. 2004. SERT: Self-Explanation Reading Training. Discourse Processes, 38, 1-30.

Meyer, B.J.F. & Rice, E. 1982. The interaction of reader strategies and the organization of text. Text, 2, 155-92.

Meyer, B.J.F., Brandt, D.M. & Bluth, G.J. 1980. Use of top-level structure in text: Key for reading comprehension of ninth-grade students. Reading Research Quarterly, 1,101.

Meyer, B.J.F., Talbot, A., Stubblefield, R.A. & Poon, L.W. 1998. Interests and strategies of young and old readers differentially interact with characteristics of texts. Educational Gerontology, 24, 747-71.

Michaels, J.W. & Miethe, T.D. 1989. Academic effort and college grades. Social Forces, 68, 309-319.

Moreno, R. & Mayer, R.E. 1999. Cognitive principles of multimedia learning: The role of modality and contiguity. Journal of Educational Psychology, 91, 358-368.

Mousavi, S., Low, R. & Sweller, J. 1995. Reducing cognitive load by mixing auditory and visual presentation modes. Journal of Educational Psychology, 87, 319-334.

Nersessian, N.J. 1992. How do scientists think? Capturing the dynamics of conceptual change in science. In R. N. Giere & H. Feigl (Eds.), Cognitive models of science: Minnesota studies in the philosophy of science (pp. 3-44).

Minneapolis, MN: University of Minnesota Press.

Novak, J.D. & Cañas, A.J. 2006. The Theory Underlying Concept Maps and How to Construct Them. Technical Report IHMC CmapTools 2006-01. Pensacola, Fl: Florida Institute for Human and Machine Cognition.

O'Reilly, T., Symons, S. & MacLatchy-Gaudet, H. 1998. A Comparison of Self-Explanation and Elaborative Interrogation. Contemporary Educational Psychology, 23(4), 434-445.

Osman, M.E. & Hannafin, M.J. 1994. Effects of advance questioning and prior knowledge on science learning. The Journal of Educational Research, 88(1), 5-13.

Peck, K.L. & Hannafin, M.J. 1983. The effects of note-taking pretraining and the recording of notes on the retention of aural instruction. Journal of Educational Research, 77(2), 100-107.

Peeck, J. 1980. Experimenter-provided and learner-generated pictures in learning from text. Paper presented at the annual meeting of the American Educational Research Association, Boston. MA.

Peeck, J. 1987. Role of illustrations in processing and remembering illustrated text. In D.M. Willows & H.A. Houghton (eds.), The psychology of illustration.The psychology of illustration.145). New York: Springer-Verlag.

Peper, R.J. & Mayer, R.E. 1986. Generative effects of note taking during science lectures. Journal of Educational Psychology, 78, 34-38.

Perfetto, G.A., Bransford, J.D. & Franks, J.J. 1983. Constraints on access in a problem solving context. Memory & Cognition, 11, 24-31.

Peverly, S.T., Brobst, K.E., Graham, M. & Shaw, R. 2003. College adults are not good at self-regulation: A study on the relationship of self-regulation, note taking, and test taking. Journal of Educational Psychology, 95(2), 335-346.

Plant, E.A., Ericsson, K.A., Hill, L. & Asberg, K. 2005. Why study time does not predict grade point average across college students: Implications of deliberate practice for academic performance. Contemporary Educational Psychology, 30, 96-116.

Pressley, M., Symons, S., McDaniel, M.A. & Snyder, B.L. 1988. Elaborative interrogation facilitates acquisition of confusing facts. Journal of Educational Psychology, 80(3), 268-278.

Pressley, M., Wood, E., Woloshyn, V. E., Martin, V., King, A., & Menke, D. 1992. Encouraging mindful use of prior knowledge: Attempting to construct explanatory answers facilitates learning. Educational Psychologist, 27 (1), 91-109.

Ramsburg, J. T., & Youmans, R. J. (2014). Meditation in the Higher-Education Classroom: Meditation Training Improves Student Knowledge Retention during Lectures. Mindfulness, 5(4), 431–441.

Rasco, R.W., Tennyson, R.D. & Boutwell, R.C. 1975. Imagery instructions and drawings in learning prose. Journal of Educational Psychology, 67, 188-192.

Reed, S.K. 1987. A structure-mapping model for word problems. Journal of Experimental Psychology: Learning, Memory, and Cognition, 13, 124-139.

Reeves, L.M. & Weisberg, R.W. 1994. The role of content and abstract information in analogical transfer. Psychological Bulletin, 3, 381-400.

Reynolds, J.H. 1966. Cognitive transfer in verbal learning. Journal of Educational Psychology, 57, 382-388.

Reynolds, J.H. 1968. Cognitive transfer in verbal learning: II. Transfer effects after prefamiliarization with integrated versus partially integrated verbal-perceptual structures. Journal of Educational Psychology, 59, 133-138.

Rickards, J.P. & August, G.J. 1975. Generative underlining strategies in prose recall. Journal of Educational Psychology, 67, 860-865.

Riding, R.J. & Rayner, S. 1998. Cognitive styles and learning strategies. London: David Fulton.

Riding, R.J., Grimley, M., Dahraei, H. & Banner, G. 2003. Cognitive style, working memory and learning behavior and attainment in school subjects. British Journal of Educational Psychology, 73, 149-169.

Risko, E. F., Anderson, N., Sarwal, A., Engelhardt, M., & Kingstone, A. (2012). Everyday Attention: Variation in Mind Wandering and Memory in a Lecture. Applied Cognitive Psychology,26(2), 234–242.

Robin, A., Foxx, R.M., Martello, J. & Archable, C. 1977. Teaching note-taking skills to underachieving college students. The Journal of Educational Research, 71, 81-85.

Robinson, D.H. & Kiewra, K.A. 1995. Visual argument: Graphic organizers are superior to outlines in improving learning from text. Journal of Educational Psychology, 87, 455-67.

Robinson, D.H. & Molina, E. 2002. The relative involvement of visual and auditory working memory when studying adjunct displays. Contemporary Educational Psychology, 27, 118-131.

Ross, B.H. 1984. Remindings and their effects in learning a cognitive skill. Cognitive Psychology, 16, 371-416.

Ross, B.H. 1986. Remindings in learning. In S. Vosniadou & A. Ortony (Eds.), Similarity, analogy and thought (pp. 438-469) New York: Cambridge University Press.

Ross, B.H. 1989. Distinguishing types of superficial similarities: Different effects on the access and use of earlier examples. Journal of Experimental Psychology: Learning, Memory, and Cognition, 15, 456-468.

Sanchez, R.P., Lorch, E.P. & Lorch, R.F. Jr. 2001. Effect of headings on text processing strategies. Contemporary Educational Psychology, 26, 418-28.

Scevak, J.J. & Moore, P.J. 1990. Effective processing of visual information. Reading, 24(1), 28-36.

Schuman, H., Walsh, E., Olson, C. & Etheridge, B. 1985. Effort and reward: the assumption that college grades are affected by quantity of study. Social Forces, 63, 945-966.

Schwartz, D.L. & Bransford, J.D. 1998. A time for telling. Cognition & Instruction, 16, 475-522.

Schwartz, N.H. & Kulhavy, R.W. 1981. Map features and recall of discourse. Contemporary Educational Psychology, 18(2), 222-239.

Schwartz, NH, Ellsworth, LS, Graham L & Knight, B. 1998. Accessing Prior Knowledge to Remember Text: A Comparison of Advance Organizers and Maps. Contemporary Educational Psychology, 23, 65-89.

Skuballa, I. T., Dammert, A., & Renkl, A. (2018). Two kinds of meaningful multimedia learning: Is cognitive activity alone as good as combined behavioral and cognitive activity? Learning and Instruction, 54(February), 35–46.

Snowman, J. & Cunningham, D.J. 1975. A comparison of pictorial and written adjuncts in learning from text. Journal of Educational Psychology, 67, 307-11.

Spyridakis, J.H. & Standahl, T.C. 1986. Headings, previews, logical connectives: Effects on reading comprehension. Journal of Technical Writing and Communication, 16, 354.

Stalbovs, K., Scheiter, K., & Gerjets, P. (2015). Implementation intentions during multimedia learning: Using if-then plans to facilitate cognitive processing. Learning and Instruction, 35, 1–15.

Szpunar, K. K., Khan, N. Y., & Schacter, D. L. (2013). Interpolated memory tests reduce mind wandering and improve learning of online lectures. Proceedings of the National Academy of Sciences, 110(16), 6313–6317.

Tabachneck-Schiif, H.J.M. & Simon, H.A. 1998. One person, multiple representations: An analysis of a simple, realistic multiple representation learning task. In M.W. van Someren, P. Reimann, H.P.A. Boshuizen & Te de Jong (eds.), Learning with multiple representations (pp. 197-236). Kudlington, Oxford: Elsevier Science.

Thagard, P. 1992. Analogy, explanation, and education. Journal of Research in Science Teaching, 29, 537-544.

Thiede, K.W. & Anderson, M.C.M. 2003. Summarizing can improve metacomprehension accuracy. Contemporary Educational Psychology, 28 (2), 129-160.

Thomas, G.S. 1978. Use of student notes and lecture summaries as study guides for recall. The Journal of Educational Research, 71, 316-319.

Tindall-Ford, S., Chandler, P. & Sweller, J. 1997. When two sensory modes are better than one. Journal of Experimental Psychology: Applied, 3, 257-87.

Tirre, W.C., Manelis, L. & Leicht, K.L. 1979. The effects of imaginal and verbal strategies on prose comprehension by adults. Journal of Reading Behavior, 11, 99-106.

Van Meter, P. 2001. Drawing Construction as a Strategy for Learning from Text. Journal of Educational Psychology, 93 (1), 129-140.

Van Meter, P., Aleksic, M., Schwartz, A. & Garner, J. 2006. Learner-generated drawing as a strategy for learning from content area text. Contemporary Educational Psychology, 31, 142-166.

Verdi, M.P., Johnson, J.T., Stock, W.A., Kulhavy, R.W. & Ahern, P. 1997. Organized spatial display and texts: Effects of presentation order and display type on learning outcomes. Journal of Experimental Education, 64(4), 303-317.

Verdi, M. P., & Kulhavy, R. W. (2002). Learning With Maps and Texts : An Overview, Educational Psychology Review, 14(1), 27-46.

Verdi, M.P., Stamm, J., Johnson, J.T. & Jamison, M. 2001. Map edges: Focal points for facilitating text recall. Contemporary Educational Psychology, 26, 211-26.

Wagstaff, R. & Mahmoudi, D. 1976. Relation of study behaviors and employment to academic performance. Psychological Reports, 38, 380-382.

Wallace, W.P. 1965. Review of the historical, empirical and theoretical status of the von Restorff Phenomenon. Psychological Bulletin, 63, 410-24.

Weisberg, R., DiCamillo, M. & Phillips, D. 1978. Transferring old associations to new situations: A nonautomatic process. Journal of Verbal Learning and Behavior, 17, 228.

Wilhite, S.C. 1989. Headings as memory facilitators: The importance of prior knowledge. Journal of Educational Psychology, 81, 115-7.

Willoughby, E., Wood, E., McDermott, C. & McLaren, J. 2000. Enhancing learning through strategy instruction and group interaction: is active generation of elaborations critical? Applied Cognitive Psychology, 14(1), 19-30.

Willoughby, T., Desmarais, S., Wood, E., Sims, S. & Kalra, M. 1997. Mechanisms that facilitate the effectiveness of elaboration strategies. Journal of Educational Psychology, 89 (4), 682-685.

Willoughby, T., Wood, E. & Khan, M. 1994. Isolating variables that impact on or detract from the effectiveness of elaboration strategies. Journal of Educational Psychology, 86, 279-89.

Winn, B. 1987. Charts, graphs, and diagrams in educational materials. In D.M. Willows & H.A. Houghton (eds.), The psychology of illustration, Vol 1: Basic research. SpringerVerlag (pp152-198).

Winn, W.D. & Sutherland, S.W. 1989. Factors influencing the recall of elements in maps and diagrams and the strategies used to encode them. Journal of Educational Psychology, 81(1), 33-39.

Woloshyn, V.E., Paivio, A. & Pressley, M. 1994. Use of elaborative interrogation to help students acquire info consistent with prior knowledge and info inconsistent with prior knowledge. Journal of Educational Psychology, 86, 79-89.

Woloshyn, V.E., Pressley, M.& Schneider, W. 1992. Elaborative-interrogation and prior knowledge effects on learning of facts. Journal of Educational Psychology, 84(1), 115-124.

Woloshyn, V.E., Willoughby, T., Wood, E. & Pressley, M. 1990. Elaborative interrogation facilitates adult learning of factual paragraphs. Journal of Educational Psychology, 82(3), 513-524.

Zimmer, H.D. 2004. The construction of mental maps based on a fragmentary view of physical maps. Journal of Educational Psychology, 96(3), 603-610.

24771155R00152